Rural Labor Movements in Egypt and Their Impact on the State, 1961–1992

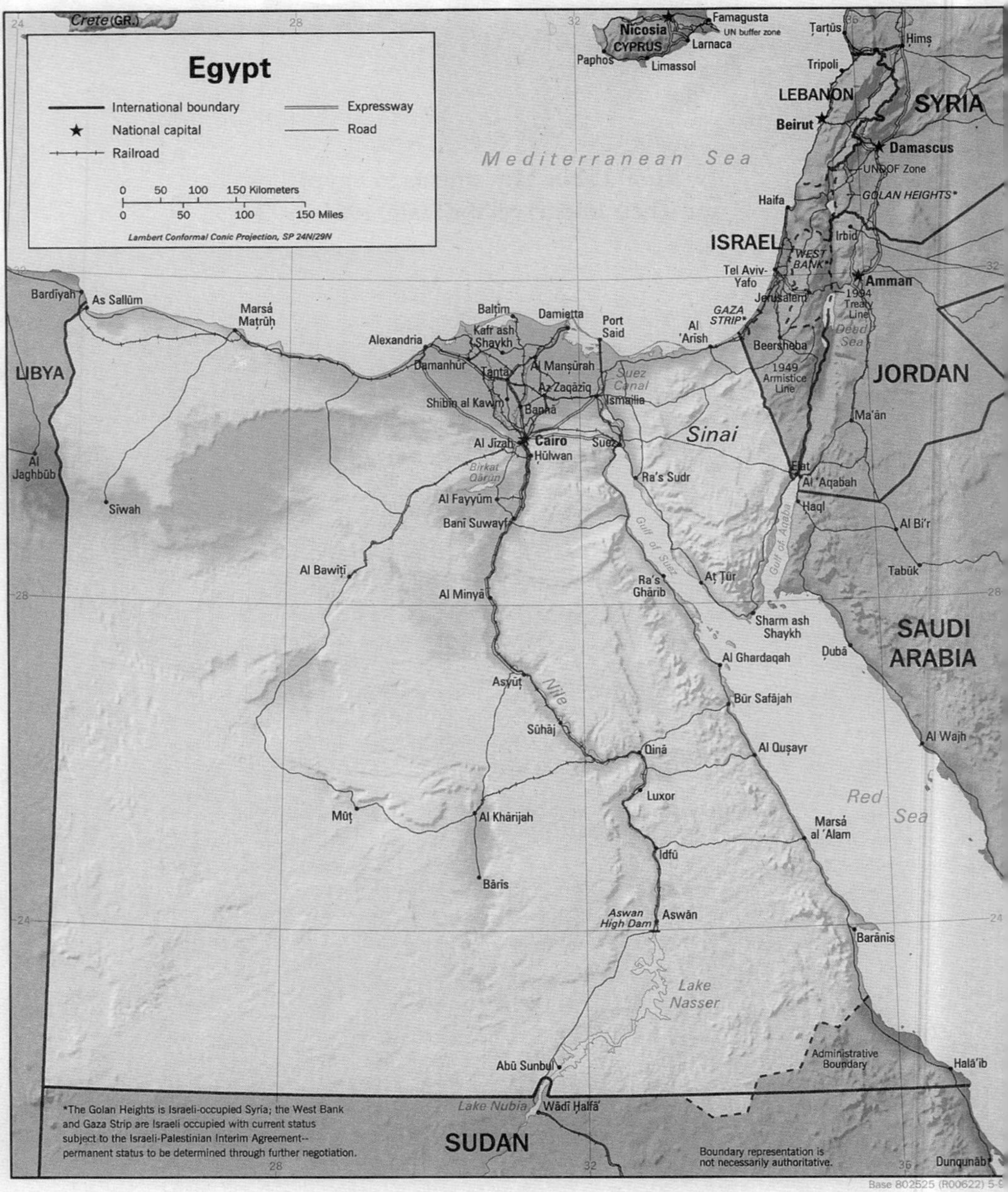
Egypt
International boundary
National capital
Railroad
Expressway
Road
0 50 100 150 Kilometers
0 50 100 150 Miles
Lambert Conformal Conic Projection, SP 24N/29N
Mediterranean Sea
Crete (GR.)
Nicosia
CYPRUS
Famagusta
UN buffer zone
Larnaca
Limassol
Paphos
Tartūs
Ḥimṣ
Tripoli
LEBANON
SYRIA
Beirut
Damascus
UNDOF Zone
GOLAN HEIGHTS*
Haifa
ISRAEL
WEST BANK*
Irbid
Tel Aviv-Yafo
Amman
Jerusalem
1994 Treaty Line
Dead Sea
GAZA STRIP*
Beersheba
1949 Armistice Line
JORDAN
Ma'ān
Bardīyah
As Sallūm
Marsá Maţrūḩ
Baltīm
Damietta
Port Said
Al 'Arīsh
Alexandria
Kafr ash Shaykh
Damanhūr
Ţanţā
Al Manşūrah
Az Zaqāzīq
Suez Canal
Ismailia
Shibīn al Kawm
Banhā
LIBYA
Sinai
Al Jīzah
Cairo
Ḩulwān
Suez
Al Jaghbūb
Birkat Qārūn
Ra's Sudr
Eilat
Al 'Aqabah
Al Fayyūm
Ḩaql
Sīwah
Banī Suwayf
Al Bi'r
Gulf of Suez
Gulf of Aqaba
Al Bawīţī
Aţ Ţūr
Tabūk
Ra's Ghārib
Al Minyā
Sharm ash Shaykh
SAUDI ARABIA
Al Ghardaqah
Dubā
Asyūţ
Nile
Būr Safājah
Sūhāj
Qinā
Al Quşayr
Al Wajh
Luxor
Red Sea
Mūţ
Al Khārijah
Marsá al 'Alam
Idfū
Bārīs
Aswan High Dam
Aswān
Barānīs
Lake Nasser
Administrative Boundary
Abū Sunbul
Halā'ib
Lake Nubia
Wādī Ḩalfā'
SUDAN
*The Golan Heights is Israeli-occupied Syria; the West Bank and Gaza Strip are Israeli occupied with current status subject to the Israeli-Palestinian Interim Agreement--permanent status to be determined through further negotiation.
Boundary representation is not necessarily authoritative.
Dunqunāb
Base 802525 (R00622) 5-9

Rural Labor Movements in Egypt and Their Impact on the State, 1961–1992

James Toth

The American University in Cairo Press

First published in Egypt in 1999 by
The American University in Cairo Press
113 Sharia Kasr el Aini
Cairo, Egypt

This edition published by arrangement with the
University Press of Florida

Dar el Kutub No. 15563/98
ISBN 977 424 517 2

Printed in Egypt

To Virginia

CONTENTS

ILLUSTRATIONS

DIAGRAMS AND TABLES

ACKNOWLEDGMENTS

This study about migrant farm workers in Egypt and their impact on the state has involved many migrations of my own: first to Cairo; then to the New Lands in what was once North Taḥrīr Province with village workers from Minūfiya Province; then to Kafr al-Shaykh province in the northern Delta; and then to the "15 of May" city outside Helwan, south of Cairo. A few years later I migrated back to Egypt to direct an international program in community development in al-Minyā. Later I taught anthropology at the University of Alexandria and then conducted additional research on the workers' union in Bāb al-Lūq, Cairo. Finally I traveled once again to Cairo to teach at the American University in Cairo. The frequent-flyer miles have certainly added up. I seem to have one foot planted in the United States and the other in Egypt—this "wishbone effect" has become a familiar part of my experience. This book has benefited greatly from all those I met during these numerous migratory trips—especially the workers themselves.

The fieldwork for this study received research support from two grants from the U.S.-Egypt Binational Fulbright Commission: a 1980–82 pre-doctoral dissertation grant and a teaching-research grant in 1991–92, in affiliation with the University of Alexandria. I also received two affiliations and a grant from the American Research Center in Cairo (ARCE), in 1980–82 and 1992. I particularly wish to thank Amira Khattab of ARCE for arranging numerous research permissions. More material was acquired during the two years (1984–86) I was employed as the field office director for Save the Children's community development program in al-Minyā, Egypt. An AUC Faculty Research Grant in 1995 funded additional fieldwork in al-Minyā, and an AUC Support Grant financed the preparation of this volume.

This study began as a Ph.D. dissertation I wrote at the State University of New York at Binghamton, where the intellectual atmosphere of anthropology, sociology, the Ferdnand Braudel Center, and the Program for South West Asia and North Africa proved extremely exciting and stimulating. In particular I wish to thank Richard Moench, Martin Murray, Richard Antoun, and Safia Mohsen for their advice, which greatly improved my efforts.

In 1990–91 I spent a year teaching at the University of New Hampshire in Durham, where, with the wonderful help of Barbara Larson, Steve Reyna, and Deborah Winslow I began developing new interpretations of this material and placing it in a different and broader theoretical context. We were not always in agreement, but the enlightened discussions we had helped me considerably in clarifying a number of new approaches.

At the American University in Cairo, all my colleagues in the Department of Anthropology, Sociology, Psychology, and Egyptology were tremendously congenial and encouraging. I would particularly like to thank Nicholas Hopkins, Cynthia Nelson, Donald Cole, Soraya Altorki, and Ted Swedenburg (now at the University of Arkansas) for helping me think through this undertaking. I also wish to thank Mona Abou-Zeid for her assistance in conducting research on the migrant workers' labor union.

In any writing endeavor, and this one is no exception, critical readers identify problems and issues that would otherwise go unnoticed. Roger Owen, Nathan Brown, Martin Murray, Nicholas Hopkins, and Barbara Larson offered copious comments, criticisms, and a large portion of their time, which helped enormously in improving the quality of this study.

The editors at the University Press of Florida have been very supportive. Walda Metcalf helped by accepting my original manuscript. Her successor, Meredith Morris-Babb, has been encouraging but uncompromising in demanding quality writing and reasoning. I also wish to thank Michael Senecal for his meticulous copyediting.

Over the years of living in Egypt and conducting research on its society, two individuals in particular stand out for giving their time, friendship, knowledge, insights, and courtesy. Unfortunately, Adil Afifi passed away before he could see this work in print. He was the director of the migrant labor program in the Egyptian Ministry of Labor. Without his assistance, none of the initial field research could have been completed. Ahmad Ramzi Abd-El Shafy continues to be the first and only real Egyptian populist I have met. His own love of Egypt and its people comes out at every meeting we have. He is a real gentleman, whose friendship and respect continue to inspire me.

Finally, I wish to express my deepest gratitude to my wife, Virginia Danielson, to whom this book is dedicated. I am profoundly indebted to her for her intellectual and marital companionship. For some time she has had to put up with a migrant husband such that a substantial share of my professional migratory career has relied extensively on her care and support.

Much research has been carried out to trace the different historical phases that the bourgeoisie has passed through, from the commune up to its constitution as a class.

But when it is a question of making a precise study of strikes, combinations and other forms in which the proletarians carry out before our eyes their organization as a class, some are seized with real fear and others display a transcendental disdain.

Karl Marx, *The Poverty of Philosophy*

1

Regulating Rural Workers and Social Pyramids in Egypt

Even before 1980 when I arrived in Egypt to conduct anthropological research on migrant farm workers—called *ʿummāl al-tarāḥīl* in Egyptian Arabic—the nation had already experienced a number of explosive events. Three years earlier, just before my first trip in 1977, Cairo had suffered violent street riots in January that had left seventy-seven dead, 214 wounded, and thousands under arrest. Six months later, the halls of government were still echoing the tense anxiety generated by this spontaneous outburst of popular unrest. During that first summer while I persistently tried to learn Arabic, Shukrī Muṣṭafa and his Islamist group *Jamāʿāt al-Muslimīn*—known to journalists as *al-Takfīr wa al-Hijra*—kidnapped Muḥammad al-Dhaḥabī, a former minister of religious endowments, who died when security police attacked the group's hideout. The ringleaders were later executed by hanging. The following November, Egypt's president, Anwār al-Sadāt, made a complete *volte face* by visiting Israel and speaking to the Knesset in Jerusalem, thereby asking Egyptians, albeit unsuccessfully, to follow suit and totally reverse thirty years of intense animosity.

Four years later, in 1981, after only a year into my actual fieldwork, an assassin's gun cut down Egypt's president—in part as retribution for the events of 1977, in part as immediate retaliation for the massive arrests made a month before in September, and in part for the ugly urban riots that had exploded in the woebegone slum of al-Zāwiya al-Ḥamrā' earlier that June. The assassination prompted a stunned, silent response that I heard contrasted ominously with the massive public wailing and outpouring displayed over the death of Egypt's first president, Jamāl ʿAbd al-Nāṣir. Throughout the 1950s and 1960s, ʿAbd al-Nāṣir had been ardently revered by many, especially by those at the bottom of Egyptian society. Yet when he died in September 1970, his star had decidedly dimmed, for without question, the devastating defeat of the Six-Day war of June 1967 had undermined his popular authority and eroded the strength of the entire country. In order to revive the nation and heal the wounds that this defeat had opened, his successor, al-Sadāt, launched a second war in 1973—a victory Egypt still celebrates every October. It was during the eighth anniversary of that war, on October 6, 1981, that al-Sadāt was assassinated. Yet this was not to be the end of Egypt's social turbulence.

In 1984, just two years after finishing my fieldwork, I was back in Egypt again. This time I was managing a major community development program in al-Minyā, a province south of Cairo in the heartland of what was becoming a hotbed of Islamic radicalism in Egypt. Halfway through my two-year tenure, the twelve-year boom in the international petroleum market burst, oil gluts flooded the globe, and those hurt by the fall in petroleum prices began grumbling even louder for equity and justice. Development projects were swirling all around us in the Saʿīd, but somehow they made little impact and brought little satisfaction. Their tranquilizing function seemed transparent to those who wanted more.

Having now resigned myself to becoming an *ustādh al-tarāḥīl,* an itinerant professor, I again returned to Egypt, where in 1991 I taught anthropology at the University of Alexandria. Just the year before, Egypt's third president, Ḥusnī Mubarak, had ordered Egyptian troops to the Gulf to fight another Arab nation, thereby strengthening Egypt's close ties to the United States at a time when a more flexible diplomatic stance toward Europe and Japan seemed a more suitable option. Then, just six months after Operation Desert Storm, Cairo finally but reluctantly signed a major financial agreement with the International Monetary Fund (IMF), which, by eliminating consumer subsidies and reducing social services, was guaranteed to upset the private economies of millions of its citizens and generate substantial social unrest. Then in 1994 I was once again in Egypt, this time with colleagues at the American University in Cairo discussing the character of an Islamic radicalism that seems to have plunged the country into an undeclared religious civil war.

At first, these electrifying events seemed completely unconnected to those *tarāḥīl* workers I had originally set out to study. These rural workers were considered the "lowest of the low," while Egypt's history appeared to be made solely by those at the top. Any causal connection between the bottom and the top seemed inconceivable. Nothing in my discussions with these workers and their bosses, or with government officials and intellectuals, or in my reading of the secondary sources—even those few relevant volumes that actually did examine Egyptian labor—acknowledged any determinant link that might exist between these two strata. The state—that national institution that simultaneously keeps the classes separate but still interacting—appeared far too powerful and way too remote to be bothered by those insignificant masses it claimed to dominate.

Still, the question remained intriguing: Was Egypt's recent development the organized outcome of the sophisticated plans of these omnipotent and omniscient government officials? Or was it the chaotic clutter brought about by unexpected jerks, stammers, and stutters made in urgent response to massive popular pressure from Egypt's working classes? To answer it required venturing outside my own field of anthropology to examine the problem from the perspective of several different academic disciplines.

A Social Pyramid of Elites and Workers

In integrating the microscopic, ethnographic perspective of anthropology with the abstract, macroscopic outlook of political science, economics, and history, questions arise over how possible is it for the common, everyday people anthropologists usually study to influence the course of national and even international events. Could their ordinary, seemingly innocent acts, engaged in with no grand purpose in mind, actually accumulate in the end to seriously affect the political and economic history of an entire country?

In examining Egypt's history since 1960, it is hard to imagine that the scramble and scurry of rural laborers could have any appreciable impact on the transcendent forces of national and international leaders, superpower machinations, the Cold War, the intractable Arab-Israeli conflict, and powerful international banks, corporations, and governments. Mighty matters of domestic policies, regional domination, and global hegemony seem to dwarf any impact their modest acts might make.

This period saw the rise of Jamāl ʿAbd al-Nāṣir to the pinnacle of anti-hegemonic Arab nationalism within the Middle East; beheld the conversion of his successor, Anwār al-Sadāt, to accept the principle of western superpower domination; and witnessed the difficulty of Egypt's third president, Ḥusnī Mubarak, to steer between the Scylla of Westernization and the Charybdis of Islamic militancy. Was this history merely a tale of contending elites, including or opposing these eponymic leaders? Or was it a story of the top hopelessly reacting to rumblings and grumblings, riots and crises, initiated by those at the bottom, where an untold narrative remained hidden in order to discount their agency and thus avoid even more disturbances?

If indeed even ordinary middle-class citizens are increasingly unable to influence momentous national and international events, how then could those at the very bottom of a social hierarchy in a country that itself is on the periphery of global capitalism be expected to carry any weight? For the profound marginalization of *tarāḥīl* migrant farm workers reduces their influence to such an imperceptible level that macro-level investigators need not regard them, and microscopic analysis, such as in anthropology, may harmlessly dismiss the broader consequences of their actions. Yet the gnawing question still lingers: Could the cumulative actions of these *tarāḥīl* migrant farm workers ever make a substantial difference? Could their aggregate movement have had any effect whatsoever on where their country had been and where it was going? It seemed a bold proposition, since the connections between top and bottom remained obscure.

For the theories of national elites that many political scientists, economists, and historians employ, together with their research methods, which remain heavily concentrated on interviewing or documenting Cairo-based officials, professionals, and intellectuals, disregard any impact from those outside and below such lofty circles. Instead, they seem to operate with a model of a social pyramid that dangles precariously in midair without a proletarian base, dominated by an all-powerful, monolithic government in the capital city.

Elite theory either simply dismisses as "immature" the influence of those at the bottom[1] or else, if considered at all, assumes a submissive relationship to those at the top. Instead, politics, conflict, and history solely depend on the elites' alliance with a state that attempts to limit their autonomy. Should these elites be otherwise unfettered, they could then, in Weberian fashion, generate the economic advancement and historical development the country needs.

Urban elites in Egypt are considered the easier to govern, yet even those in the countryside are viewed as either securing or forfeiting their village autonomy because of their connections to Cairo. Numerous studies of rural Egypt, such as those by Leonard Binder, Simon Commander, Bent Hanson, James Mayfield, Amr Mohie-Eldin, Samir Radwan, Alan Richards, Gabriel Saab, Robert Springborg, and John Waterbury, employ a theory of elites and a monolithic government to examine Egyptian history and political economy. Only a few go beyond privileging this upper strata and its supposedly strong state to study the far greater number of ordinary people at the bottom, who may well oppose and even undermine government action.

Yet studies of Egypt's underclass are flawed because they go in one of two divergent directions. On the one hand, workers in the countryside are treated as marginal and inert members of homogeneous peasant communities who are denied separate and distinct interests of their own. Even though a plurality of rural Egyptians still work in agriculture, a large majority of these do not rent or own land, or even have access to enough land, to remain fully occupied within this sector. Yet agricultural production is still seen as performed by landholding households that combine property, management, and labor into single, family-based enterprises (Hopkins 1993; Weyland 1993). Rural wage labor remains incidental, or, if recognized at all, is treated in Chayanov fashion merely as family members hiring out to local landowners (Richards 1982; Brown 1990). Further class transformations are seen to take place outside the village, as rural workers who lose their property vanish by migrating straightaway to urban areas (Waterbury 1991).

Thus enmeshed in an outdated concept of peasant family production, many scholars fail to appreciate the differentiation of village members into workers and employers, and fail to detect the outside labor nexus of landless and near-landless laborers. Rural workers are either swept into the dustbin of peasant studies or else are summarily dismissed as urban migrants.[2]

On the other hand, workers in the cities are treated only within an institutional context that is limited to large-scale bureaucratic enterprises and service sectors and hierarchically organized unions and political parties. Those who are employed in less formal enterprises and who are mobilized into nonoccupational or unauthorized associations are ignored. In the institutional approach, formal organizations bear the full burden of achieving better working and living conditions. Measuring their successes and failures is thus considered imperative in evaluating the strength of labor's struggle against capitalism. Yet without a broader social analysis that looks beyond archival documents and official interviews to conducting ethnographic fieldwork among the workers themselves, scholars have little idea of how the informal relationships that originate outside the factory walls, union halls, and political parties can also advance these objectives when formal organizations fail to work.

For it is the larger informal sector that serves as the migrant's first introduction to the city and that imperfectly shields the formal workforce from its rural counterparts. And it is the more common network of informal affiliations that increasingly attracts workers as the official political system breaks down. Neglecting these connections has led scholars to underestimate the importance of the reserve labor army of rural and ex-rural workers and their mobilization in explaining the dismal political clout of organized factory workers against the state (Posusney 1991); the discrepancy between industrial organization and political doctrine (Goldberg 1986); and the political astuteness of those otherwise dismissed as exhibiting false consciousness (Beinin and Lockman 1987).

Thus, studies of rural workers perceive them as members of an integrated, homogenous peasantry, while studies of urban workers identify laborers as members of separate, specialized organizations. Yet if rural workers were treated like their urban counterparts and were seen as distinct laborers in their own right, and if urban workers were treated like peasants and were seen as having informal occupations and social relations, we would then get the best of both possible worlds.

Accordingly, any analysis of *tarāḥīl* migrant farm workers has to take a third course. It needs to reconcile these different approaches by examining social relationships that are both formal and informal, specialized and multipurpose, bureaucratic and paternalistic, hierarchical and collegial. It also must recognize that a vast chasm exists between middle-class, urban-based labor leaders, state officials, and educated chroniclers, on the one hand, and the vast majority of unskilled and unschooled rural workers, on the other, such that only through ethnographic fieldwork that goes beyond institutional studies will it be able to successfully restore the proletarian base to Egypt's floating social pyramid.

Unfortunately, common *tarāḥīl* workers fall analytically between the cracks of scholarly discourse. As a result, they are disregarded by both scholars and national elites and are dismissed as irrelevant and unimportant. What, after all, can be expected from those like *tarāḥīl* migrant farm workers who are located at the very bottom of society and are considered the "lowest of the low"?

Yet in Egypt, agriculture continues to be the largest economic sector. Back in 1960, when this study begins, migrant farm workers represented the largest single category of Egyptian workers, including as many as 30 percent of the entire national labor force (see chapter 5). This number was three times greater than the next largest sector of service employees and six times greater than the number of industrial workers. However, per capita income in agriculture was just one-fifth of that earned in industry. It seems clear, therefore, that *tarāḥīl* workers were more numerous but more destitute. This means that their cumulative endeavors to find better incomes and more rewarding employment ought to be a major, dynamic force in determining Egypt's economic growth.

Even so, their efforts have remained largely ignored,[3] for many scholars have declared these workers immune to the forces of struggle, the production of history, and serious analytical treatment. The present study seeks to remedy this indifference and correct this omission by bringing rural workers squarely into the analysis of Egypt's recent history. Filling the cracks in scholarly discourse requires clarifying the otherwise obscure connections between the very few elite at the top and the vast majority of workers at the bottom and then devising a better measure of labor's strength by evaluating the impact of these *tarāḥīl* workers against a hypothetical model of capitalist development.

Regulation Theory

What is needed therefore is a theory that integrates both macro-and micro-level perspectives, identifies the determinant relationships among social actors, and outlines the likely trajectory of capitalism's historical development. A number of theories satisfy these requirements, yet marxism remains one that offers a dynamic approach by hinging its analysis to "class" as the objective structure, to "class agents" as the subjective element, and to "class conflict" as the motor force of historical development.

Unfortunately, marxism has remained more faithful to its Kantian roots sustained by the Second International, with their parallel and unconnected movement of objective conditions and subjective agency. While various interpretations have claimed to combine this dualism through praxis, they have instead tilted in favor of one or the other without achieving an analysis whereby material conditions and social agents are united dialectically through class struggle.

After World War II, the humanist thrust under Jean-Paul Sartre established a major preoccupation with subjective consciousness and individual human will, replacing material production with subjective effort as the motor force of history. Yet it verged on becoming a social psychology, for without strict economic considerations, these marxists were unable to demarcate class boundaries, and therefore were unable to identify which agents were the actual makers of history. In the 1960s, the structuralism of Louis Althusser formulated a rigid edifice that inserted a marxist totality into linguistic and structuralist theory, yet eliminated any reference to subjective agency whatsoever. Instead, agents simply became "structural supports" or "Träger," acting out the dictates of transcendent structures that reduced class conflict to a multiplicity of interlocking components and reduced historical movement to vectorial noncorrespondence. Thus, one interpretation championed human will and subjectivity without objective conditions, while the other advocated transcendent structures devoid of imaginative human actors. In both, the antinomies of object and subject remained detached, operated separately, and seldom interacted dialectically. Both lacked an operative theory of praxis that could unite objective circumstances and subjective appraisals. Each removed history from the outcome of conditioned working-class agency and abandoned it instead to the forces of philosophical speculation.

However, in recent years, an approach called *regulation theory* has emerged out of the ashes of an Althusserian structuralism unable to resolve the question of just who creates history and a Sartrean subjectivism unable to determine the material conditions under which this happens, all nourished since 1973 by a prolonged period of economic uncertainty in the West. The central problem in regulation theory is to understand how contemporary societies change over time by analyzing different phases of capitalist development. This issue of transformation, of capitalist crisis and breakdown, had once topped the marxist agenda before it became distorted by the Russian Revolution's notion of party vanguardism and Western marxism's idea of false consciousness. However, regulation theory could not simply adopt a model of unalterable decline and deterioration forged in the more heady days of nineteenth-century competitive capitalism. Bourgeois economists such as John Maynard Keynes, Joseph Schumpeter, and Michael Kalecki had long since developed more sophisticated theories that explained why periods of crises alternated with periods of stability. Accordingly, there was not going to be just one final breakdown of capitalism but rather a series of economic failures and catastrophes, separated by periods of relative balance and calm. Social change was conceived of not as anarchy, or the absence of the laws of capitalist development, but rather as the very realization of these laws: crises were part and parcel of capitalist development, not its negation. The question for regulation theory then was how to account for these fluctuating periods of crisis and stability, and how societies were to move from one to the other.

Regulation theory became identified principally with studies conducted by French political economists beginning in the mid-1970s following the publication of Michel Aglietta's pioneering study, *A Theory of Capitalist Regulation: The U.S. Experience.* It then spread throughout Europe to include similar approaches established in Germany, Holland, Norway, and even the United States (Jessop 1990). Early regulation theory borrowed considerably from the workerist theories developed by marxists in the Italian autonomist movement, which lasted from 1960 to 1977. This perspective gave regulation theory a substantial focus on labor's activities at the actual site of capitalist production.[4] However, by 1980, regulation theory had moved away from a labor theory of value and its initial concern for workers' agency and had become more a form of radical Keynesianism that instead emphasized a nonmarxist price-theoretic. Yet here I wish to focus more on the earlier version, with its strong concentration on labor's role in history.

This approach understands the movement of history as the direct product of human agency *pace* Sartre, but one explicitly mediated by a particular production system and the current configuration of social conditions. Human agency thus operates specifically within the confines of the structured social relationships contained in the capitalist valorization process that encompasses the organization of production, the apportionment of wages and profits, and the circulation and consumption of commodities, all under the contested authority of the state and its hegemonic institutions. History then becomes something that is initially generated by the interaction of society's two antagonistic classes—labor and capital—a movement that comes about as a series of distinct but contingent phases that ultimately grow out of the daily struggles taking place between workers (as such, but also as consumers and citizens) on the one hand, and managers, merchants, and officials on the other.

However, regulation theory avoids the vulgar economism of the Second International by rejecting the assertion that political and ideological superstructures are determined by, or simply reflect, the economic base. Instead, it deliberately reverses causality by arguing that the daily struggles taking place between labor and capital are controlled, or *regulated,* by an ensemble of social institutions specific to a particular society and history.[5] This means that the fundamentals of capitalism—the separation of labor from private property, the wage relationship, but in particular, the appropriation of surplus value—do not have the same appearance in all places and for all times. As essential elements of the superstructure, the various forms of property and wage relations, along with other socially and historically constituted institutions, critically shape and contour the relations of value appropriation that form the heart of the production processes that constitute capitalism.

It is the dialectical interaction between labor-capital conflicts and their bilateral control or regulation that embodies the microscopic activities of ordinary workers that ethnographers study and that then generates the macroscopic dynamics of national and international developments examined by political scientists, economists, and historians. Regulationists call these conflicts over the valorization of capital, which includes the contingent realization of production, profits, wages, and consumption, the "regime of accumulation." The mutual management and modulation of these contests, which include all the institutional relationships that shape the regime of accumulation, is designated the "mode of regulation."

Production is certainly the most important element in the regime of accumulation. Its labor process includes all the ingredients of production—material, tools, organization—but it essentially boils down to the two major antagonistic agents, workers and employers, who explicitly or implicitly negotiate over production requirements.[6] Yet there is more than just the labor process involved here. For in order that production be valorized, and that capitalism and labor continue without interruption, final consumption becomes conceptually necessary. Thus the attempts to realize a socially determined consumption norm or standard of living also create tensions that involve negotiations between workers *qua* consumers, and merchants.

The regime of accumulation then is a set of social relationships that establishes an uneasy parity between effort, wages, and consumer prices such that the specific amount of effort workers render earns them a certain amount of wages, which in turn purchases a set amount of goods and services that reconstitute their ability and skills. Conflicts can erupt in the regime of accumulation when workers gain more control over their own efforts, income, work conditions, and consumption than employers, supervisors, merchants, or state officials would otherwise wish. This steady tug-of-war can either reduce production and the profits it generates or else reduce income and the standard of living it supports, depending on the relative strength and success of the institutional controls that mutually regulate these conflicts. Laborers could then become incapable of working sufficiently and quit, and businesses could lose their market share and go bankrupt. Propagated throughout a sector or even over an entire economy, such interruptions in the valorization process can result in economic crises. New institutions and new controls then emerge to limit these crises or reverse them by enhancing the position of labor and capital. Thus, when the "effort = wage = price" formula becomes too unbalanced and old institutions fail to contain these struggles, major crises can occur that are often resolved when new institutions arise to more efficiently regulate the antagonistic relationship between labor and capital.

When the effort to earn an adequate wage is too great, when the income to purchase consumer items is too meager, when the cost to sufficiently reconstitute labor is too high, then workers find themselves in a tight predicament. Are they ever able to control and alter this effort = wage = price formula to their own benefit, or is labor completely powerless? In spite of the formal authority of those in command, strenuous work demands do generate slowdowns, "laziness," and absenteeism; low wages do provoke job searches, unionizing, and strikes; and high prices do beget theft, moonlighting, and child labor. Is labor, then, ever totally subordinate? The answer is no, for no matter how much labor is subsumed under capital, workers still retain some ability to alter the regime of accumulation and modify its effort = wage = price equation, for valorization invariably involves mutual relationships that are not always unilaterally defined and controlled by managers, merchants, and officials (Littler and Salaman 1982:60).

The effort = wage = price relationship that characterizes the regime of accumulation is controlled by the mode of regulation, which contains different economic, political, and social institutions. Aglietta stressed such institutions as private-property relationships, wage-payment methods, technology, and the market relations among businesses, to which can be added other economic practices such as supervisory mechanisms, workforce composition, credit and finance, and labor-market opportunities. Political institutions can include government, international organizations, civil society, and civil disorder, while social institutions might include such cultural constructs as kinship, age, collegiality, and gender.

The mode of regulation, through its constituent institutions, mutually shapes the core struggles that occur within the regime of accumulation. Depending on the relative strength of these institutional controls, the conflicts between labor and capital can tilt the effort = wage = price equation either to the benefit of capital and greater surplus accumulation or else in favor of labor and its interests, in which case new institutions might emerge that attempt to rebalance this formula in support of capital. This then creates a new mode of regulation that reconstitutes the entire society.

Yet of all of the institutions in the mode of regulation, it is the state that proves to be the most dominant in contouring the constant conflict between labor and capital (Jessop 1990:160–61). For it is the state, with its organization of bureaus and departments, its instruments of persuasion and coercion, and its formulation of national policies and programs—themselves responses to other struggles occurring elsewhere in the national and international economy—that constitutes the most fundamental institution in the mode of regulation. So very often it is these political struggles over controlling the valorization process—in practice, of workers *qua* citizens versus state officials and the government policies they apply—that critically regulate and control the volatile tensions that lie at the center of capitalism.

But the state is neither monolithic nor omnipotent, notwithstanding its greater ability not only to shape the conflicts between labor and capital but also to shape how these contests are perceived by both sides. Just as labor is never completely subordinate to capital, neither is it totally dominated by its government. Seldom is the state itself so coordinated that its different parts come together as one united institution formulating consistent practices and policies that reflect unvarying class interests. Moreover, were the state able to unilaterally dominate those it ruled—through its uncontested hegemony over the instruments of outright coercion and doctrinal persuasion—then capital's reproduction would occur without opposition, and the creation of new institutions in the mode of regulation to control labor's antagonism would prove unnecessary (Jessop 1982:chap. 1). Social change would cease, since the all-powerful state would not condone any deviation from its own plans. Such an instrumentalist (and despotic) model of the state ultimately invalidates all notions of struggles and the national transformations they provoke. However, state authority is instead contingent, countered and challenged by its citizens using those institutions and practices that enable them to resist the coercion and reject the persuasion wielded by their national government.

The concept of regulation is closely related to the notion of reproduction found in Althusserian marxism. Yet the structuralists' preoccupation with reproduction frequently turned analysis into an implicit form of social self-perpetuation and functionalism (Connell 1979:317). However, regulation can also *transform* society—and often produce some very radical transformations at that.

Thus the term *regulation* refers here to attempts at controlling the essential struggles between historically and socially constituted class agents found in capitalist valorization, and the perpetuation and/or transformation of society's economic, political, and social institutions as the contingent outcomes dependent on how successful these attempts turn out to be. Old institutions disappear and new ones emerge so that by means of the ongoing struggles between workers and employers, merchants, and officials, and their institutional regulation, societies move uneasily from periods of social stability to moments of crises and then pass on to establish new social orders.

Regulation theory argues against the Althusserian perspective of an invariant, undifferentiated capitalism left undisturbed by social agents and class conflict. Instead it views the likely history of capitalist development as passing through a set of distinct but contingent phases that unevenly combine specific "regimes of accumulation" and particular "modes of regulation."[7] There are basically two regimes of accumulation, *extensive* and *intensive*, and two modes of regulation that Aglietta identified according to what he saw as their principal institutions of *competitive* and *monopolistic* market relations. Their respective combination results in two main phases of capitalist development. Each phase is characterized by equilibrium and labor quiescence, but the transition between them is marked by crisis and unrest. Temporal movement is achieved through labor's agency and the constant pressure of concrete class struggles.

Extensive accumulation means accumulating profits by extending the time laborers actually spend working—whether by lengthening the workday or else by reducing dead, unproductive time inside the job. This technique became known in the core as Taylorism. Although the appearance of Taylorism differed from one country to the next, it followed the initial period of primitive accumulation or petty commodity production that marks capitalism's birth. Its eponym derives from the popularizer of scientific management, Frederick Taylor, whose scientific time-motion studies established the most efficient physical movements for labor that could maximize production and profits.[8] His methods included work speedups, lengthening the workday, and pushing workers harder, often by employing harsh, arbitrary supervisors. A relentless competition among businesses further accelerated the drive for profits and the reduction of wages, unimpeded by a lax, laissez-faire state.

By contrast, *intensive* accumulation involves making profits by using modern machinery to rationalize production. This is labeled Fordism. Elements of the Fordist regime of accumulation such as the automated assembly line appeared in the United States as early as 1905, but the entire phase did not emerge full-blown until after World War II, when mass consumerism, state welfare policies, and legalized union representation all came together. It is named for Henry Ford, the inventor of the conveyor-belt assembly line, which could impersonally speed up the labor process despite labor's own wishes. Moreover, efficient production permitted Ford to pay workers higher wages, which then could be used to purchase the very cars they built. Thus Fordism became synonymous with mass production and mass consumption, advanced technology, planned obsolescence, legalized unions, high wages, government subsidies, welfare, and Keynesian pump-priming.

In the United States, the transition from Taylorism to Fordism was achieved through an assorted variety of job actions and labor unrest. Workers demanded higher wages, shorter hours, less despotic supervisors, and union recognition. Companies unwilling or unable to satisfy these demands closed down, moved to less restrictive regions in other parts of the country, or else moved overseas. The growing gap between the overproduction of high-priced goods and the underconsumption of low-paid workers widened considerably. Without independent unions, no effective channel was available to articulate labor's demands that could otherwise narrow it. This helped provoke the Great Crash of 1929, which inaugurated the Great Depression of the 1930s that then spread worldwide. The United States was able to recover during the New Deal, which recognized labor unions, legislated reduced work hours, subsidized unemployment, and expanded markets overseas. Other countries, however, were less fortunate, and instead installed strong fascist forms of state intervention that could traverse the transition. The vast military spending prompted by World War II witnessed the advent of military Keynesianism. Later the armistice ushered in a period of monopoly capitalism coupled with U.S. global hegemony. Bought off, labor in the core remained quiescent, basking in the warmth of its new social contract guaranteed by the state and the core's market superiority. In the periphery, however, the intense exploitation of an already pauperized workforce ignited a large number of national independence movements frequently under the direction of charismatic, authoritarian leaders.

Since 1973 or so, the singular superiority of the United States has vanished and has been replaced by the precarious, multicentric hegemony of Japan, Germany, and the United States. This period of economic uncertainty marks the beginning of postmodernity or post-Fordism, where caught in another transitional period, it is still unclear as to what the next major phase of capitalist development will be like.

Unfortunately regulation theory remains fixated on developments in the core and has spent much less effort on considering the periphery. Attention to a broader global dimension, therefore, remains embryonic. It is perhaps easy to say that the history of the periphery is primarily determined in Washington, London, or Paris (and now Tokyo and Berlin as well), but it is also necessary to point out that the history of the core is also influenced by developments arising outside its constituent countries. For as Alain Lipietz pointed out (1987:48–55), peripheral nations represent more than just a "thermostat" that simply alerts the core to its own impending problems. They do have histories of their own, with their own trajectories and phases. But without considering such autonomous developments, any analysis of global Fordism will continue to be parochial and incomplete. One initiative, however, has proven useful in tracking the history of countries like Egypt by outlining the possible phases of peripheral capitalist development and suggesting how labor's agency might encourage or inhibit their emergence.

Lipietz himself proposed (1982:40) three different phases of capitalist development for noncore economies. These include:

1. The "export promotion" of local raw materials typically found in colonialism. Here workers are subjected to what Lipietz called "bloody" Taylorism: the violent enforcement of low wages, harsh labor conditions, arbitrary supervision, and abject poverty by a bloated state apparatus that starkly contrasts with the lean, laissez-faire political system once found in core Taylorism.

2. The "import substitution" of peripheral industrialization that took place in the 1930s and 1950s when capital left the core during recessionary periods. Here, a small, privileged segment of well-paid laborers works in a peripheral Fordism of secondhand technology. But the home market remains stunted, and thus mass consumption remains limited since most consumers still work in an informal sector of small-scale enterprises or a petty-commodity sector of "peasant" production.

3. The "export substitution" of trading manufactured goods back to core markets. Peripheral Fordism persists, but unlike before, local industries since 1973 no longer compete against those in the core but instead coordinate their production with multinational corporations.

Since the early 1970s, global Fordism has established a new international division of labor with three levels of worldwide production: (1) conception, planning, and engineering; (2) complex manufacturing with skilled labor and relatively high equipment costs; and (3) unskilled assembly, requiring little knowledge and less investment. Over the last two decades, level-3 industries in the core have shut down—or deindustrialized—and have relocated to sites of cooperative Fordism in the periphery. This movement has created the "economic miracles" of such newly industrializing countries (NICs) as Brazil, South Korea, Taiwan, Hong Kong, and Singapore.[9]

Businesses have taken advantage of cheap labor and market proximity in the periphery to establish factories whose level-3 activities now complement level-1 and level-2 operations in the core. Financing has come from expanded oil revenues recycled through multinational corporations and international banks. Their markets lie principally in re-exporting back to the core and, to a lesser extent, to other peripheral countries. However, this export orientation has retarded the development of mass production oriented toward local needs. Consumption is met instead through foreign imports whose high prices exacerbates the national balance of trade and exasperates local, impoverished consumers.

It is this global economy, with its phases of peripheral Taylorism and competitive and cooperative Fordism, that provides the context in which we can situate Egypt's last half century of economic growth and national development. And it is within this national history that we can begin to locate the *tarāḥīl* workforce and evaluate the impact of its tense, dialectical relationship with capital and the state. Regulation theory provides the conceptual ability to do this.

It prompts us to explore how the microscopic ethnographic details of the laborers' relationships and struggles with capital and the state are connected to the macroscopic outcomes of Egypt's economic and political transformations taking place during the administrations of ʿAbd al-Nāṣir, al-Sadāt, and Mubarak. The analysis begins by understanding the ordinary production and consumption activities of these migrant farm workers that lie at the heart of the regime of accumulation. Then it looks at how these laborers and those who ostensibly dominate them control and shape these struggles by using the institutional resources provided in the mode of regulation. In particular it examines the state policies and programs that presumably play a large role in determining how these struggles affect the wider society outside the laborer's work site and household.

Our attention is thus focused first on the fundamental struggles found both inside the labor process and in realizing preferred standards of consumption. It then becomes a question of how these workers' immediate conflicts with managers, merchants, and officials, at once amplified throughout the agricultural labor force and duly supplemented by other agents, can have important, long-term consequences for Egyptian development. Finally, and despite the fact that these unskilled workers do not have a coordinated strategy of deliberate social change, it is still possible for us (by using regulation theory) to evaluate their impact on this development by comparing Egypt's actual history to the proposed set of possible phases of peripheral capitalism.

We shall see as the dialectic between valorization and regulation unfolds just how important *tarāḥīl* migrant farm workers were in creating Egypt's recent history and in affecting its adjustment to global Fordism.

The Contingent Outcomes of Accumulated Labor Actions

Unfortunately, Egypt did not benefit greatly from deindustrialization and the rise of peripheral Fordism—thwarted, as this study shows, by a rural and ex-rural labor force that felt the intense social polarization such transitions generated. For as capitalism advanced in Egypt, it was the actions of rural and ex-rural workers that prevented it from advancing to more efficient forms of capitalism.

Over the past forty years, Egypt's economy has been handicapped by the widespread exodus and relocation of *tarāḥīl* migrant farm workers. This movement was triggered by numerous work site conflicts over defining wages and effort. Gender-based wage disparities in the village and corruption-based speedups at migrant work sites provoked rural laborers to "vote with their feet" and leave farming and then casual migrant employment altogether for urban construction jobs. Yet once lost to migrant labor, *tarāḥīl* workers also became lost to agriculture, its complement in Egypt's rural division of labor. Migrant employment had provided agriculture with a reservoir for its surplus of seasonally unemployed workers, hiring them when farm work slackened in the village and discharging them back into agriculture as employment needs arose back home. Without this economic sponge to absorb and release workers, agriculture, which had previously relied on their availability in periods of high labor demand, began to experience major production problems.

The agricultural sector, in addition to providing employment for the largest single segment of Egyptian workers, also grows food for an expanding population and produces important export crops such as cotton for the nation's hard-currency requirements. After 1960, however, agriculture did not supply nearly enough food, and importing expensive foodstuffs drastically inflated Egypt's trade bill. Moreover, since Egypt's industrial sector remained weak, export crops continued to bear the greatest burden of earning the foreign currency needed to pay for imported food, foreign equipment, and investment dollars. The difference between low exports and high imports forced Egypt time and time again to borrow funds to make up the financial deficit.

As a result, Egypt's balance of payments declined and its national debt increased. International credit arrangements momentarily resolved this predicament, but default remained an ever-present possibility. Yet, even short of this calamity, distortions in the national economy developed serious problems that compounded and propagated themselves into higher and higher realms of national and international finance and politics, gradually leaving behind the real origins of Egypt's financial crises. It is the aim of this study, however, to solidly anchor these national crises and developments over the last forty years in the actions and movements of its producers and consumers by examining the impact of one essential segment of its workforce.

Since this rural workforce did represent the largest single division of Egypt's working class, what these workers did should have made a significant impact on economics and politics. This suggests that as the local struggles between them and their superiors accumulated, this buildup was to have important repercussions on the agricultural economy that then were propagated throughout the entire society and its political economy.

Yet can *tarāḥīl* migrant farm workers be "blamed" entirely for Egypt's economic and political woes? No, for these problems certainly stemmed from a number of different pressure points and constraints. But, indirectly, unintentionally, and without acknowledgement, these laborers made a major contribution to generating these dilemmas. The contribution was indirect because by simply redirecting and removing their laboring efforts, they caused agricultural production shortages, which in turn contributed to food deficits, export declines, a widening gap in Egypt's balance of payments, and a higher national debt. It was unintentional because, in committing separate, individual, innocuous acts, they nevertheless still cumulatively weakened Cairo's ability to finance economic growth and to maintain political legitimacy. And it was unacknowledged because the proliferation of individual acts seldom prompted a serious recognition in government policies or scholarly studies of rural labor's crucial importance in agricultural production and national development. Thus, without any grand plan in mind, these workers inadvertently set in motion a series of mishaps that eventually combined to thwart and stifle Egypt's national advancement.

At the same time, these workers' movements were also spontaneous reactions to mistimed and poorly designed policies that the Egyptian state formulated for High Dam construction, desert land reclamation, crop marketing, institutional expansion, labor organization, overseas migration, economic reforms, social entitlements, and uncontested domination. But without the essential core struggle at the actual site of production over effort, wages, and perceived standards of consumption, the subsequent movement of workers might never have gone in the directions it did. For as employers reduced the wages workers spent on socialized existence and increased the physical effort that wore down their stamina; as merchants raised the price of the consumption needed to reconstitute that labor; and as officials sought to govern these capitalists, promote development, and insure its own hegemony, workers felt compelled to alter this constellation of control over their lives and seize the new opportunities opened up by the blunders made by state policy planners. This need not have been the case—for nothing is inevitable—but as this study demonstrates, *tarāḥīl* migrant farm workers who simply wanted better incomes and better employment did—indirectly, unintentionally, and without acknowledgment—critically undermine Egypt's economy as they left a trail of labor shortages, production failures, and civil disorders in their wake.

Such individual tactics, James Scott once recognized (1985:301), could possibly have a multiplicity of lasting, long-term consequences despite the immediate, subjective intentions of their contributing agents.[10] Economic actors often engage in actions that, by themselves, have only immediate instrumental consequences, but that also cumulatively and imperceptibly nibble away at the economic condition of the country. Individually, these actions are of little significance; collectively, however, they can take on much larger dimensions. No grand strategy of social change need be invoked—usually that is the domain of intellectuals and political organizers in any case—but simply the recognition of the aggregate effects of numerous acts of quiet discontent and determined resolution.

Anthony Giddens has pointed out (1984:11) that "the further removed the consequences of an act are in time and space from the original context of the act, the less likely those consequences are to be [the] intention[al]" ones. He argued that as long as actions remain within the range of the agent's immediate control, intentions and consequences remain closely and causally linked. Only as agents relinquish control do the consequences of their actions fall outside and go beyond the bounds of their original intentions. And only then do other contingent events, generated by yet other social agents, enter into the making of history.

Thus the actions of individual rural Egyptian workers were innocent enough by themselves. Yet propagated throughout the rural labor force, the singular result became amplified all the more. Then, as these effects spread throughout society, the addition of further actions committed by other agents caused the original outcome to take on new directions, dimensions, and magnitude. Granted, many others were undeniably responsible for Egypt's national development, not just rural workers alone. So, when appropriate, these other contributions will be acknowledged and included. But it remains the purpose of this study to focus primarily on the struggles and actions of *tarāḥīl* migrant farm laborers that, when duly multiplied, had a crucial impact on Egypt's economic and political development.

Framework

In order to understand how *tarāḥīl* migrant farm workers unexpectedly contributed to making Egypt's recent history and to shaping its national development, this study begins by examining the struggles taking place inside the rural regime of accumulation and the methods of control each side employed to regulate these nuclear conflicts. This involves not only describing the workers' way of life, standard of living, and the labor processes in both village agriculture and migrant labor, but also identifying the asymmetric relationships and negotiations involved in mutually defining the effort = wage = price formula. Initially these institutional relations remained local, for direct state intervention was relatively absent from rural valorization before the 1960s. Once the state did step in, however, local conflicts diminished while the struggles between workers and their government acquired greater importance. State policies formulated since 1960 repeatedly altered the equation between labor and capital. This paramount struggle between the government and those who opposed its regulation then became an important motor force in creating Egypt's recent history.

Chapter 2 describes a composite migrant labor trip out to work sites on the perimeter of Egypt's northern Delta region, where I conducted fieldwork in 1980–82. Here the emphasis is placed on introducing *tarāḥīl* migrant farm workers, describing their life and livelihood, and distinguishing the variety of social and economic relationships that keep these laborers at the bottom of Egypt's social pyramid. The next chapter examines why poor village farm laborers in Egypt repeatedly take up *tarāḥīl* migrant work. It first "normalizes" their abject situation by showing it to be a common feature of capitalist agriculture and then demonstrates that rural workers in Egypt are channeled into this occupation by the limitations imposed by seasonal unemployment, debt, gender stereotypes, and the country's economic underdevelopment. Pivoting into their alter identity, chapter 4 considers how migrant workers exercise some control over valorization by using "weapons of the weak" and other stealth techniques, which enable them to overcome their hardship and poverty despite the detrimental ubiquity of corruption. The momentary success of these controls appeared to be recent—emerging from the labor-management negotiations I observed in the early 1980s—but it masked the harder work and stagnant wages caused by corruption, which was provoking widespread dissatisfaction with *tarāḥīl* labor.

Thus, chapters 2 through 4 discuss the rural regime of accumulation and the local mode of regulation found in the countryside, bridging both village agriculture and migrant labor camp activities. They represent the situation I found in the Delta, but one that is replicated throughout the Egyptian countryside, both north and south. This general picture provides insights into the myriad of tactics and techniques that regulated the valorization process at home and afar and that conditioned village lives and camp experiences. Yet despite the double-sided nature of these controls, they remained insufficient to prevent first a wholesale flight of farm workers escaping the unsatisfactory conditions of village agriculture, and then later a widespread exodus that rejected the drudgery of both farm and migrant employment and seized upon new urban job opportunities that rural workers believed could improve their lives.

After 1960, these struggles and their regulation became "nationalized" and were henceforth elevated to a higher level. The conflicts between labor and capital ceased to have merely local consequences and began to acquire a broader, more national dimension. Chapters 5 through 8 examine the outcomes when Egypt's mode of regulation came to include a greater regulatory role for the government. For in its zeal to stabilize and safeguard the national economy, the state ironically came instead to transpose and transform it.

Four important years are examined: 1961, 1964, 1977, and 1992, when the course of Egyptian development was strongly influenced by *ʿummāl al-tarāḥīl* and their contentious relationship with the state. Chapters 5 and 6 analyze the outcome of the surge of rural workers who left agricultural employment behind in the 1960s and increasingly took up full-time migrant labor in building the High Dam at Aswān and reclaiming new agricultural land in Taḥrīr Province. Chapters 7 and 8 examine the results of the large-scale movement of *tarāḥīl* workers who, later in the 1970s, deserted *both* complementary types of employment, farm *and* migrant labor, for similar but more rewarding construction jobs in Egypt's expanding cities and towns.

In 1961, the timing of farm workers moving into migrant labor could not have been worse. National programs and policies in infrastructure, nationalization, price controls, and organization-building combined to remove large numbers from the countryside without leaving any recourse for understaffed village employers. This caused a national agricultural crisis that for years thereafter continued to weaken Cairo's ability to promote steady economic growth. In 1964, the state wanted even more migrant workers and so created a national labor union that championed their rights. Although its bureaucratic disarray may have contributed to its ultimate failure, its initial successes nonetheless momentarily removed even more workers from the countryside, compounding earlier agricultural problems and confounding Egypt's regional ambitions in 1967, which required a sound economic recovery.

Thus, chapters 5 and 6 document the decline of Egypt's agricultural and national economies, generated in good part by rural labor's physical exodus from the countryside in response to both village conflicts and state plans and projects. In 1974, the declining national economy turned around, spearheaded by skilled urban construction workers emigrating abroad, who were then replaced at home by large numbers of rural laborers dissatisfied with both farm and migrant employment.

Once *tarāḥīl* workers left both agricultural and migrant labor and moved into urban areas, they ceased to be a significant force in the countryside except insofar as their growing scarcity continued to generate production problems in the village and at migrant-labor work sites. This study might have come to an end simply because there were, relatively speaking, fewer workers left. Yet the practices of *tarāḥīl* labor continued to influence these workers even after they arrived in the cities and towns. Our study then joins them in the urban informal sector and the shantytowns to understand how their rural experience shaped their city life and how these workers continued to affect Egypt's development. Chapters 7 and 8 describe the further deterioration of class relations and government legitimacy, aggravated by ex-rural workers who, having now migrated to the cities, nonetheless continued to be economically and politically disenfranchised.

After 1974, Egypt's new Open-Door investment policy failed to create the number of jobs and growth in incomes that ex-rural workers and their families so urgently needed. In places like Cairo, but also in cities and towns throughout the country, class differences intensified under the pressure of rapid price inflation. When material circumstances deteriorated even further, this disheartened mass of workers erupted into riots in January 1977. Later on though, other, more organized disturbances took place, increasingly under the more solemn auspices of the Islamist movement. Stringent financial difficulties after a recession in 1985 meant that budgetary assistance from the state would be unlikely. This was especially true in Egypt's southern region, the Saʿīd, where I conducted additional fieldwork in 1984–86 and since 1994. Worried about the increasing violence there, the government launched a concerted attack in 1992 against those southern adversaries who preached practical solutions. Ex-rural Saʿīdīs, like their colleagues elsewhere, also suffered from government neglect, but now they began fighting back by supporting religious associations that appealed to the values, experiences, and social background of many former migrant farm workers.

These chapters seek to demonstrate that Egypt's recent history has been critically affected by the movements of rural workers from both the north and the south. But they also appear as "studies in negation" that evaluate the tangible outcomes of *absences*, of something not there. For it was the absence of adequate income, comfort, and control in either of their rural jobs, together with the absence of an alternative to the constant movement between agriculture and *tarāḥīl* labor, that made these workers particularly discontented and ready to find better, more rewarding possibilities elsewhere. It was then the absence of farm and migrant workers in the countryside after 1961 that undermined the agricultural and national economies, and it was the absence of occupational and political opportunities for ex-rural workers in urban areas after 1974 that undermined the state and its plans for national development. For as *tarāḥīl* migrant farm workers struggled to reverse the absences created by those at the top, they indirectly, unintentionally, and without acknowledgement negated their country's ability to sustain long-term economic growth and political legitimacy.

How then can we evaluate the lack of national transformation? For nothing says that it is inevitable that Egypt's economy should remain underdeveloped, nor that it should automatically become an Arab tiger. By comparing Egypt's current situation with the phases proposed by regulation theory, this study concludes that it has been the movements of *tarāḥīl* migrant farm workers that have significantly contributed to preventing Egypt's successful transition to cooperative peripheral Fordism. Labor shortages, agricultural failures, food deficits, export declines, balance-of-payment and trade problems, the unraveling of Arab socialism, a recession in 1965–66, the June 1967 war, emigration, urban migration, mounting poverty, the 1977 Cairo bread riots, intensified religiosity, and Islamic radicalism in the Saʿīd have prevented the state from achieving a capitalist development that, while it may be more efficient for capital, nonetheless promises to be even more detrimental to Egypt's working classes. *Tarāḥīl* workers played a major role, along with other agents, in these events that thwarted the economic growth and development that the Egyptian state so eagerly desired.

History does not stop, but, luckily, narratives do. For the moment, peripheral Fordism in Egypt has not been realized. In the last forty years, the mode of regulation that once kept rural labor's struggles over the effort = wage = price formula localized in the villages and migrant campsites changed in response to the interest of other class and international forces such that these conflicts began to overflow the bounds of local production and consumption to take on a national scope. This expansion in turn temporarily stymied the smooth, sophisticated plans of state officials. Yet the continued quest for better jobs and lives, coupled with the uncertain multicentric hegemony of the 1990s, may well provide Egypt with the motor force and the space it needs for further capitalist development.

2

Tarāḥīl Migrant Farm Labor

The Egyptian countryside exhibits a technical division of male labor that consists of two distinct branches—farm work and *tarāḥīl* migrant labor. Yet these categories are not mutually exclusive. Indeed, it is the motion across their permeable boundary, the "casual" movement back and forth between these two branches, that gives Egyptian agriculture both its resilience and its fault lines. Many impoverished rural workers uneasily occupy both realms of farming and internal migration. The designation "migrant farm worker" attempts to capture this dual identity.

Tarāḥīl labor is a type of "casual" employment that involves gangs of unskilled males,[1] recruited from the same village, who travel together to distant production sites far from home for several weeks at a time. They are hired indirectly by companies through intermediate labor brokers (*muqāwilīn al-anfār* [singular: *muqāwil;* subjective plural: *muqāwilūn*]), who advance them their low wages on credit but who then frequently demand unpaid "free days" for interest. Since job sites are remote, transportation, food, and shelter must be provided in order to ensure the migrants' survival. This opens up even greater opportunities for exploitation and abuse.

Ostensibly, the term "casual" means that rural workers engage and disengage in *tarāḥīl* labor by free choice, contingent on just individual circumstances and preferences. Yet this "freedom" conceptually masks the real limitations placed on locally improving village incomes, specific restraints imposed by seasonal unemployment, perpetual debt, and debased wages added onto a widespread pattern of polarized land ownership and insufficient rural investment and job generation.

Tarāḥīl migrant laborers are employed in part-time construction work, reclaiming desert land, excavating and repairing irrigation canals, building and rebuilding railroads, laying telephone lines, digging building foundations, and paving roads. Despite the varying character of different employ-

1. *Tarāḥīl* work crew excavating a canal, Kafr al-Shaykh, December 1981.

ers, most activity is still extremely repetitious: bending over to dig dirt, weed crops, rake fields, excavate pits, lift rubble, shovel asphalt, and many other forms of arduous stoop labor. Work is monotonous, extending over hours, days, months, years, and even lifetimes. *Tarāḥīl* labor is exhausting, and living conditions away from home are harsh. Piece-rate wages are low. For these reasons, *tarāḥīl* work becomes a good illustration of rural peripheral Taylorism.

The famous Egyptian author Yūsif Idrīs once described *tarāḥīl* workers in his novel *al-Ḥarām* as "miserable human refuse obliged to leave their homes in order to find work, in order to eat and make some kind of life for themselves" (1984:11).[2] Yet despite its inferior status, migrant labor is not an unimportant component of Egyptian agriculture. It constitutes a very necessary part of farming because it provides a critical labor reserve for its workers. Like a sponge, *tarāḥīl* labor absorbs rural workers in seasons of unemployment and releases them back when local labor demands pick up once again in the village. Low migrant wages supplement seasonal employment in village agriculture, which is also low paying—all in accord with the principle of capitalism, which states that employers deduct from a worker's wage that which is earned from other employment. Thus it is the very "casualness" of this movement between village farming and distant migration that allows Egyptian agriculture to continue operating successfully by providing rural workers with extra income from other employment. This in turn allows farm employers to pay low wages and thus to maintain or even to expand their own personal profits.

This chapter introduces *tarāḥīl* migrant farm workers by examining how this double identity shapes their way of life. Since village farm work is relatively well known, and is discussed later in chapter 3, the emphasis here is primarily on the labor-camp experience itself. It describes a typical work trip, a composite of several *tarḥilāt* I joined during my fieldwork. The stint starts from the period of their unemployment in the village and ends with their exhaustion in the work camp and eagerness to return home.

Since wages and costs are foremost factors in their lives, workers are very attentive to matters of pounds and piasters. But in order to safeguard this income and the standard of living it supports, they also give great consideration to the social relationships they are immersed in, for they enable workers to subtly manipulate the effort = wage = price formula. This chapter places more stress on the wage = price relation, which links labor's income and consumption, and leaves the detailed analysis of the effort = wage connection—the heart of the labor process—for chapter 4.

Many of the personal attachments forged in the labor camps are fashioned by the mutual familiarity but the unequal benefit of paternalism, a Janus-faced mechanism of labor control that vertically juxtaposes those who hire and supervise workers and those who toil and live together. The *muqāwil* and those who act on his behalf are patrons who provide services to clients in exchange for their commitment and who take part of their earnings in exchange for their continued employment. Workers, for their part, are linked together horizontally by strong bonds of kinship, friendship, and age. These bonds create a powerful group unity that protects workers from extreme exploitation and allows them to survive the work trip and beyond.

Numerous instances of patron-client paternalism and fraternal solidarity infuse the methods that control Egyptian migrant efforts, wages, and prices, an arrangement that uneasily straddles the hazy distinction between the formal subsumption of labor contained in peripheral Taylorism and its real subordination found in peripheral Fordism. That is, the paternalism and the solidarity of *tarāḥīl* employment allow workers greater command over their laboring efforts and consumption than does a more rigid, bureaucratic form of supervision, although the coexistence of these two different management styles indicates the extent to which this control is presently in dispute, a struggle that in recent years, those who remain migrant farm workers have been winning.

Sixty Days of Toil

Men and boys regularly leave home on *tarāḥīl* work trips when village agricultural production slows down and local employment dries up, when family debts mount, and when farm employers threaten or enforce wage cuts. They engage in migrant labor so that they can earn extra income and maintain what is already a precarious standard of living. Yet these workers do not leave without hesitation, for, after all, the labor camp is desolate, the toil is unrelenting, the conditions are dismal, and the diversions are dreary. The familiar social rhythms of daily village life are abandoned and replaced by unavoidable supervisors, distrustful strangers, tasteless food, and unfamiliar terrain. Many are accustomed to this movement and do not complain outright. But when they return home, their silence often translates into actions that indicate just how unsatisfactory they consider this work to be. Others, however, are resigned to the hardship, for their immediate future entails more trips, more work, and more exhaustion, interrupted only by the relief of temporarily coming back home to their village once again. This adversity becomes evident when the character of a *tarāḥīl* trip is examined in detail.

A migrant work trip begins, in a sense, with the end of the last one. Once home, workers spend from ten to fourteen days doing chores around the house, helping an uncle sell vegetables in the market, assisting a brother or father in the fields, repairing the house, feeding the animals, delivering cotton to the cooperative association, or visiting a distant relative in a nearby village who knows of better employment. Old acquaintances are renewed and family relations are strengthened. Sleep, work, gossip, errands, tasks, bicycle rides, visits, weddings, job hunting, and pranks fill their days until the appointed time for the next departure arrives.

Men and boys signal their intention to participate in the next work trip by receiving an advance on their wages. Shortly thereafter, they gather in the center of the village and leave by dilapidated bus or truck to live an austere existence in labor camps of cement barracks or canvas tents for two months.[3] Then they return to their village, where they rest and continue to work for one or two weeks before they either leave once again for another distant migrant job or remain home longer in order to keep working in and around the village. Significantly, in recent years, more and more workers have begun disregarding *tarāḥīl* work after the stint is over or once the crop is cultivated.

Estimates of annual migrant income are difficult to calculate because of the irregularity of *tarāḥīl* employment. In 1985, Egypt's annual per capita income amounted to $US430.00 (World Bank 1989:90). In 1980, my first year of fieldwork among *tarāḥīl* workers from Minūfiya Province, the prevailing farm wage for men in Minūf District was £E1.20 a day. The government public sector paid migrant workers 80 piasters (£E0.80) a day, but wages could rise to as much as £E1.60 with overtime. Private sector wages were higher—anywhere from £E2.00 to £E6.00 a day—but for much more arduous work. The workers I interviewed typically made three two-month migrant trips per year and were employed for half the remaining days back in the village. Assuming no deductions for poor work, absenteeism, or incurred costs—not really a credible presumption but it allows for a generous estimate—their income fluctuated around £E210 a year. Translating this into dollars is difficult since the "soft" Egyptian pound prior to 1991 was exchangeable at many different legal and illegal rates. Still, a rough estimate based on a basket of minimally necessary consumer goods places the two at near equivalency, or $US1.00 = £E1.00. The income of a *tarāḥīl* worker therefore was almost half the 1985 national average—itself already a fairly low figure.

Still, in Minūfiya and throughout the Delta and rural Egypt, those men and boys who, for the moment, have no permanent work or obligations and no immediate prospects for them, are signed up by brokers, sub-brokers, or foremen. These *muqāwilūn al-anfār* have contacts and contracts with construction firms, the Irrigation Ministry, and road-paving and bridge-building companies. When these operations need unskilled workers, they give the brokers their orders, and these recruiters in turn enlist men for work, either directly or through yet other, smaller *muqāwilīn*. Brokers receive commissions from these firms based on the total wage bill. They also profit by frequently retaining a portion of the wages and demanding unpaid work in addition to manipulating subsistence prices, shelter and transport costs, and credit rates to their benefit.

Public-sector land reclamation companies owned by the government work differently. They are required by law to use instead the services of the Labor Ministry's district Employment Offices unless these offices are unable to supply enough workers. These offices operate as institutional and therefore impersonal brokers, but this merely displaces the burden of actually hiring workers onto the local representatives in the village, the labor-gang foremen, *al-ruʾisāʾ* (singular: *al-raʾīs*), who make the arrangements and pay advances but lack the higher prestige, independent position, and income of full-scale *muqāwilīn*.

The laborers I talked with only signed up with local, village-based brokers. Directly contacting *muqāwilīn* who operate in other villages or towns is risky. In finding more permanent types of employment, such outside connections are frequently used, but they are, nevertheless, ones personally known to the job hunter, his family, or his sponsors. However, because of the nature of *tarāḥīl* work, brokers or sub-brokers are always local village men well familiar to the workers and thus men who remain predictable. The relationship between brokers and workers involves multiple bonds built over years of living together. Should transgressions occur, workers and brokers together can resort to a myriad of common village friends and relatives to resolve the difficulties.

Large independent labor brokers who pay out wage advances receive large amounts of money for this purpose from employers. This means that frequently they are either landowners or storekeepers, for companies only accept property or store goods as collateral for the enormous sums given for advances and final payments.

Such brokers are not unique to rural Egypt. They are frequently found where there are enclave economies or, to use Jeffery Paige's typology (1975:79), distant migratory labor estates. Ostensibly, the *muqāwil* merely matches the labor supply from agriculture with labor demands from companies. Indebtedness, however, becomes a strong mechanism for prying workers away from other sources of income, such as farming, and for prodding uncommitted laborers to appear at the site of production. Most, if not all, *tarāḥīl* workers are indebted or, if too young, then their parents are. Debt especially ensures that laborers will work for particular brokers *cum* creditors and not enter other forms of "casual" employment such as local day labor.

Yet indebted *tarāḥīl* workers remain rather reluctant workers. Employers who contracted through *tarāḥīl* labor brokers told me they found that these exploited workers were reluctant to work far from home, even for the "precious" wages that, after all, might also be earned in other occupations. So something and someone has to prod them into laboring. *Muqāwilūn* thus operate in these dual-sector economies where the agricultural sector of small family plots and waged farm work offers other income options. Only the poor, low-income members of this sector have need to resort to the wage advances and consumption loans that then obligate them to perform *tarāḥīl* work.

At home, the squeeze on prices, wages, interest, and income compels village workers and small farmers to supplement their earnings through *tarāḥīl* employment. Yet the squeeze on migrant wages and camp consumption also compels them to return back to local agriculture, where they have kinship relations or property ties. The village labor brokers I knew were never so powerful that they alone could engineer such price and wage constrictions—they relied in fact on a state that established low agricultural commodity prices, and government and private companies that fixed low migrant wage levels. Still, they were large landowners and big local merchants who could and did influence local wages, consumption prices, and usurious interest rates to force impoverished and indebted laborers into performing *tarāḥīl* work.

However, after 1960, the bonded labor and servile deference that once were key attributes of *tarāḥīl* labor began to disappear. As new job opportunities appeared, income and consumption fell less under the immediate control of village brokers. Workers and their families found other ways of increasing income, sustaining their standard of living, and settling consumption loans and debts. By 1981, when I did my fieldwork, the mode of regulation had changed, such that rural workers gained greater control over their effort = wage = price relations. As a result, the *muqāwil*'s grip over local valorization eased, along with his coercion and harsh exploitation. *Muqāwilūn* began offering no-cost loans—wage advances without demanding free days—and other services to entice workers to join their *tarāḥīl* work gangs.

Most workers I met asked for and received wage advances from the *muqāwil* or *ra'īs* to provision themselves while on the job and to support their families back home. The remainder of their pay, if any, comes after the trip is finished—minus deductions for days not worked, sick time, faulty work, and for consumption loans incurred along the way. In the case of the government's Employment Offices, the advance is usually most of the next wage, an amount fixed by law. By 1981, wages had risen from 80 piasters to £E1.00, so that a forty-five-day trip brought in £E45.00 and workers received up to a maximum of £E40.00 in advance. For the public sector Nile Bridgework and Road Co., the daily wage for a forty-day trip was £E1.60, 60 piasters more than in land reclamation. Out of a total of £E64.00, £E60.00 was paid as advance money. With private companies, wages varied between £E2.00 and £E3.00 a day. On one quite typical occasion, the daily wage was £E2.40, or £E96.00 for a forty-day trip. The advance was £E70.00. The Minūfī workers I interviewed spent on average 40 percent of this advance on trip provisions, 50 percent on family support, and 10 percent for pocket money and expenses while away from home.

Very seldom do the broker's foremen not deliver advances to the workers, but should this happen, the dishonesty is rarely punished. However, such brokers or foremen might quickly lose workers' loyalties and their clientage. This lack of support can then translate into a loss of status. Other brokers and foremen, in fact, might actually take up the cause and force the dishonest recruiter to hand over the payments in order to gain new, faithful workers. At the other end, laborers who accept their advance but who do not show up for work are expected to return the money. If not, they are hounded by the foreman until they or their relatives pay up. The close intimacy of the village makes such deceptions difficult. Though judicial courts are available, they seldom appear as viable options for settling disagreements. So then once these advances become settled and the trip is scheduled, workers then make preparations to embark.

On departure day one morning in May 1981, *tarāḥīl* workers from Kafr ʿAbdū, a small village north of Minūf District township, showed up early with family, friends, and packages. When the government Employment Office bus used to transport workers and their belongings rumbled and lurched at mid-morning into an open area of the village, it encountered crowds of people and parcels ready for loading. Wives, sisters, and mothers brought food in straw baskets, clothing, soccer balls, utensils, lamps, cooking burners, kerosene, radios, tools, blankets, and cassette players and hoisted them up into the bus. A silent roll call was taken and a head count was made. A representative of the Employment Office returned the workers' identity cards, which had been collected earlier when advances were paid to the foreman. Boys under eighteen received temporary work cards, and these were kept by the foreman to give to the company supervisor at the work site. After several loud honks on the horn and some false starts, the bus finally departed for the New (reclamation) Lands located on the edge of the Delta near Alexandria.

The three-hour trip started at ten in the morning, but due to delays, stops, breakdowns, and wrong turns the migrants did not arrive until after two in the afternoon—definitely too late to put in a full or even a partial day's effort. Anyway, by this time, the company reception office had closed, the supervisors had gone home, and the supply depot was no longer handing out provisions. Nevertheless, some initial contacts were made, with the labor supervisor at his home for registration; with the field engineer at his bunkroom to arrange for the first day's assignment, and with the camp director who was awakened to unlock the storeroom and hand out sleeping mats and blankets. However, a late arrival at the work site could also entail delays that could jeopardize the first day of work, forfeit a day's wage, and spell discomfort for the first night away from home.

Once at the land reclamation company, the government bus stopped first at the supervisor's home or office (the latter was technically called the Reception Office) in al-ʿAmariya, thirty kilometers outside Alexandria. The supervisor lined up the workers, took their identity cards to register them as "Man," "Big Boy" or "Small Boy," and assigned them to a particular labor camp. Because wages differ for those under sixteen ("Big Boys") and again for those under twelve ("Small Boys"), senior workers preferred that their younger companions be registered one notch up from their actual, age-defined category. (These wage differentials only exist in land reclamation work. Other employers do not make such distinctions.) Later, then, once the identity cards were returned and before work actually began, a £E2.00 to £E5.00 payment per dependent to the supervisor usually succeeded in registering the twelve-year old as a "Big Boy" and big boys as "Men." Such changes were not automatic, for obvious age discrepancies could not be entirely dismissed. But, usually, satisfactory arrangements could be made, with the help of a small gratuity on the side.

After a few workers bought groceries in town, the bus left al-ʿAmariya and delivered the gang to its assigned camp. Unlike workers in the private sector, those in public-sector land reclamation live in unfurnished, but permanently built cement shelters. On arrival, the workers spilled out of the bus, cleaned up the barracks, received their two blankets and one mat from the camp director or his assistant, and carved out their territory along the inside perimeter of the barren shelter by piling up baskets, boxes, and blankets on the concrete floor. Here they created their homes for the next sixty days. Workers who were already in the camp from other villages remained at a comfortable distance and watched. Workers from the same village lived together, taking up the whole barracks or staying off to one side.[4]

Clusters of kinsmen and friends from the same village band together at the work site for mutual safety and support. Relatives, family members, and good friends sleep and cook as a unit around the same hearth (actually a gas-burning Primus stove). Although all gang workers know each other since they are from the same village, these individual hearths are even more intimate. Here members work together, sleep together, cook and eat together, relax with each other, and support each other in day-to-day companionship. Working among friends and family rather than with unknown

2. *Tarāḥīl* labor barracks, Mariout Land Reclamation Company, July 1981.

and possibly suspicious strangers—for reasons, then, of companionship and security—is very important to *tarāḥīl* laborers toiling at isolated and distant work sites.

Later that year, in December, another gang of *tarāḥīl* workers from an adjacent village in Minūf, Dair ʿAmmiya, was employed by the privately owned ʿAzzāzī Construction Co. on a project in the northernmost province of Kafr al-Shaykh. They did not receive the same camp benefits as their neighbors. Private-sector employment entails a much greater variety of job sites, even within the same company. Since job contracts regularly end and operations move on, laborers do not sleep in permanent barracks but are sheltered instead in cheap canvas tents. Private firms like the ʿAzzāzī Co. further reduce costs and raise profits by neglecting shelter, bedding, and food for its unskilled workers and by transporting them in rickety old trucks instead of more comfortable government buses.

If workers arrive on time, the company engineer meets them and passes out tents, which they pitch next to each other near the work site. Like the workers from Kafr ʿAbdū, those from Dair ʿAmmiya also separate into hearth or tent groups according to kinship, marriage ties, and friendships. But while these tent groups are more detached than barracks, their canvas walls offer no obstacle to visiting and socializing. On this particular day, however, workers arrived late, and the engineer had already gone home. So they were forced to sleep that first night out in the open, suffering from the cold seasonal rain and freezing temperatures.

An important characteristic of *tarāḥīl* work gangs in 1981 was the extremely skewed age distribution apportioned to the public and private sectors. In the public sector, an overwhelmingly large number (65.4 percent) were young men and boys under twenty-three years of age. A much smaller number (21.4 percent) were old men over forty.[5] Yet the young are so inexperienced that ineptness limits their competency, and the old are so feeble that frailty hinders their effort. Both groups were channeled into lax public-sector employment. The dearth of men between twenty-three and forty (13.2 percent) appeared ominous for the public sector since it indicates the flight of the strongest and brightest workers. Those who have the greatest experience and shrewdness (which increases with age) and who have the greatest strength and endurance (which declines with age) are middle-aged men. But these workers were finding employment in the more demanding private sector. This consigned the poorest quality workers to the public sector.

Young workers use *tarāḥīl* employment to earn income between jobs back home and while waiting for permanent employment after they complete compulsory military service. In 1981 they had more job options—and had begun to exercise them—but for those who lack land or access to land, nonfarm skills, and congenial personal networks, migrant farm labor is

3. Migrant laborers' tents, canal excavation, Kafr al-Shaykh, December 1981.

their only alternative. Old men, on the other hand, perform *tarāḥīl* labor because they cannot afford to retire, but they also cannot continue doing difficult and strenuous village farm work either. Many elders first engaged in full-time *tarāḥīl* work because of the limited nonfarm employment they encountered years earlier when they were young. Many had built up seniority over the years, which gave them easier supervisory positions. In public land reclamation, the very small number of middle-aged workers who do remain in *tarāḥīl* labor become enterprising migrants such as foremen, task-group leaders, and service workers who do not qualify as desperate workers without alternatives. Or, they are, as ordinary laborers, either among those momentarily without work and needing income or else among the few permanently consigned to repeatedly shift back and forth between village farming and distant migration. Their relative scarcity, however, indicates that the current generation of *tarāḥīl* workers would not be sufficiently replaced.

When migrant laborers go on work trips, few if any travel alone without relatives, for village gang members are all related to each other through complex networks of kinship ties. Even the old "loners" sleeping off by themselves in a hearth of one are nonetheless distantly related to many of the younger workers who reside in different hearths. Even when the unity of the group is otherwise disrupted, this kinship gives the work gang a resilient solidarity that helps members endure the hardship of difficult *tarāḥīl* labor and facilitates their departure when better employment opportunities open up elsewhere.

Senior workers are regularly accompanied by junior relatives. First, these companions ease the seniors' overall work load. Since old workers perform the heavy tasks of *tarāḥīl* labor at much lower energy levels, they soon become dependent on the services of their sons or nephews to complete unfinished task assignments and to avoid pay deductions. Without the help of junior workers, seniors either lose wages for inferior work or else suffer greater health problems from exhaustion. Young laborers, on the other hand, prove to be the most energetic and ambitious workers in the labor gang. Being in far better physical condition than their fathers or uncles, they work much harder. Once they finish their own assignments, these potential rate-busters are channeled instead into finishing the morning quotas their seniors are unable to complete and then into engaging in (increasingly rare) afternoon overtime opportunities. Furthermore, young migrants are also responsible for all of the small chores—preparing food, buying extra supplies, fetching water, washing dishes, finding wood, and preparing fires—that release the old men, often exhausted after even a minimum day's work, from having to do the countless number of incidental tasks necessary for life support in the labor camps.[6] This also conveniently reduces the pressure on company budgets to provide these essential services.

Second, many senior workers are foremen or task-group leaders, who require a retinue of loyal supporters to uphold their authority in dealing with workers, labor brokers, and company supervisors.[7] For despite their small numbers, old workers, with their greater experience and knowledge, still dominate the labor gang by taking charge of plans and supervision for the entire group. Young men and boys dutifully carry out these directions. Senior workers provide the brains of the outfit, negotiating with supervisors over work assignments and bargaining for reduced quotas. Juniors supply the brawn to get their own work done and, if need be, to finish their elders' quotas as well. Seniors are expected to argue with vigor and shrewdness since junior labor gang members rely on their finesse to obtain lighter work loads. Seniors can facilitate the temporary absence of workers from the job site and defend them should their shirking anger co-workers and supervisors. Without this support, the elders cannot adequately organize the gang or arrange for reduced work loads and better incomes. Without this protection, junior workers can not sustain their stamina and income.

Thus, age and kinship curtail potential disruptions in *tarāḥīl* work and forge a strong, collective solidarity. Still, tensions can arise in this imbalance between brawn and brain, in exchanging the junior's completion of unfinished labor quotas for the senior's efforts in bargaining for light loads. For when management assigns the labor gang a standard task, the average amount of labor for each worker is already more than a normal person can accomplish. But then when the juniors are delegated even more work than their seniors, these young workers are pushed to the limits of their strength and endurance. Sharing incomes enables the old to consume the wages of the young even while youthful exertions exceed those of their elders. These inequities undeniably benefit the seniors to the clear disadvantage of the juniors.

However, this asymmetry is never permanent and is rebalanced once *tarāḥīl* trips are over. The key to understanding this rebalancing is to recognize how junior workers find new employment or receive new promotions in their migrant jobs. These advancements take place by means of the personal recommendation and sponsorship of older relatives.

For when juniors want to assume easier labor-gang positions like guard, vendor, task-group leader, or subordinate foreman, or to find better, more permanent employment elsewhere, seniors prove very useful. Their

4. Workers' foremen discussing work plans, Mariout Land Reclamation Company, July 1981.

knowledge of new job opportunities and their connections to friends and distant relatives who have, or know of, job openings expedite the search for better employment. Fathers sponsor sons, uncles recommend nephews, older brothers endorse younger brothers, older cousins support younger cousins.

Thus juniors gain in the long run by cooperating with seniors because their heavier work loads are exchanged for later assistance in getting jobs, better positions in migrant employment, and access to resources and information unobtainable through more formal channels. Kinship thus establishes a reciprocity that eliminates potential gerontocratic exploitation. For seniors, kinship eases management's harsh demands for more effort, while, for juniors, kinship opens up opportunities for future employment. This bond becomes a way of adding years to the future of senior workers and of quieting junior workers who grumble over the demands placed on their immediate labor.[8]

The unity that kinship fashions is relatively different from the solidarity found among workers in the core industrialized countries. There, individualism and technology breed independence, separateness, and isolation, which weaken group unity and expose workers more to the harshness of Taylorist speedups and stretch-outs. Seldom do laborers work just with friends, neighbors, and relatives. Since they do not, and in place of these personal relationships, workers rely instead on impersonal labor unions, government regulations, and job action against employers to improve low wages and bad working conditions. Grievance procedures, courts, and government arbitration play a bigger role than kinship. In Egypt, where such autonomous institutions have not yet completely succeeded in helping workers and therefore have not yet totally replaced family and kinship relationships, *tarāḥīl* workers use these more informal connections to soften the blows that would otherwise go unrestrained. Here kinship creates a social cohesion that proves relatively unassailable by management.

Workers from the same village live together with the foreman or *raʾīs* at the apex of their crew. He is the singular contact person, not only between workers and labor brokers and Employment Offices, but also with company supervisors, engineers, and administrators. The labor-gang foreman is not just an occasional *tarāḥīl* worker, or even a part-time farmer or seasonal laborer. In fact, he occupies the only full-time position in *tarāḥīl* work, making his entry and exit much less irregular than for common workers. He skillfully balances two sets of concerns—those of his workers below and those of his employer and broker above—often playing one set against the other, while still maintaining influence and earning profit for himself. And by upholding this pivotal authority, the foreman and the labor gang discourage direct bureaucratic management from displacing the more informal yet more advantageous patterns of paternalism.

The *raʾīs* receives daily job assignments, allocates work, distributes company food, helps sick workers, conceals absent laborers, and is accountable to workers for protecting their welfare and to the company for completing their tasks. With the workers from Kafr ʿAbdū, an older, senior worker with respect and experience and a younger but middle-aged worker with energy and enterprise operated together as co-foremen. They were father-in-law and son-in-law. Tasks were split between them: the younger dealt with the immediate supervision of workers and daily issues, while the older planned for upcoming assignments, negotiated work loads, wages, and overtime, and handled logistics for provisions. In the next workers' camp, another team consisted of two middle-aged brothers who similarly apportioned their duties.

Under the government Employment Office, foremen receive additional pay, varying from 3 to 25 piasters a day extra depending on the district and province. In Minūf District, for example, the foreman from Kafr ʿAbdū received £E10.00 for every fifteen workers he signed up. On the other hand, a foreman working for the Nile Co., a public-sector construction firm, received an additional regular salary for his services. In the private sector,

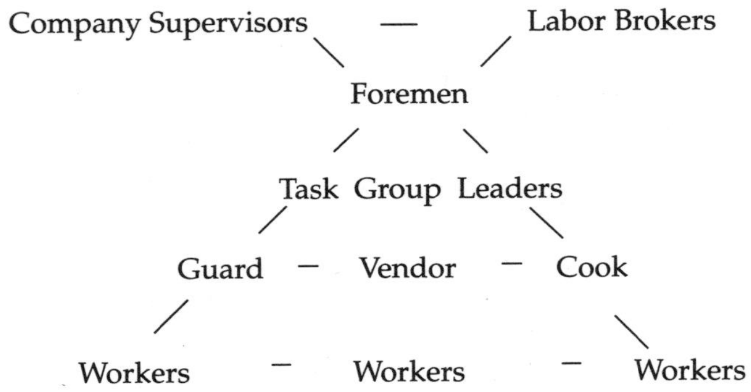

Fig. 2.1. Hierarchy of patron-client relations in *tarāḥīl* labor

workers from Daīr ʿAmmiya frequently gave £E8.00 to £E10.00 to their foreman for emergency expenses, such as sending home a sick colleague, paying for an occupational accident, or bribing a supervisor. Not spent, it was otherwise paid back to the workers in payments of £E2.00 or £E2.50 every two weeks as a secured form of savings.

Tarāḥīl work crews contain a number of positions that do not involve strenuous physical labor. Every village gang has its own guard, who is assigned to watch over the belongings workers keep in the barracks or tents. With the land reclamation companies, the formal labor contract permits three nonworking service personnel. Two of these are the foreman and the guard. The third is a worker assigned the duty of cooking the morning and evening beans and potatoes in the camp kitchen and who is often responsible for carrying in drinking water and kerosene from the nearby village. The guard and cook are usually senior workers, occasionally sick or tired men, but sometimes favorites of the foreman or his relatives, or even young boys. The foreman also assigns senior workers to supervise individual tasks when the work gang is split up and allocated different jobs. These smaller task groups contain, in addition to the nonworking task leader, a water carrier who might or might not work depending on his age and status.

A part-time vendor provides for the workers' consumption needs at most of the work camps. With the labor gang from Kafr ʿAbdū, he was a senior worker who brought along a trunk filled with cigarettes, razor blades, candy, tobacco, cans of jam, meat, fish, and tomato sauce, and other small items commonly used in the camp. On other trips, he was the cook, or perhaps an ordinary laborer, or even just the *ra'īs* himself. Should the vendor be the cook, repeatedly restocking his supplies becomes more easily integrated into his regular chores, which take him to nearby villages and towns. It is a post that is selected by the *muqāwil*, although it is not officially authorized by either contract or company. Trunk vendors, while posting cheaper prices than those offered by neighboring grocers, nevertheless represent a variant of the "internal store" that in Taylorism helps control labor by controlling the level of prices and debts relative to wages. The camp vendor, then, becomes one of the labor control mechanisms that manipulates the effort = wage = price formula and keeps laborers working.[9] His local monopoly is reinforced further by the antipathy and price gouging of nearby merchants, an unpredictable relationship that limits the migrants' independent access to consumption goods.[10]

Only when the production site is more or less continuously occupied do harmonious commercial relations prevail outside the camp, but then they usually involve just the foreman or the vendor himself. It is infrequent that workers shop at local stores or nearby consumer cooperatives since they cannot purchase government-subsidized foodstuffs because their subsidy booklets and credit are only acceptable back home. Fortunately, those workers who are not provided with company food or are not willing to buy from their vendor are resupplied from home halfway through, or thirty days after the start of, the work trip. This midtrip provisioning requires the laborer to work for a local broker who is familiar with the worker's family and home residence. But it also serves as a way for workers to break the grip of the camp vendor's control.

It seems clear from all these personal arrangements (see fig. 2.1) that a number of paternalistic, patron-client relationships control the production and consumption of *tarāḥīl* workers. Paternalism provides a mutuality that simultaneously benefits both patrons and clients, although, routinely, the patron gains more while the client gains less. For brokers and foremen, paternalism helps to recruit workers whose numbers remain limited because of competition from village rivals and from other employment opportunities. In the past, they used coercion to force laborers to work in specific village gangs. More recently, however, they began offering better credit, prices, and mediational services to attract migrants. For rural laborers, paternalism helps them find other jobs and earn additional income. Workers offer the loyal support, obedient compliance, and credit, price, and wage concessions that preserve the labor broker's economic and political position in the local community and that maintain the foreman's occupational status with respect to his own immediate patrons. In pre-Fordist economies, such paternalism proved to be a quite common and useful institution of labor control. It was a more mutual, personalized way of regulating the regime of accumulation.

The organization of *tarāḥīl* work conforms in general to a modified pattern of what John Buttrick (1952) once called "inside contracting," whereby companies rely on independent brokers and foremen to transmit their work orders instead of depending on their own immediate bureaucrats. Even though laborers toil exclusively on company-owned property and with company-owned equipment, the foreman remains the person chiefly responsible for a major portion of organizing and supervising the labor process and consumption. Nevertheless, this pattern of "inside contracting" becomes altered when company supervisors appear at the work site and use their formal authority to directly allocate labor quotas or distribute food and supplies. The fine, indiscernible line separating "inside contracting" from direct management parallels the fluctuation between the formal subordination of labor established under Taylorism and labor's real subsumption to capital found in Fordism.

The formal subordination of labor to capital emphasizes the tangible control workers still retain over the labor process despite the fact they are formally separated from the means of production. Under real subsumption, however, workers forego any control over production that they once might have had (Burawoy 1985:87, 93). *Tarāḥīl* work represents a form of employment that awkwardly straddles the boundary between the two. Its ambivalent nature is reflected daily in contests over authority between workers' foremen and company supervisors. The outcome of this tug-of-war depends initially on the relative strength and support of the negotiating parties and ultimately on such institutions as the state. First in the early 1960s and then again in the early 1970s, the government formulated policies that began to alter the relationship between labor and capital. But because the state was weak—notwithstanding its claims to the contrary—*tarāḥīl* workers were able to delay the appearance of new bureaucratic controls in favor of the more familiar style of paternalism. The persistence of "inside contracting" and its paternalism in 1981 provides strong evidence of the leverage workers were still able to retain.

Yet in distant labor camps, *tarāḥīl* workers seldom realize just how much control they actually hold, although they do their utmost to survive—itself a modest victory of sorts, given the harsh work, low pay, and dismal living conditions so far away from home.

Once the workers arrive at the job site, arrange their work camp, and stake out territory, they begin devouring the prepared food they carried along with them. Meals from home always taste better, but once the leftovers are consumed, workers cook their own meals over the Primus burners they bring with them: rice with sugar, and beans in tomato sauce with garlic, finally degenerate to cheese, bread, canned sardines, macaroni, or just plain, ungarnished beans.

On their first day on the job—and for the next sixty days—everyone wakes up at dawn, eats a small breakfast of dried bread, cheese, maybe some beans, and then marches off to work by seven o'clock. The foreman knows the assignment from talking to the supervisors the day before, for seldom are company employees awake at this hour. At times, work involves weeding a grape vineyard with a crew of thirty men, or digging irrigation channels for bean plants with another companion, or harvesting watermelons with five other workers. Or, the workers pile dirt on the roadside for street paving, spread it to grade the roadbed, or deliver curbstone. Perhaps a dozen men are assigned to clean an asphalt mixer, dig a canal, or lift out buckets of dirt for the foundations of a building. (The efforts workers exert in the labor process are examined in detail in chapter 4.) Work continues until one or two o'clock, when supervisors stop work. After this, overtime tasks can be assigned, although after 1971, such opportunities declined drastically. A mid-day lunch is usually inserted somewhere in the work schedule. By sunset, the day's work comes to a halt. From sunup to sundown, workers are engaged in strenuous labor activities. Now they are exhausted.

Once back in camp, men and boys begin preparing the evening meal, which is cooked on their Primus burners or in the camp kitchens. Dinner is quickly devoured by the famished workers. Laborers from Daīr ʿAmmiya had to provide strictly for themselves, while those from Kafr ʿAbdū received food from the company as part of their contract.

Yet much of the food from the land reclamation companies is so meager and of such poor quality that many prefer to eat what they bring or what they purchase from the camp vendor. Frequently the complimentary flour and shortening distributed under the auspices of the UN World Food Programme and intended for use in company bakeries are embezzled from the workers by company employees who sell them on the black market. Rations are then replaced by cheaper ingredients in order to provision the workers. The result is a quality of bread so bad that a week's supply of six loaves per person, small as that seems, lasts only two days before becoming inedible. Workers then dry it out in the sun to prevent mold before they pack it away in sacks and take it home later for barnyard consumption. Instead they go to the nearby village and buy commercial bread for 1 piaster a loaf.

Elsewhere, *tarāḥīl* workers only consume what they receive from home or purchase locally. In general, consumption on *tarāḥīl* trips is much less than if workers stayed at home. Family support and village obligations reduce what income remains, forcing workers to severely cut their own maintenance costs. So, very often, the wage = price relation works against them. The high cost of living and their low wages results in greater debts and greater exhaustion.

Men and boys endure sixty days of this, broken only by the mid-trip provisioning or a day off. Occasionally a day or two of pay is lost because of technical bottlenecks. Inactivity because of rainy weather receives only a half-day's pay. When work is performed poorly or incompletely, when supervisors find scapegoats to protect themselves, or when work discipline strays too far out of line, employers withhold a day of pay. Old workers are particularly prone to losing a day's wages for bad work because of their infirmed condition; that it does not happen more often is due to the help from the young workers completing the old men's assignments. A supervisor's aggravation is frequently placated by the mediational efforts of the foreman, who tries to remain on good terms with management to prevent scapegoating and to cover up poorly performed work. Occasionally the foreman gives in to the supervisor's demands for more work just to keep life tranquil, even though, all the while, he represents the interests of those under them whose cooperation and reenlistment remain necessary in order for him to keep his privileged position.

Fatigue and sickness frequently keep workers from expending sufficient energy on the job. Only the really severe cases, however, have their wages deducted. If the problem is critical, workers seek local medical assistance, but, as in the rest of Egypt, they are discouraged by the same problems of professional condescension and high expense that in general deter the poor from consulting physicians. Company medical care is nonexistent. Despite claims I heard from land reclamation administrators that health services were always available, the many empty clinics testified to the lack of adequate first-aid facilities.

Sometimes men who are ill show up for work—present and accounted for—but perform little if any actual labor. Found crouching down in the fields between rows of grapes, standing in front of a filled basket of dirt no one ever hauls off, or getting lost in the shuffle while men and machines fly around from task to task, workers are able to avoid work if they are sick. In turn their companions toil more to compensate. Task-group assignments are the joint responsibility of the team. Workers who finish help those who are slower and all leave together. Healthy workers do the work of those who are sick or absent. Those whose health is in a very serious condition remain in the barracks or tents. They often switch jobs with the guard or cook, whose presence in the camp goes unchallenged. And even if not, the workers' guard is always around to conceal those inside their shelters from those outside. If unhealthy workers are able to avoid detection by company supervisors, their wages are not likely to be penalized.

Laborers recruited through the government Employment Offices are supposedly paid the remainder of their wages if they are hospitalized or excused by doctor's orders. These workers also are technically permitted two sick days without losing pay, but they are seldom granted. Workers employed by private companies do not even have the benefit of these official exemptions. Often those temporarily unemployed because of their poor health take advantage of their patron-client relationship with their labor broker to at least borrow money to keep going until they can recover and work once again.

Occasionally workers simply leave the job site and temporarily return home, thus losing, perhaps, a day or two of pay. But just as the sick can hide, so too can the truant. Furloughs often go unnoticed except by fellow workers and the foremen. Depending on the absentee's relationship with the *raʾīs* or, less often, to the company supervisor—for here it does not pay to be popular or be noticed—an absent worker can get lost in the shuffle of task assignments, of camp service personnel, of companions compensating for work not done. As long as the number of absent workers is not flagrant, one or two missing is not noticed by the company or punished by losing wages. Jan Breman (1985:250–251) has reported that migrant workers in south Gujarat, India, often leave camp prematurely, departing surreptitiously at night in order to avoid employers discovering their absence until it is too late. He concluded that this happens more often in labor groups that lack brokers and their on-site representatives, the foremen. In Egypt, foremen keep the gangs together. What averts a wholesale flood of "home leaves," then, is the condition that foremen have to supply a quorum of workers and that colleagues will eventually not compensate further for absentees without additional pay.

Finally, on that sixtieth day, everyone wakes up at dawn as usual, but this time, they relax and wait for the bus or truck to return them home. At other times, work trips are extended another sixty days and the workers do not go back, or else they go to the village for two or three days at some other time. Some go home and do not return, finding other, better jobs once they are back. Some return to farming. Some have to go into the army. Some finally receive that job the government promised them. Some return to school. Some who quarreled with the foreman or broker—usually over money—switch to another foreman and work gang if problems are not so critical, to another broker if matters are really bad, or to completely new jobs. Sometimes, it is Ramadan and men do not want to leave home so they can fast in comfort. Sometimes it is Ramadan and they *do* want to leave so they can ignore fasting without opprobrium. Sometimes it is cold and rainy during the winter months, too inclement to work and keep an old body and soul together. Borrowing money from a local grocer, landlord, or labor broker, they can, for the moment, afford to relax, recuperate, and avoid another *tarāḥīl* labor trip. Many, however, eventually return, although recently, many more began finding better, more rewarding employment elsewhere.

Throughout these work trips, *tarāḥīl* laborers are involved in many social relations of paternalism and solidarity that regulate their work site struggles over production and consumption. To rural workers, they are simply concerned over effort, wages, and prices so that they can survive until they return home and so that they can endure until either they have to travel once again or else find another job. To the analyst, they are altering the regime of accumulation more to their advantage. Yet as much as these contests over valorization are conditioned by life in the labor camp, so too are they patterned by practices back home. Many migrant workers, especially the "loners," spend a lifetime moving back and forth between work on the farm and work in the labor camp, yet their anchor always remains the village. It is here that their departure is determined; it is here that they return. Although over the last thirty years many workers have left both the village and the camp for new lives in the city, their rural roots continue to haunt them, shaped by their dual identity as *tarāḥīl* migrant farm workers.

3

Exporting Unskilled Farm Labor

The Egyptian village represents the fundamental point of departure for *tarāḥīl* laborers. Its rhythms and respites, its attachments and diversions—and, of course, its production—bind workers strongly to their home communities. Yet village life is far from idyllic. Low wages, high prices, and heavy toil regularly interrupt this rustic charm with large doses of capitalist reality. Rhythms get interrupted by work and respites become just momentary interludes between jobs. Attachments turn exploitative and diversions prove expensive.

For at the center of village life lies the labor process that underwrites the lifestyles of both rural workers and farm employers. The Russian agronomist A. V. Chayanov wrote in the late nineteenth century about the self-contained peasant farm, managed by the household head and staffed exclusively by family members. Not that this ideal does not exist in Egypt, but balancing the fine line of neither hiring in nor hiring out has for some time been overturned by secular, polarizing trends in the rural economy. Landless and near-landless workers now hire out to village employers who possess more land than they can manage with just their families' labor alone. Once the capitalist wage relation is inserted, these two agents develop different, even opposing interests. There is a zero-sum game here, for a worker's wage and an employer's profit are inversely related: the more of one, the less of the other. The wages that employers pay are subtracted from their gross crop sales, as are other production inputs. Large farmers may well bargain with suppliers over the costs of seed, fertilizer, pesticide, equipment, land rents, and credit, but it is labor that proves to be the biggest and the most variable cost of all. Employers use a wide variety of methods to lower these costs; workers for their part do all they can to raise their income. Since the payment form of piece rates ties wages to effort, compensation can certainly rise, but at the cost of greater exhaustion. Workers

5. A village in Minūfiya Province, 1981.

therefore also attempt to conserve their energy so they can continue to work, but also so they can enjoy the fruits of their labor, as shriveled as these might be.

This chapter examines the variety of institutions and methods that both these economic agents draw upon in order to control the effort = wage relation found in the agricultural labor process. The options available to *tarāḥīl* migrant farm workers are limited, or were in the past, by a mode of regulation that compelled them to shift back and forth between farming and migration. *Tarāḥīl* employment paid low wages, but its limited duration allowed workers to return to the village when farm work resumed. When it stopped, workers left again on *tarāḥīl* trips. Yet village agriculture also paid low wages, which were driven down even further by an "innate" rivalry between men and women. Farm and migrant incomes together seldom allowed workers to live comfortably. When they were insufficient, workers borrowed money, and the burden of debt often forced workers into *tarāḥīl* labor even against their wishes. *Tarāḥīl* work was thus an "option" in effect mandated by three important village institutions: seasonal unemployment, permanent debt, and gender competition.

Low wages in rural Egypt are generally blamed on the excessively large numbers of redundant workers, who reduce economic efficiency by clogging the agricultural labor market. Yet modern agriculture, like all capitalist operations, demands a significant proportion of unemployed to keep wage costs down. For agriculture to remain profitable, temporary workers must be hired and fired promptly, and this means moving workers rapidly in and out of production. But where do these workers come from? In core countries, they are shipped in from distant communities; in the periphery, they live right next to the production site. This gives countries like Egypt the illusion of redundant labor, but—were the boundaries of production drawn correctly—one that it shares with the core.

Egypt may have a large rural population, but laborers, no matter how many there are, must work for a living, unless they depend on family members—in which case they do not appear in the active labor force of the national census—or unless they depend on the state, as with welfare capitalism. This has not yet happened in Egypt. But if workers are not employed in agriculture, then to earn an income they must eventually be employed somewhere else. Once these alternatives are examined carefully, the excessively large numbers of redundant workers disappear. Meanwhile, basing employers' lifestyles, state policies, and scholarly analyses on illusory hordes of jobless farm workers is often confounded by their substantial employment in other, nonagricultural sectors of the rural economy.

Egyptian agriculture—the heart of the nation's economy—exhibits similarities with other capitalist activities and with other patterns of modern agricultural production. These involve private property, profit maximization, market control, and labor disputes. Farming itself varies seasonally, causing the supply and demand of its inputs (including labor) and yields to fluctuate as well. Then there are other traits, which are reserved only for peripheral economies. These include low wages, limited revenues, debt labor, market imperfections, and state intervention, which are the results of the countries' vulnerable position in the global economy. Finally, there are differences that are uniquely Egyptian. Here I refer to Egypt's long history of class polarity, outside domination, state hegemony, and agricultural fecundity. *Tarāḥīl* workers encounter all of these limits in their daily lives, sometimes mastering and taming them, other times being subjected to their whims.

Capitalist Agriculture and "Surplus" Labor

Low wages, marginalist economics argues, are the outcome of the law of supply and demand which predicts that as the number of supposedly unskilled (and therefore easily replaceable) workers increases, their wages ought to decline proportionately. Egypt's countryside is seemingly one where the number of surplus rural laborers is so big that it drives wages down to their opportunity cost. Such a theory, though, requires a perfectly free and competitive market without any obstacles from "combinations" that restrict the labor supply and cause wages to rise. Yet workers in Egypt are far from being disembodied commodities who are incapable of joining together to press employers into raising wages above the cost of recruitment. Such collective pressure does take place, albeit locally, emanating from among small groups of workers in the village or the labor gang. Here the law of supply and demand operates much less effectively, confounded by the insertion of real economic agents into the otherwise lifeless price curves of abstract economic theory.

Yet of far greater importance is the assumption of "vast numbers" of redundant, surplus workers whose aggregate existence reduces wage levels to minimal proportions. It is more than what Bent Hanson once called a "red herring" (1972:27); it also a misreading of the Egyptian countryside as a result of theoretical and methodological blinders. Scholarship has recently recognized the labor shortages presently besetting Egyptian agriculture (Taylor-Awny 1987), but even earlier, rural workers kept themselves in short supply, and precisely at those moments when observers and planners proclaimed their numbers excessive and unnecessary. This means that the relevance of a theory of surplus labor lies less in the domain of economics than it does in the realm of ideology, for arguing that vast numbers of workers exist in the Egyptian countryside has done more to keep wages low than the actual numbers themselves.

Beside concealing the fact that capitalism in general creates armies of unemployed so as to keep labor costs low, this theory goes on to specifically depict rural Egyptian society as overpopulated, overprocreative, and backward. Perpetuating this illusion for Egypt has had advantages for capital, the state, and those who promote both: it vindicates employers in paying low wages, absolves officials in miscalculating state development policies, and justifies scholars in underestimating Egypt's agricultural vigor.

Egypt became a textbook example of endemic surplus labor, along with two other gems from the former British colonial empire, India and Jamaica. Determining the exact percentage of redundant rural laborers remains one of the most thoroughly analyzed topics in the economics of Egyptian agriculture ever since Wendell Cleland first estimated (1936:35) during the height of the Great Depression that 80 percent of Egyptian rural workers were chronically unemployed or underemployed, and therefore constituted a large mass of expendable surplus labor. Since then, numerous neo-Malthusian economists such as Bent Hansen, Charles Issawi, Robert Mabro, Donald Mead, Amr Mohie-Eldin, Patrick O'Brien, Samir Radwan, Gabriel Saab, Doreen Warriner, and the International Labour Organisation in Geneva have either raised or lowered this single percentage, but, in applying a strict marginalist model of economic efficiency, few if any of these analysts questioned the axiom of "redundant labor."[1]

After the Korean War, the development theories of the British economist W. Arthur Lewis further fueled this discussion. Lewis argued that redundant workers could be effortlessly and harmlessly removed from the countryside, shifted to urban locations, and used to staff cheaply the new factories that eager U.K. and U.S. investors would finance. Coming at a time when the core economies of the United States and Europe were bogged down in a postwar recession, Lewis's theory of "Economic Development with Unlimited Supplies of Labour" (1954) justified a new, more profitable wave of foreign investment and peripheral Fordism. Yet the existence of *tarāḥīl* labor ought to have been the first clue that in Egypt, seasonally unneeded farm workers were not then necessarily unemployed, for the rural division of labor was and is much more complex than these economists imagined. Nor were rural workers simply inert, expendable inputs easily siphoned off without damaging agricultural production and then relocated to the cities in such large numbers that urban life would not suffer either. Not only did rural laborers have other options besides the binary choices of "farm work" or "no work," but other sectors of the Egyptian economy were already exploiting this seasonally available labor force. Economists never took into account *tarāḥīl* work and thus missed the point that unemployed or underemployed agricultural workers were not necessarily redundant and nonessential.

The question of "surplus" labor boils down to an observer problem, for what appears to Western eyes as redundant labor is a necessary aspect of capitalist agriculture, regardless of whether a country is "developed" or "developing." In the core, farm communities typically are sparsely settled landscapes where large numbers of outsiders are brought in temporarily to work when crop operations increase and are then shipped back to their distant homes when fieldwork is finished. In the periphery, however, agricultural villages are already densely populated communities where the large numbers of local laborers live right in the immediate vicinity of their work sites and are therefore visibly identifiable. But later, when village farm work decreases, they are sent to distant migrant work sites and are brought back home when local agricultural activities pick up again. Such movement seems to have escaped the attention of these agricultural economists.

The difference then reduces to a question of boundaries. Were the boundaries of Long Island potato production, for example, extended to include its labor sources, then the frame of analysis would stretch well beyond New York to the crowded communities of Florida, the Caribbean, and Latin America. Doing so would produce a picture of surplus labor here as well. In Egypt, however, the boundaries of crop production encompass just the local village, although the centers of ownership, control, and finance extend to Cairo and Alexandria and beyond to include Europe and the United States. The dilemma of surplus labor, then, becomes more a chimera in the minds of neo-Malthusian observers rather than an issue that concretely affects rural unemployment. Fitting Egyptian agriculture into the mold of marginalist economics ultimately breaks the cast.

In both Egyptian farming and agriculture in core countries like the United States, shifting workers in and out of production is essential for earning profits. Whether this means importing outside laborers to the work site or exporting local laborers away from it, capitalist farming is unfeasible without such continuous motion, for it is just this physical movement that gives modern agriculture its low costs and high profits. But in further examining Egyptian *tarāḥīl* labor and U.S. farm employment, the two patterns appear as the inverse of one another. Because Egypt occupies a subordinate position in the capitalist world economy, it is the export of unskilled farm labor out of the village that proves necessary, giving *tarāḥīl* work trips a vital function in agricultural production.

In the United States, the need for extra farm workers at certain peak periods of the agricultural cycle is met by importing unskilled laborers from distant, unseen barrios, large city slums, and peripheral foreign countries like Haiti and Mexico. When work is finished, U.S. farmers discharge these extra hands, sending them back to their original homes far from the actual work site. The crucial bottleneck here becomes one of *importing* sufficient numbers of workers so that crop operations can proceed without interruption. This is accomplished by paying laborers wages higher than those they receive at home. Although farm wages in the United States are low, they are nevertheless still high enough to attract migrants and immigrants who as paupers back home are compelled to resort to distant employment. Being at the core of capitalist production means that relatively low wages can still attract an indigent workforce.

At the other end of the international spectrum, however, in a country like Egypt, farm wages, rather than attract a destitute workforce, actually *expel* impoverished workers from the village. Wages are so low that no one from outside the countryside would come to work in farming. Importing labor becomes impossible without coercion (e.g., slavery). But then why bother when there are already enough workers in the countryside—sometimes, it seems, more than enough.

Instead of importing its extra labor force, then, Egypt finds its seasonally necessary workforce right at home, living in the thousands of villages dotting the Egyptian countryside. In this sense, Egypt already grows its own labor force right in its own backyard and contains a *local* workforce that is substantially large enough to supply sufficient numbers at the peak of agricultural demand. Here, the separation between farm production and labor reproduction found in the core does not exist. But then the critical bottleneck becomes one of *exporting* the large numbers of workers when work finishes in the village and laborers are no longer needed, before they begin pressuring local employers for additional wages. *Tarāḥīl* employment becomes one such way to occupy these workers, to provide them with additional income, and to remove them from the village so as to avoid troublesome demands for greater compensation. The solution thus becomes one of paying farm workers such low wages that they are compelled to find additional employment like *tarāḥīl* labor just so they can earn a decent income. These two opposite solutions are reinforced by the fact that the strong U.S. economy can afford to pay relatively high farm wages, while the weak economy of Egypt cannot.

Another difference between Egyptian and U.S. farm migrants pertains to the specific nature of work actually performed during migration. In the United States, itinerant migrants do farm work, although once they return home, they may take up other temporary jobs until the agricultural season starts up again. In Egypt, on the other hand, migrants do construction and desert development when working away from home, although once they return to their village, they may engage in local farming until the season ends or another *tarāḥīl* work trip is launched.

Both types of migrant labor deal with unskilled employment, but one becomes the mirror image of the other. Although this distinction may appear minor, it cannot be overlooked, for *tarāḥīl* labor provides Egyptian workers with new nonfarm skills and information networks acquired through informal job training and meeting new colleagues while on work trips. Later, when they wish to leave farming and migrant labor altogether, they have the skills and connections to find new nonfarm jobs. This makes migrant labor an important "bridge" between village farming and full-time construction work in nearby cities and makes finding new jobs easier. This becomes important in understanding their subsequent exodus and its impact on Egypt's national economy. On the other hand, migrant work in the United States represents a dead-end job. When workers want to leave such unskilled employment, there is nothing else to do with the training but continue doing farm work.

Seasonal Unemployment

Tarāḥīl employment therefore is not agricultural, but farming still dictates its basic seasonal rhythms. Workers stop farming to go on a migrant labor trip and return to it when the trip is over. Old men retire from farming to engage in *tarāḥīl* work, and young men sandwich in a migrant work trip between seasons on the family farm. The ebb and flow of the agricultural labor process, its meager wages, and the necessity to find complementary employment all give rise to *tarāḥīl* labor.

Modern agricultural production is not like other capitalist activities, for it depends on Mother Nature for its key ingredients. The supply of these elements—sun, temperature, water—vary over the course of the year. Thus as the seasons change, so too does agriculture. Since farming requires more work at certain times of the year than at others, the demand for agricultural labor is not evenly distributed throughout the year. Although some farm employment in Egypt is permanent, the vast majority is not. Rural workers are, at times, pawns to these seasonal fluctuations, resigned to alter their activities as the year proceeds. But large farmers do not pay enough to support temporary workers when they are inactive, and small farmers frequently find their cash flow erratic until harvest sales are finally transacted. Unskilled farm work, income, and wages, then, all become highly seasonal.

As the months advance, so too does the number of unemployed workers rise and fall. The calendar year begins with the most minimal of agricultural work but with the highest demands for local nonfarm labor. January is the month for canal cleaning, as the barrages are raised, water levels are lowered, and men and boys clear out the mud, muck, and vegetation from the past year. Much of this is done by teams of local wage workers employed by the Irrigation Ministry, which, in turn, reduces the number employed in migrant labor to its lowest seasonal level. February is the start of the cotton season, although increasingly, many fields remain planted with animal fodder either as a short crop before cotton or else as a long-term crop illegally competing with cotton. Wheat, already planted in November, lies growing in the field. In May and June, it is harvested, mostly by men, which again reduces the ranks of migrant labor. Rice is then planted in the nursery and a month later is replanted in the fields, mostly by women. Summer corn and sorghum are then planted, to be harvested in the fall. Throughout the months of late June and July, teams of women and children are drafted by the local agricultural cooperative association to hand pick boll weevils off the cotton leaves and scoop them out of the soil. Cotton picking commences in September, although in recent years, delays in planting and declines in the availability of labor have postponed cotton harvests until October or even November in order to allow it time to ripen and to receive the necessary three passes to complete the harvest. Immediately after cotton leaves the ground, plots are planted with fodder and nearby fields are prepared for winter wheat. By year's end, with its rainy weather and cold days, local farm work slows down until time comes once again for canal cleaning. One economist summarized the peaks and troughs in the following manner: "[T]here seem to be two clearly distinguishable seasonal peaks for agricultural households: one in May–June and one in September. The first peak is related to the wheat harvest and maize sowing [male]; the second to cotton harvest [female]. The slack season occurs from the middle of October to the middle of February" (Hansen 1969:304).

There is also nonseasonal work, such as animal husbandry, perennial vegetable production, and infrastructure building, evenly distributed throughout the year. The three graphs in figure 3.1 demonstrate the seasonality of work (Hansen and El-Tomy 1965:405–7).[2] Significant here is the pivotal month of September, which represents a critical period for employing women in export cotton agriculture.

Men's farm work shows a constant demand from April to July, then slows down by half in the subsequent months, and rises only slightly in December or January. A small peak pops up in February at the beginning of cotton season. It is in the troughs, though, when *tarāḥīl* migrant labor is expected to absorb seasonally unemployed males who need additional wages. Demand for work from women and children also rises in April but remains high, exhibiting actual shortages from July through September. Although their participation falls off precipitously in November, they do not become recruits for migrant work gangs. But channeling men into *tarāḥīl* employment and restricting women from entering migrant labor is not just a statistical quirk, as we shall see shortly.

Very often, as agricultural activities slow down to a halt, men and boys

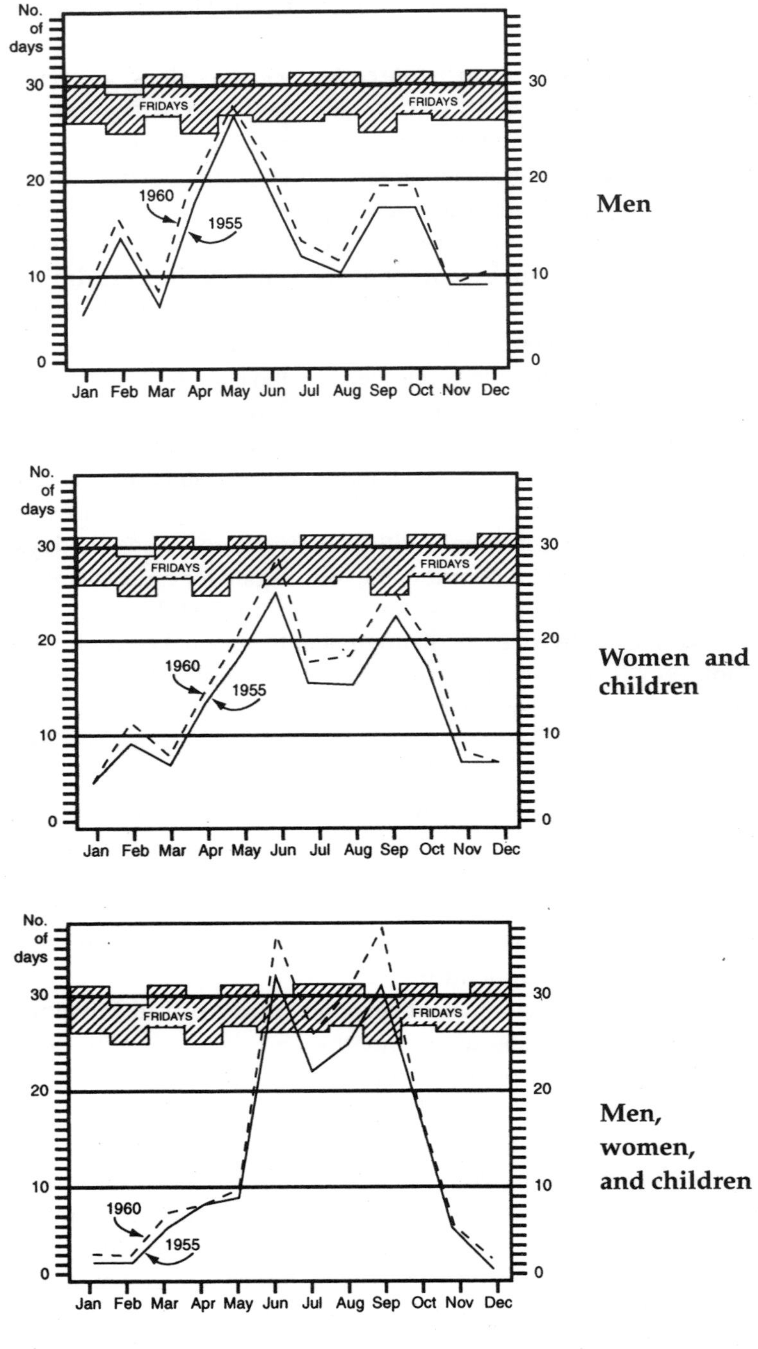

Fig. 3.1. Labor demand for men, women, and children, by month, 1955 and 1960.

begin to look around for opportunities in *tarāḥīl* employment. Then, as family finances begin to tighten, relieving seasonal unemployment becomes even more urgent. Sitting in village coffee houses, talking with relatives, calling on friends, or receiving guests, they hear that the local labor broker is hiring workers. With empty time on their hands and with no other immediate prospects available, many respond by indicating their commitment to travel once again to distant work sites. Thus periods of protracted seasonal unemployment in the village, accompanied by troublesome financial constrictions, are mitigated, however reluctantly, by males leaving on *tarāḥīl* labor trips.

The Farm Debt Crisis

Farm employers pay wages just for the time workers spend in the fields and no more. Merchants buy crops at the lowest possible price. Both expect other jobs to compensate farm workers and small farmers for shortfalls in income. *Tarāḥīl* trips often provide the extra earnings that employers and merchants are unwilling or unable to pay laborers and small cultivators. But sometimes other jobs are just not available, or else they are too demanding. Either way, those without alternative sources of income can borrow money from local landlords or grocers to sustain them and their families during periods of unemployment. When work does resume, however, it seldom compensates workers sufficiently so that their debts can be settled completely.

Fearful that loans may be recalled, workers try to postpone the final day of compensation, but then they fall prey to the demands of their creditors. Frequently these money lenders are also *muqāwilūn* who intimidate insolvent workers into joining their *tarāḥīl* labor gangs in order to repay their debts. Pre-trip wage advances then merely turn into additional loans. Migrant wages offset these loans, but not enough so as to avoid further debt.

Chronic indebtedness eventually leads to bonded labor. Until recently, when workers could independently settle their obligations, the compulsion of repaying these debts often determined as much whether workers participated in migrant labor as did seasonal unemployment. For as the outside demand for unskilled labor increases, more *tarāḥīl* trips are organized and scheduled at times that clash with wage work in the village. Unable to evade their creditor's wishes, rural workers are required to leave home regardless of the abundance of jobs in local agriculture.

Unpaid debts get carried over and end up accumulating over a worker's lifetime. When the household head dies, these liabilities can become particularly irksome. Creditors immediately recall their loans, and a man's heirs must often sell all or part of their inheritance to accommodate these demands. This, more than any blind obedience to Islamic inheritance laws, accounts for land fragmentation in rural Egypt. But being dispossessed of sufficient land means relying less on farming and more on local wage employment and eventually participating in *tarāḥīl* work trips. If the demand for *tarāḥīl* labor is down, workers are forced to borrow. If age or infirmity means postponing the next trip, debt levels rise even higher.

Yet even while property disappears entirely from the household domain, relatives in the larger extended family may still continue to own or rent agricultural land. Workers resort to these connections of birth and marriage in order to remain employed. Kinship conceals the asymmetric relationships of production with a veneer of equality by offering employment under conditions more favorable than working for strangers, although the work is usually performed without wages and compensated only in kind. Still, as the amount of land in the larger kinship group shrinks, kinsmen are forced to rely more and more on impersonal wage labor. Proletarianization is not an immediate slide into landlessness, for even with limited incomes, Egyptian small-plot farmers do all in their power to remain solvent.

The complete loss of land frequently means that ex-farmers also lose many of their social ties to the village. One of the few remaining solutions is to migrate permanently to the cities, especially when nonfarm jobs in the village are nowhere to be found. *Tarāḥīl* employment serves as a "bridge" between the rural dispossessed and the urban laborer. Those who remain on this "bridge" are workers who are unwilling or unable to relocate to the cities since they lack the skills and/or personal contacts necessary to find urban employment. Many, especially the older ones who grew up before the 1952 revolution and did not have much schooling, possess few other skills besides farming to sell.

Tarāḥīl labor remains a viable option and has been one for as long as the Egyptian countryside contained a class of rural workers dispossessed of sufficient amounts of land, or access to land, that could provide an adequate income, and where the rural economy offered extremely limited opportunities for nonfarm employment. *Tarāḥīl* labor was, until the last thirty-five years, the end result of family debt, forced land sales, and the relative absence of local alternatives. Credit from accommodating labor brokers helps workers in periods of unemployment and helps them delay departures when critical farm tasks have to be performed or when sickness prevents even a minimum of effort. Yet credit always has its obligations, and laborers are frequently compelled to repay their family debts by going on *tarāḥīl* work trips even when local employment becomes available.

Since the 1960s, however, bonded labor has virtually disappeared from the Egyptian countryside as workers have settled their liabilities through new, nonfarm occupations, so that when household heads die, accumulated debts no longer require forced land sales and incapacitate entire families. Occupational diversification within the family has relieved the immediate urgency for those who remained small farmers or rural workers to engage in *tarāḥīl* labor at inappropriate times of the year.

Diversifying incomes sources is a common mechanism found among agricultural families that ensures that a variety of jobs reduces the risk that any one occupation by itself might fail to generate sufficient income. Finding employment in other sectors, however, does depend on its availability, individual abilities, personal information and connections, and the family development cycle. But farm families continuously compare the emerging skills and pursuits of their members against the prevailing trends of the outside labor market, and adjust their consumption and standard of living accordingly. Families may well scrimp and save in order to elevate a particularly bright teenager into a valuable career. I found many a *tarāḥīl* worker related to people in well-off positions.

At no time has such diversification been altogether impossible, although there were lean years, such as the 1930s, when it was extremely difficult. Yet even before the recent emergence of new jobs in continuous *tarāḥīl* employment, urban construction, informal enterprises, and services, there were local nonfarm activities in trade, crafts, transport, building, and repair work. Occupational diversification does not mean that family members can simply stop moving back and forth between agriculture and casual *tarāḥīl* work. But it does mean that even when crop sales are down, farming is slow, wages are small, or *tarāḥīl* trips are postponed—all of which increase the family's overall debt burden—loans are no longer the potent force they once were that compel workers to leave their villages against their wishes.

Engendering the Agricultural Labor Process

Tarāḥīl labor is not inevitable. Seasonal unemployment can be relieved by more loans, and debts can be settled by family members employed in nonfarm occupations. But despite these prospects, workers still join *tarāḥīl* trips because it is what men can do. For example, even when debt was more important and used throughout the rest of the year to compel workers to leave the village at the wrong time, it seldom became a lever to pry them into departing during such a crucial month as September. For it is this month when brokers, landlords, and merchants all shared a financial interest in harvesting cotton at the cheapest cost possible and who therefore hesitated to initiate *tarāḥīl* work trips. Yet even though village work was readily available, men and boys left these jobs to women and children, and instead joined government-organized *tarāḥīl* labor gangs.

For when men disregard their pride and perform women's work, and when women disregard their seclusion and do men's work—yet both receive low wages despite the effort they expend—then their ability to alter the effort = wage relation and to realize a socially determined standard of living is substantially reduced. Thus it has been a gender division of rural labor, with its battle of the sexes and low wages, that has injected a dynamic into Egyptian agriculture that parallels the racial and ethnic segmentation of workers in the core.

Confronted with labor's collective opposition, capitalist employers often divide the workforce into different social or technical segments in order to strengthen their control over production and to undermine labor's collective solidarity. This divide-and-rule method, if successful, allows capital to fabricate a mutual rivalry that then lets employers lower wages to the level earned by the most denigrated segment. Mutual cooperation can restore labor's unity, but this often intensifies capital's efforts to keep the workforce divided (Cleaver 1979:108–113). One way of substantially dividing workers is to convince them that their differences are based on the immutable attributes of race or gender. Ineluctable biology thus acts to separate workers, weaken their solidarity, usurp control over production, and debase the wages that workers earn.

In Egypt the gender division of labor divides the workforce, plays males against females, and allows employers to lower wages while invoking gender stereotypes to justify their actions. *Tarāḥīl* trips enable male workers to resist these reductions, but they also undermine labor's collective ability to press for higher incomes. Men are channeled instead into *tarāḥīl* labor, while women are prohibited from such employment. This reinforces the same gender images that are used to divide the labor force in the first place and to defend the resulting low wages.

The gender division of rural labor is certainly a familiar institution in the Arab world, although it is rarely recognized as a means of regulating the labor process. Richard Antoun once remarked (1968:682) that through the gender division of labor "certain tasks are performed exclusively by men and others exclusively by women." A keen observer of Egyptian agricultural labor, Amr Mohie-Eldin, also commented (1982:251) that "since

Table 3.1. Composite gender division of labor in rural Egypt

Women	**Men**
Nonfield work	*Nonfield work*
Family management and internal relations	Family management and external relations
Food and meal preparation	Fathering
Mothering	Building
Housework	Canal cleaning and maintenance
Cattle and poultry husbandry	Cleaning stable and collecting manure
Cleaning stable and collecting manure	Crop sorting and preparation
Crop sorting and preparation	Crop transport and storage
Crop transport and storage	Major irrigation work
Small-scale trade	Large animal husbandry
Processing dairy products	
Light irrigation work	
Field work	*Field work*
Planting crops	Preparing land
Resetting rice	Plowing
Thinning wheat and cotton	Harrowing
Weeding	Planting crops
Cutting clover	Hoeing
Harvesting cotton and wheat	Thinning
Shucking corn	Weeding
Harvesting, threshing, and winnowing rice	Fertilizing
Winnowing wheat	Insecticide spraying
	Daily crop maintenance
	Cutting sugarcane and corn
	Harvesting wheat and cotton
	Threshing and winnowing wheat

women and children carry out separate activities at different times of the year, we do have two distinct categories of labor, male and nonmale (women and children). Moreover, I assumed," Mohie-Eldin continued, "that social institutions are so rigid that the possibilities of substitution are nearly absent." Another scholar, Nicholas Hopkins, also concluded (1983:194) that "[t]he household is the locus of the [rural] sexual division of labor, so that certain jobs are defined as 'male' or 'female.' Thus if the household does not have enough adult males to do its 'male' tasks, it has a shortage of labor; if it has more, it has a surplus."

Thus the concept implies fixed sets of complementary skills where each gender has his and her own exclusive sphere of distinct tasks and activities, equally important in their contribution to agricultural production. Yet in

Table 3.2. Percentage of women working on agricultural tasks

Activity	Delta	Saʿid
Plowing	49.7	10.9
Harrowing	49.7	41.3
Drilling	54.5	41.3
Cultivating	62.9	33.7
Irrigating	62.3	34.8
Fertilizing	56.9	38.0
Resowing	64.1	34.8
Thinning	65.8	34.8
Hoeing	55.7	37.0
Insecticide spraying	55.7	38.0
Reaping	67.7	38.0
Transporting crops	70.1	27.2
Packing crops	65.3	41.3
Milking	73.2	55.2
Raising poultry	79.0	81.5
Home crafts	64.1	45.6

using such terms as "equal," "exclusive," and "fixed," this concept conceals more than it reveals. For it masks an unequal gender relationship that is more appropriately labeled a social "hierarchy" rather than an intrinsic "division." It further suggests a separation of tasks so rigid that two distinct types of labor appear to operate in isolation from each other. Moreover, it implies a determinism that depends on assuming innate "natural" attributes for each sex. However, as we shall see, the gender division of labor is explained not so much by biology, despite this popular interpretation, but instead by capital accumulation in the village and control of the effort = wage relation.

Engendering the different activities in Egyptian farming has not received unanimous agreement. Firsthand observations frequently clash with stated customs. Although Egyptians may, like their census, deny female participation in agriculture,[3] social scientists have somewhat succeeded in drawing a wavering boundary between men's and women's work. The list in table 3.1 combines observations and informant statements from a number of sources (Toth 1991:217–19) in order to provide a composite of gender chores in rural Egypt.

It seems clear then that men are expected to perform the hardest tasks in agriculture and women are responsible for physically easier chores in and around the homestead. But women are not merely relegated to housework and animal husbandry alone. They also work in the fields alongside men, cultivating such crops as wheat, cotton, corn, clover, and rice.

Although women do all these tasks for hire outside the family farm as wage laborers, they seldom do so in a permanent capacity. They engage in permanent nonwage work at home, and then temporarily hire out at peak seasons to village farm employers (Hanafi 1973:30). This proves important in considering the withdrawal of female wage labor from the ranks of the temporarily employed.

Regionally, the Saʿīd exhibits lower female participation rates than the Delta, supporting the claim that a more patriarchal division of labor exists in southern Egypt. An FAO study (cited in Hammam 1986:171) concluded that although countrywide female participation rates, listed in table 3.2, well exceeded the 6.2 percent found in the national census, those of the Saʿīd were, on average, two-thirds the levels in the north.

Yet however important it may be to engender specific farm activities, labeling particular tasks as inherently tied to one particular gender seldom remains fixed in practice. It is, of course, necessary to outline the gender division of labor, but to stop merely at this descriptive level proves inadequate. For the boundary between men's and women's work is not a physiological certainty. Instead it is a cultural misrepresentation since despite the belief in innate gender differences, it is repeatedly crossed by both male and female workers. This in turn is profitably exploited by employers who manipulate the gender division of labor for their own economic ends.

For even though a sharp asymmetry is embedded in the strict "men's work/women's work" distinction at the cultural or folk level, it is repeatedly contradicted by a large number of crossovers and a growing homogeneity of the rural workforce within the agricultural labor process itself. Mechanization merely reinforces this uniformity when it eliminates strenuous tasks. Thus a contradiction exists between stereotypes of gender differences on the one hand and actual gender interchangeability on the other.

This difference between cultural discourse and production practices is mediated by the fact that women's wages in Egypt (as elsewhere) are much lower than those for men. The presumed but erroneous "equality" in the gender "division" of labor is belied by a consistent historical record of unequal pay. Women receive anywhere from one-half to two-thirds the wages of men, and children receive one-third to a half of men's pay. Moreover, these proportions have remained constant over time despite actual increases or decreases in the absolute magnitude of the wage itself (Hansen 1969:308; Saunders and Mehenna 1986:109; Rugh 1985:281).

Farm employers do not discourage crossovers, but then they reinforce gender distinctions by citing them when employing men to perform women's work—and compensated with women's lower wages—or when hiring women to do men's work—but still paid their lower rate. Men's wages already abut the limits of acceptability, so that further increases are only reluctantly conceded. If, however, men are assigned the simpler, supervised tasks customarily labeled "female," the lower wage they are forced to accept—should the outside labor market be constricted—can reduce employers' costs. Similarly, women's wages are already low to begin with. If they cross over the gender line to do "male" tasks, then even a slight increase in their wages would still give the employer a net advantage over employing men. Dividing the labor force according to gender thus reduces all wages to those paid to women even while men's extra efforts go unrewarded and women's efforts are intensified to match those of men.

However, men resist such debasement—not so much because of its threat to their masculinity (although this often shapes their discourse) but because of its threat to their income. Lowering wages while still demanding the same effort or more unfavorably alters the effort = wage relation to these workers' detriment. In trying to rebalance the formula, male laborers may switch to other jobs if possible—that is, if the technical division of labor permits. Often, when village wages for men fall to the unacceptable level of women's pay, men ask *muqāwilīn* for wage advances and join the next *tarāḥīl* work trip. *Tarāḥīl* labor has existed as a local alternative to farm employment for over a hundred years and provides the option that makes rejecting women's work in the village possible. Women, too, withdraw their labor from outside waged employment, since their effort = wage relation is often debased by hiring even lower-paid children. Frequently they turn their efforts inward into the home and into home-based animal husbandry for the more profitable work there or, at least, to ease the burdens of wage and domestic double time. Both justify their actions, as do employers, by referring to customary conventions of standard gender behavior.

Gender stereotyping, like all discrimination, offers shortcuts to hiring by reducing the cost of screening out information about workers' potential performance, which in turn can improve profitability (Thurow 1975). By decomposing the labor force into its different social identities, employers believe they can gain quick insight into the dependability of workers. Defiance and compliance are important qualities that employers seek to estimate because this enables them to predict whether laborers will demand higher wages and slack off if such demands are not met or met only slowly.

As Ester Boserup once observed, "Women are preferred to men in jobs because they are willing to accept lower wages and more often accept unauthorized deductions, false accounts and delayed payments" (1970:80).

In Egypt, pugnacity and docility in requesting higher wages are believed to differ according to gender. Frequently women are intimidated into accepting what is paid out and so are preferred as workers because of their presumed submissiveness. This mitigates against wage hikes, which could otherwise impinge on employers' profits and family income. Men, on the other hand, repeatedly make strident, more unacceptable pay demands.

Such demands become even more difficult to dismiss or evade when workers and employers both live in the same community. Here proximity can be a disadvantage. One solution, justified by citing gender differences, is to send male discontents out on *tarāḥīl* migrant labor trips and replace them with compliant, village-bound females. Wage entreaties are stifled by removing male workers from the village. Women do not participate in *tarāḥīl* migrant labor and, in terms of labor discipline, need not.

During my fieldwork, brokers, employers, and workers frequently justified excluding women from long-distant migrant labor by pointing to the strenuous activity required to earn *tarāḥīl* wages and the need to protect women from strange men at distant work sites. Yet this argument falls apart because migrant labor often repeats many of the hard farm tasks both genders perform at home, and because on *tarāḥīl* trips, women would reside with the same men they see every day in the village—their husbands, fathers, brothers, and sons. Still, it proves more profitable to employ women at home to do the work that men leave behind when they go on migrant labor trips because women are cheaper to hire and more easily intimidated. So they are strongly discouraged from leaving on migrant labor trips. This restriction provides a good example of how directing women into particular jobs and barring them from others reduces their bargaining strength (Stevenson 1978:96).

The idea of labor-force homogeneity—that men and women can work equally hard—is disagreeable to employers, for it presents a unity that defies manipulation and debasement, and undermines their control over production. Yet when the labor force becomes divided into different social or technical divisions, employers enjoy greater command. Labor's mutual cooperation becomes more difficult when workers are convinced that their differences are innate, even biological. Rather than recognize their common interests, men are instead channeled into gender-based *tarāḥīl* employment, which reinforces their gender identity and diffuses their united opposition.

Workers in core countries like the United States have also experienced similar trends toward homogeneity, especially when technological improvements in the late nineteenth century reduced the demand for skills that had once divided the labor force into various craft trades (Gordon, Reich, and Edwards 1982). This homogenization solidified the workforce but weakened management's ability to play one segment of workers off another. Therefore, capital either artificially divided up the labor process through Taylorism or else exaggerated already existing social differences based on ethnicity, race, and gender. These distinctions limited labor's ability to coalesce and weakened its resolve in confrontations with management.

In contrast to the wide social diversity found in the United States, Egypt displays a much greater uniformity. Ethnic and racial distinctions are not found in rural Egypt, although segmentation according to religion (Weyland 1993:99) and region (Richards 1982:62–63) does happen. But the stress on gender is more pervasive, for it substantially divides the local workforce and, much like the ethnic and racial divisions found in core economies, dilutes workers' ability to define wages or resist their reduction. It allows employers to weaken labor's solidarity and to consolidate their own domination. Gender distinctions instill a type of labor discipline that undeniably benefits employers.

Presumed female docility not only averts annoying wage demands but also undercuts male defiance by moderating the latter's wage requests. If men persist, employers can either threaten to reduce their wages to the level of women's pay or replace them with women altogether. Mutual resentment of one gender toward the other then diverts attention away from those who actually divide the workforce and reduce wages. Instead, men push women back into the house, justified by beliefs concerning seclusion and natural abilities, and leave on *tarāḥīl* work trips. For their part, women resist their household isolation by ignoring male bluster, visiting and socializing together, and influencing other women—and men—through domestic quarrels and disputes (Collier 1974). Discontent is thus diverted into a battle of the sexes. Who, in turn, would point to employers as responsible for wage cuts, real or threatened, and for undermining labor solidarity?

So, if under capitalism management divides the labor force, weakens its unity, and undermines its wage demands, it does so in Egypt by playing one gender off against the other. Men's jobs encounter wage cuts when they are performed by women, and men are paid women's wages when they accept women's work. Gender stereotypes then portray these distinctions

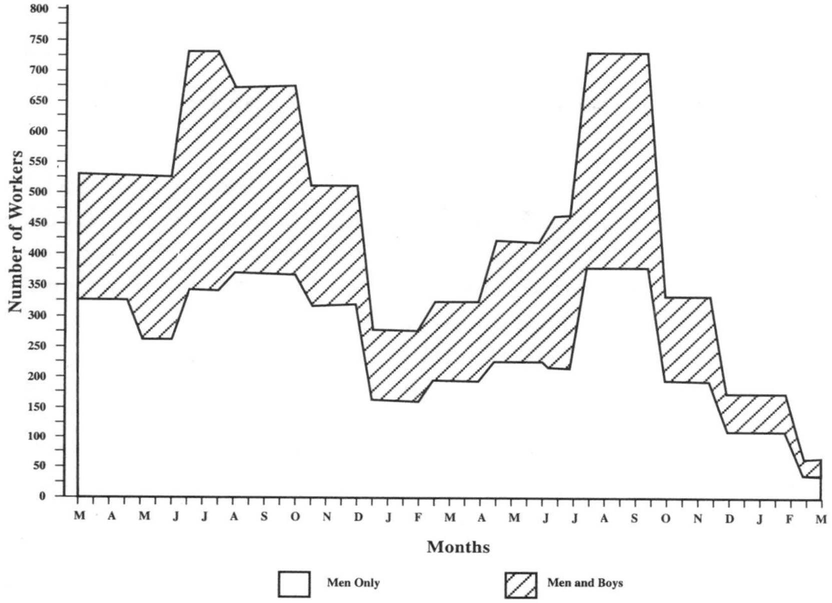

Fig. 3.2. Departures of migrant laborers, Minūf District, 1979–81.

as innate. In the ensuing battle of the sexes, wages are reduced to their lowest possible level—though not without opposition.

Evidence of this manipulated gender division of labor lies less in theoretical explanations than in discovering resistance to it by those subjected to its wage limitations. By way of illustration, a profile of *tarāḥīl* migration from Minūfiya Province for the month of September 1981 presents a curious situation unaccountable but by applying the notion that wage differences and gender stereotyping of farm tasks divide the labor force and reduce its wages to the lowest possible cost.

In September, practically the only job available in rural Egypt is cotton picking, a most labor-intensive task. While each *faddān* (1.038 U.S. acres) of cotton requires, on average, only two men, it nevertheless employs thirty-five women or children to handle the harvest. In that month, men are employed only four days of the thirty-day period; women and children, however, are in such high demand that three times their full employment is needed, often requiring extra shifts on other farms after finishing the picking on their own plots (Toth 1987:604; 1975 figures). The difference between a low supply of women and children and the high demand for their labor could otherwise be offset by employing "surplus" men—though still at wages earned by women. But from the man's perspective, he would be receiving a woman's pay for performing her tasks with the greater energy and agility expected of a man. Refusing to accept women's wages and having no other work available in the village, many men instead opt out for *tarāḥīl* labor.

In 1980, the prevailing village wage for male farm laborers in Minūf District was £E1.20 a day. Women earned 85 piasters for a day's work picking cotton. Children received 60 piasters. *Tarāḥīl* work in the government public sector paid less than the local wage—80 piasters a day—but with opportunities to earn as much as £E1.60 with overtime. Private-sector wages were higher still, but private employment in September was negligible. Since no other unskilled activity of a temporary and casual nature availed itself locally at any wage rate, many men left for *tarāḥīl* work in the New Lands instead of pitching in and supplementing women's wage work at home.

As figure 3.2 indicates, September is the month in which the largest number of workers are engaged in government *tarāḥīl* labor from Minūf. Despite the relative high demand for cotton pickers in the district, wages did not rise high enough above the levels earned by women and children to keep men at home. Instead, the harvest was lengthened into October so that enough local, nonmale labor would eventually become available to satisfy harvest requirements. Thus, in September, when the greatest demand was made of the local workforce, the largest number of male *tarāḥīl* workers left the district, leaving the remaining women and children overworked.

Without the notion that employers divide and cheapen labor along gender lines, it would be difficult otherwise to understand why male workers refused cotton harvest employment—which is defined as women's work—when jobs seemed so plentiful. Without realizing that these laborers had more than agricultural employment to choose from—namely, *tarāḥīl* jobs—it would also be difficult to understand how impoverished male workers could afford to turn down such work even with its low wages. September's labor profile demonstrates that employers manipulated these gender stereotypes in order to reduce their labor costs and to maximize profits. Cotton harvests were strapped to employ enough workers. Male workers, though, took advantage of the different opportunities within the technical division of rural labor to increase their own income. However, the relatively few workers who remained potentially threatened to ruin September's cotton harvest.

Wage differentials and sexual stereotypes thus become crucial in understanding how the gender division of labor is used and maintained. Unequal wages enable employers to debase labor to its lowest possible cost in order to realize greater capital accumulation. Stereotypes centered around character traits of male pride and female seclusion are frequently invoked to predict labor militancy and docility and to justify a gender hierarchy where a battle of the sexes distracts the rural labor force, weakens its collective efforts for higher wages, and disciplines each gender by using the other to undermine it. The social definition of women as dominated, docile, and servile serves mainly to obscure the true relations of production and to strengthen their exploitation. Men lose out, too, when the stridency of their efforts is diluted.

The gender division of labor, while fundamental to the social organization of agriculture, is not merely an innate "natural" architecture of tasks and activities grounded on fundamental definitions of what constitutes human behavior. Such reductionism is belied by the variety and frequency of rural workers crossing over the gender boundary. This gender division of labor assigns distinct chores to men and women. But this job distribution is underwritten by historically consistent inequalities in wages between the genders and justified by cultural constructions defining sex-linked behavior. These two forces combine to lower the cost of labor and raise the profits of farm employers. Men frequently reject this debasement by turning instead to migrant labor, even at periods of high labor demand. Women, too, reject this manipulation by turning inward to animal raising and housework.

The gender division of labor forms an important social institution that regulates the agricultural labor process by dividing the labor force into opposing segments that then reduces labor's ability to control the relationship between effort and wages. Yet other institutions, namely the technical division of labor and the *tarāḥīl* migrant labor market, also shape the regime of accumulation in the village such that male workers can then shift within the technical division of labor and perhaps redefine the effort = wage equation more to their favor. Understanding Egypt's gender division of labor becomes critical to explaining why, in addition to seasonality and debt, men and boys move back and forth between farm work and *tarāḥīl* labor gangs.

Together, these three institutions—seasonal unemployment, consumption loans, and particularly gender distinctions—push rural farm workers into *tarāḥīl* labor—an occupation that appears not as a "casual," serendipitous choice but as one that is partly engineered by landlords and merchants who manipulate wages, costs, and prices, but also one partly countered by workers who find village employment unsatisfactory.

Yet if men and women did not see themselves as so "naturally" different, they could cooperate and exact greater wage concessions. If male workers earned enough income just from local employment, despite its seasonality, there would be no need to incur debts or resort to *tarāḥīl* work. If the crop sales from small plots were sufficient, farmers would not have to intersperse their field chores with migrant work trips. If consumer prices were low and labor demands were mild, *tarāḥīl* wages and work would not be so dissatisfying. But these are not the case, although rural workers are seldom content to merely accept such conditions fatalistically.

Workers were once disgruntled over the combined impact of unemployment, bonded labor, and gender wars. However, in more recent years, seasonal inactivity has been resolved by part-time work in the cities, and debt crises have been checked by family labor diversifying out of farming into better-paying occupations. But it has been the persistence of the gender division of rural labor that has continued to irritate male workers, sending them first on *tarāḥīl* work trips, later compelling then to look for work on urban construction crews, but then precluding their return to agriculture despite their economic hardship in the cities. Workers began to "vote with their feet" and to disrupt the agricultural labor process and its effort = wage formula. Changes in the mode of regulation offered them new opportunities and transformed the constant tensions between workers and local elites such that these struggles soon overflowed the small boundaries of the village work site to affect the entire national economy. What had once been shackles that constrained workers' discontent became chains that restricted the emergence of peripheral Fordism in Egypt.

4

The Labor Process among *Tarāḥīl* Workers

The "regulatory" institutions that make agricultural work at home less manageable and therefore unacceptable are the same ones that give rise to *tarāḥīl* labor. Seasonality, debt, and gender rivalries, added onto unequal land ownership and insufficient job opportunities, limit the leverage and options available to village workers. The result is that males join *tarāḥīl* labor gangs and leave for distant work sites. Once in the labor camp, workers are subjected again to unsatisfactory circumstances: low piece-rate wages, high labor allocations, harsh living conditions, and top-heavy control over valorization. The last is particularly important, for it defines all the other conditions—the intensity of effort, the level of wages, the standard of living—that workers must endure.

Tarāḥīl migrants are hired as manual laborers to work on a wide variety of labor-intensive projects at many different job sites. No longer employed on family farms back in the village, they become instead part of a large, impersonal bureaucracy, inserted in the lowest tiers of company operations. Organizational layers of office managers, field supervisors, labor brokers, sub-brokers, foremen, and task leaders intervene between labor and capital to alienate these workmen from any formal influence on how production ought to proceed.

Yet despite the nominal authority of those in charge, workers are not entirely incapable of exerting some control over the labor process. For in determining the proportions of effort and wages in *tarāḥīl* labor, the resolution turns out to be far from a unilateral decision by management. Instead, it becomes a negotiated settlement, with each side advancing its interests using those methods it has available. And just as neighborliness, cooperation, diversification, and migrant employment give farm workers a little leverage over the agricultural labor process at home, so too do *tarāḥīl* laborers have their small ways of influencing the size of workloads and income at distant work sites. Here workers apply a number of covert tactics that indirectly increase wages, reduce exertion, and ensure survival. Repeatedly and collectively using these "stealth" techniques places adverse pressure on supervisors to alter their own definition of the labor process. Eventually, they can even accumulate to the point of undermining and reducing overall production. In turn, such evasions are sustained by a labor-gang solidarity constructed out of strong kinship and age relationships and tolerated by a lenient management staff worried that workers will find other jobs.

Workers and their representatives use these tactics in their negotiations over workloads and wages. Chapter 2 described the way of life that *tarāḥīl* workers experience in the camps. This chapter explores the migrant-labor process that supports these consumption patterns. It examines these negotiating techniques in detail in order to understand how they play an integral role in labor's job-site experiences, constituting an essential part of daily existence that makes both wage income and physical survival possible.

By resorting to these tactics, *tarāḥīl* workers since the early 1970s have begun to win a number of small victories in reorganizing the labor process. These were achieved because the mode of regulation now included direct state intervention and government policies such as emigration, construction, and investment, which opened new urban employment opportunities that attracted dissatisfied rural workers in search of better jobs and better lives.

Soon this new labor market began generating serious labor shortages for those businesses that employed *tarāḥīl* workers. Labor brokers and company supervisors were quick to take advantage of this scarcity. Short of workers, they over-reported high numbers of laborers on official company invoices. They then split the extra fraudulent wages between themselves and subsequently pushed the fewer number of workers even harder to compensate for the shortages. Rather than generating lighter labor quotas and higher wages, as might be expected from the law of supply and demand, these shortfalls combined with deception to lower wages and increase burdens for those workers who did arrive on-site. Such corruption was remarkably widespread and turned these migrant victories into hollow achievements, transforming their weapons of resistance into stopgap measures to withstand the greater speedups and workloads that resulted from such duplicity. Yet many *tarāḥīl* workers, taking advantage of miscalculations in state policies, responded to these deteriorating circumstances by leaving migrant labor in even greater numbers. While this exodus gave those back in the labor camps more leverage to reverse these dismal conditions, it also had the unexpected consequence of withdrawing even more labor from the countryside, thereby disrupting agricultural and economic development for the entire nation.

Bilateral Negotiations

Tarāḥīl employment is harsh, compounded by low wages, heavy workloads, and desolate work and living conditions. Ill-fed, workers generally lack the energy to finish the tasks assigned by management. Ill-sheltered, they often miss the recuperation necessary to maintain strong bodies and good health. Few make it through a work trip unscathed, returning home with broken arms, lame legs, missing fingers, gashes, aches, and, in general, broken bodies. Thus, basic survival over two months in work camps and over lifetimes of movement quite literally depends on withstanding these adverse conditions by either easing arduous work assignments—made even harder when contractors over-report their labor force—or else by surreptitiously raising wages—otherwise restricted by tight company budgets, formal bureaucratic rules, and supposed reserve armies of unemployed. Since workers are ostensibly "unskilled"—that is, they possess skills sufficiently replicated in the larger rural labor force that they can be easily replaced—they have little if any formal leverage over production and the effort = wage relation. So in order to reduce fatiguing labor allocations and to increase inadequate wages while still accommodating management's demands, workers and foremen informally and spontaneously engage in work site tactics such as "haggling," "padding," "rescheduling," and "shirking," which achieve a temporary *modus vivendi.*

Of all the economic institutions that regulate the migrant labor process, it is the pattern of remuneration that proves to be especially important, for it stipulates just how much money workers are paid for producing a set amount of products, partial products, or services. It provides the critical envelope within which workers adjust their effort and energy output to match their expected wage. *Tarāḥīl* laborers are compensated according to a simple piece-rate scheme that pays workers a daily wage once they complete a fixed amount, or "piece," of output.

Workers are subjected to enormous workloads that start early in the day, pause momentarily throughout the morning, hesitate briefly at one or two o'clock when company supervisors stop work, and may even continue into afternoon overtime stints comparable to morning assignments. What determines this amount of work—and thus the extent of strain and fatigue—

is the formal piece rate, or labor quota, *al-maqṭūʿiya*. This single number constitutes the most significant feature of *tarāḥīl* work at the site of production. Stated in terms of men per *faddān* of crop, or men per volume of dirt, or linear meters of canal excavation per person, this seemingly simple figure nevertheless is the "force" that moves men to toil by defining what is a "fair day's" effort so that workers can receive their wage.

The critical question becomes: Who actually determines the *maqṭūʿiya?* The answer is not so much a foregone conclusion as it might first appear. Certainly management has its prerogative and the formal authority to impose it, but its control is not absolute. Instead, the definition of the work quota is an outcome of constant negotiations at the job site, after work is complete, back at the labor camp off to one side, or over at the engineer's bunk room. Transactions may be quarrelsome and contentious or amiable and good-natured. Outward appearances may be deceptive: outright anger can be a sign of declining leverage, and cheerful congeniality an indication of firm control. Yet if these daily negotiations repeatedly go against the welfare of workers—due, perhaps, to a foreman's inability to bargain—then workers, in desperation, revert to more subtle techniques to covertly reduce their effort without seriously jeopardizing their daily wages. And if these tactics do not work, workers can, labor market permitting, "vote with their feet" and leave *tarāḥīl* work altogether.

Labor-quota calculations are based ostensibly on the amount of production required, the number of workers available, their daily wage, and the project's budget. The labor bill for the entire work gang is estimated at the start of the trip, but a number of intermediate adjustments allows for unforeseen slowdowns, subsequent speedups, and unplanned changes in the quota. Periodically, supervisors and foremen renegotiate how different tasks are budgeted, how they are staffed, how much work is to be done, and how extra wages are apportioned. Indicative of "inside contracting," foremen are responsible for receiving company work orders and payments, and then for organizing and supervising the task groups that are responsible for completing the assignments. Once the foreman accepts the fixed sum of money for his crew and its task, he can keep it all, minus all or part of the workers' wages, pay workers extra wages, or else spend it on adding extra laborers transferred from other crews. The first option clearly contradicts the workers' interests, so through either silent action or loud protest they pressure their foreman into implementing one of the other two options—either pay more wages or add more workers—both of which are more to their advantage.

In the raw and unrestricted private sector, laborers frequently want higher wages rather than more workers and lighter individual quotas. Task groups are often understaffed so that actual per capita quotas are high, but then so are wages—if foremen and supervisors cooperate. As middle-aged adult men, these workers are in their physical prime, but also at the peak of their consumption, with new family and community responsibilities to satisfy. They are willing to accept heavier loads if it results in higher income. Workers in the private sector are sometimes assigned the quotas of fictitious colleagues and earn more money. In one case of understaffing I witnessed, four men were assigned the work of six, with the two extra wages divided among the four. At other times, however, the extra wages were not forthcoming. Yet with quotas fixed at such a high level, few who are not at their physical best can complete the assignments. Each worker's effort strains his ability and endurance. Occasionally, the demands become so onerous that a task team's collective solidarity breaks down and subgroups compete against each other, finishing their assignments early and returning one by one, in order of their relative stamina, to their tents to eat and sleep. Afternoon overtime is rare in the private sector since its regular morning shift includes what in the public sector involves both morning and afternoon assignments. Workers are generally too exhausted to complete additional quotas.

In the milder, more constrained public sector, laborers instead prefer to add extra workers to their task teams and reduce individual labor quotas—as long as their managers acquiesce. Senior workers are often too frail to exert more effort and even bring young relatives along with them to finish their quotas. Their physical survival requires easier assignments rather than extra hard-earned wages since their consumption norm is lower than that of middle-aged adults. In this, the public sector is quite accommodating. In the late 1960s, government companies, under pressure from a newly organized *tarāḥīl* workers' union, cut their labor quotas and work hours to half those of the private sector. But in order to match the productivity of private companies, extra afternoon shifts were added offering overtime pay. All public-sector workers are required to complete the morning assignment, but afternoon overtime is optional. This enables the strongest to continue working while allowing the tired to return to camp. Old workers who are unable to toil so hard can avoid overtime, while young, ambitious workers have the opportunity, or at least had it until the mid-1970s, to earn incomes even higher than those paid in the private sector.

In order to understand how labor quotas become negotiated settlements and not just the unilateral imposition of management directives, let us put the production activities of *tarāḥīl* work under a microscope and examine

6. Starting canal excavation, Kafr al-Shaykh, December 1981.

the minute details of exactly how the *maqṭūʿiya* is established.[1] Although the tactics workers use to influence the outcome differ between the two sectors, these techniques nevertheless aim for the same results: to secure their daily wage while reducing the effort needed to earn it so as to limit the exhaustion and hardship of *tarāḥīl* labor and still bring home an income.

In the private sector, digging irrigation canals or foundations for buildings is an arduous task with workloads rarely found in the public sector. Labor quotas are evaluated daily according to the production requirements established on-site by the supervising engineer, whose experience and knowledge determines what the output should be.

Here is how one foreman, ʿAbbās ʿAbd al-Qādr of the village of Daīr ʿAmmiya, described his team's daily assignments and the negotiations for excavating an irrigation canal. The job uses the quotas given in figure 4.1, where linear and rectangular surface measurements translate into volumes of dirt excavated down into the ground. It illustrates just how labor and management initially disagreed in defining the labor process. Although eventually they reached an accommodation so that the project was completed and the workers were paid, these mutual arrangements could have broken down if the disparity had been too divergent, with management either suffering a project slowdown or a budget overrun, or both, or else

Fig. 4.1. Labor quotas for canal excavation,
ʿAzzāzī Construction Company, 1981

The figure illustrates the side view of a canal
Length is projected outward from the plane of the page.

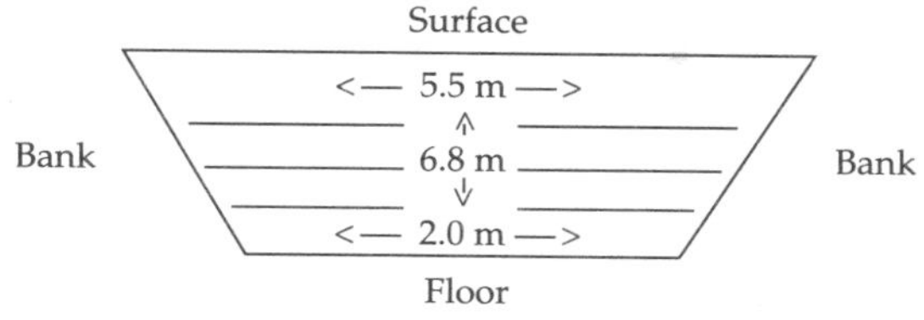

Day	Top Width (m)	Bottom Width (m)	Layer Depth (m)	Accum. Depth (m)	Engineer's quota Length 1 (m)	Engineer's quota Volume 1 (m^3)	Foreman's Quota Length 2 (m)	Foreman's Quota Volume 2 (m^3)	Volume 3 (m^3)	Layer Depth (m)	Accum. Depth (m)
A	B	C	D	E	F	G	H	I	J	K	L
1	5.5	4.0	1.7	1.7	.625	5.0	.55	4.4	5.0	1.7	1.7
2	4.0	3.0	1.7	3.4	.625	3.7	.55	3.25	5.0	2.3	4.0
3	3.0	2.6	1.7	5.1	.625	3.0	.55	2.5	5.0	2.8	6.8
4	2.6	2.0	1.7	6.8	.625	2.5	.55	2.0	–	–	–

Excavation requires that a specific volume of dirt be removed daily (col. G or I). The individual labor quota (col. F or H) is a measurement of length. It is calculated by dividing the constant traverse area of the trapezoidal canal—D(B+C)/2—into the desired volume (col. G or I). This length is the per-capita quota; it is then multiplied by 6 for one six-man team, then doubled for a 2-team strip.

The engineer's quota. The company engineer measured out a length of 7.5 m. Dividing by 2 gives a team measurement of 3.75 m, and dividing again by 6 gives an individual length of .625 m (col. F). This results in the graduated volumes listed in col. G.

The foreman's quota. The workers' foreman argued that the strip should be 6.6 m. Dividing by 2 gives a team measurement of 3.3 m, and dividing again by 6 gives a individual length of .55 m (col. H). This results in the volumes listed in col. I. Comparing col. G to col. I reveals opposing quota definitions.

Graduated quotas. Digging is graduated because each day the daily volume *decreases* by keeping the depth (col. D) constant. Each day a layer is removed, requiring 4 days to remove 4 layers (col. E). If the daily volume remained constant at 5.0 m^3 (col. J), the depth would then *increase* daily (col. K) and it would take only 3 days (col. L) to reach the floor 6.8 m below the original surface. Comparing col. L with col. E reveals that at this pace, the excavation would be completed one day earlier.

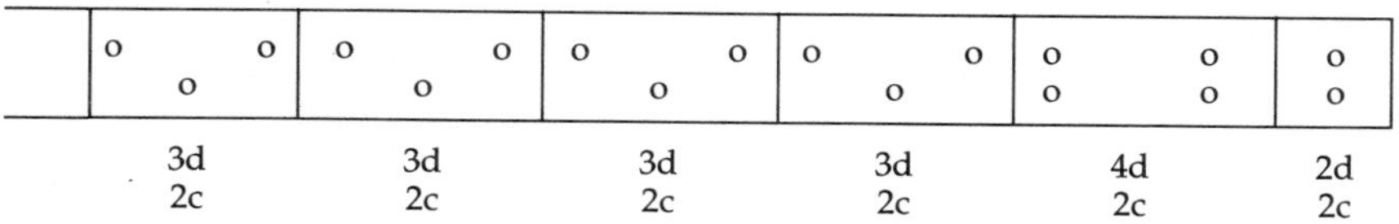

Each block is a strip which ideally requires 6 workers. The first 4 strips are understaffed, giving each member 1/6 more wages. Of 5 workers per team, 3 dig dirt (d) and 2 carry it (c). A fifth strip has a full complement of workers, 4 diggers and 2 carriers. The last strip is half the length of the others and has a smaller team of 4 workers. The entire project uses 3 supervisors (1 foreman and 2 task leaders) and 30 workers, comprising 18 diggers and 12 carriers.

achieving an early project completion or a reduction in labor costs. In turn, workers would have had to toil harder or earn less, or simply go home. Conversely, the company could have hired more laborers (if they were they available) so as to finish the project on time.

Excavation assignments involve graduated quotas. That is, the quota imposed the first day is eased each day thereafter as the work becomes progressively more difficult, since dirt is removed from further below the surface and has to be lifted to higher piles of debris. Graduated quotas constitute a compromise won in earlier labor-management confrontations. If quotas were not graduated, then management could complete the project in less time, as the example demonstrates (compare column E and L in fig. 4.1). Graduating daily quotas thus prolongs the labor process and thereby reduces daily hardship. Once the final depth is reached, workers move on to the next, adjacent rectangle and digging begins anew.

> At the canal digging project for the ʿAzzāzī Construction Company in Kafr al-Shaykh province, the daily quota measurement made me angry because I was responsible for protecting the welfare of the workers. In the late afternoon, after all the workers had finished their work, returned to camp, and fallen asleep, the project engineer Aḥmad Ibrāhīm and I would return to the work site to lay out the next day's assignment. Once, Engineer Aḥmad claimed that the real labor quota should actually be 7.5 meters, shown by way of his detailed calculations which determined that for a team of six men, the quota would be 3.75 meters or, for two teams, 7.5 meters. [See columns F and G in diagram 4.1.] Nevertheless he measured off an initial 8.5 meters [!] along a line extending straight beyond the temporary end of the emerging canal. I immediately protested and presented a counter-claim calculated from my own numbers. The measurement should really be 6.6 meters instead, I insisted. [Compare with columns H and I.] Aḥmad eventually brought his thumb back along the measuring tape to the 7.0 meter point but, despite more protests, he did not budge from there. [ʿAbbās chuckled as he dramatically recounted the drama of his indignation and his stomping off in feigned exasperation.] Despite my anger and persistence, the measurement remained standing. Engineer Aḥmad claimed, in fact, that since the higher, 7.5 meter measurement was more accurate, the workers were actually getting off lightly.

In fact, two days later, Engineer Aḥmad actually did impose the higher 7.5 meter measurement on another section. The workers on my team responded silently by leaving a huge concave bulge protruding inward across the end width of the canal where a straight line should have been. Aḥmad reprimanded me, so in turn, I ordered the workers to straighten it. So we corrected the problem by some extra digging. At the same time, Aḥmad realized the daily labor requirements were heavy, but continued nonetheless to impose high quotas. He said he felt encouraged by the speed at which the project was being completed. Further progress meant he would receive a bonus from his own boss. On my part, I was well aware that the workers were grumbling about the heavy work. Although all the workers will finish this trip as a group, I worry that once at home, many will begin looking for work elsewhere and not return with me on the next trip. If this goes too far—if too many workers leave and not enough replace them—this will reduce my own authority and position. Moreover, this would not please my boss, Maḥmūd ʿAbd al-Ḥalīm, the labor broker. If he continues to lose men, my job might be in jeopardy, but I don't think so. Eventually I guess, ʿAbd al-Ḥalīm could even replace me with a younger, more energetic foreman. For this reason, then, I continue to confront Engineer Aḥmad each day, and protest his incorrect measurements.

At the end of the day—when company supervisors stopped work, when the quota was finally completed—workers returned to their tents exhausted. They may have taken a short tea break or two, but rarely did workers eat on the job. Instead, back in the camp, they devoured their stale leftovers and canned food. Already over the last few mouthfuls they were beginning to fall asleep. At night, workers recuperated, relaxed, and talked. The younger ones played soccer, washed dishes, finished camp chores, hunted for wood and food, or else walked to the nearest village for supplies. Meanwhile, the *raʾīs* discussed the next day's assignments with the project supervisor. The next day's work repeated the day before and previewed, without much variation, the days to come. By 8 o'clock the camp was dark and silent; the only voices to be heard were those of the foreman and engineer still quarreling over the next day's tasks.

Thus the most frequent tactic for reducing workloads in the private sector is to work for a foreman who is skilled at wringing the most concessions from company managers. Each side's interest is argued with spirit. Angry shouting frequently breaks out between foremen and engineers, though this rarely provokes an irresolvable breech. Strained patronage is restored

7. Company supervising engineer, ʿAzzāzī Company, Kafr al-Shaykh, December 1981.

later over tea. The paternalistic relationship between foreman and supervisor becomes one constructed from rancor mixed with flattery, iron resolve tempered by leniency. Still, the conflict of interests is dramatized each day as the work site struggle over labor quotas continues unabated.

Such haggling, however, leaves the opposition to management directives in the hands of foremen who otherwise may have their own welfare in mind rather than the workers' interests. Yet although quota negotiations are undertaken by the workers' representatives, even their "final" resolution is not absolutely fixed. For when workers become unduly exhausted, they leave, despite close supervision, protruding concave bulges and unfinished work. And, in the end, workers who feel overworked can change to other foremen or even other labor brokers, or else, conditions permitting, leave private-sector *tarāḥīl* labor altogether.

Still, skillful "haggling" makes the difference between illness and careless accidents brought on by exhaustion on the one hand, and, on the other, endurance and surviving to the end of the two-month trip with enough strength to return. Thus, defining the labor process relies in the short term on the expert negotiating skills of foremen and engineers and how willing they are either to lose men or to lose time. But in the long run, it depends critically on whether there are other jobs available for *tarāḥīl* workers.

When migrant workers leave the private sector, some join permanent construction gangs, where the workers' continuous ties to foremen, supervisors, and employers create a labor dynamic that is different from temporary *tarāḥīl* employment. Others, however, particularly the older ones, tired from the arduous requirements of the private sector, do not want to find permanent jobs since this means breaking their ties to seasonal agricultural work back home. Yet their poverty does not permit them a leisurely retirement. Still others, the younger ones especially, see migrant labor merely as a temporary job until a more promising career appears. Few if any want to incapacitate themselves in advance. These workers, therefore, continue in *tarāḥīl* labor but gear down to a lower level of effort by moving into the public sector. Here work quotas are lower, but in recent years, the pay also became low. Yet very often, workers are even less energetic, so that even muted quotas still remain a problem.

In shifting from private- to public-sector employment, the style of tactics *tarāḥīl* workers use to control effort and wages becomes transposed. The passionate drama and direct confrontation of haggling is eliminated in favor of quiet pretense and evasion. Rarely do foremen protest their assignments since they and their workers can use other, more indirect techniques to adjust quotas and ensure survival. In place of "haggling" we find "team padding," "rescheduling," and individual "shirking." The chief reason for this inversion lies principally in the quality of supervision.

With more lenient supervision, the tactics workers cannot undertake in the private sector become more commonplace in public-sector employment. The stricter management of private companies does not permit evasive practices that explicitly alter the production process once it is in progress. Profitmaking companies pay their supervisors too well. Although the engineer on the canal project, Aḥmad Ibrāhīm, received the same monthly income, approximately £E40.00, that public-sector supervisors earned, extra bonuses more than quadrupled his base salary. Such fringe benefits encourage vigilance, but government companies are unable to pay such expensive bonuses. They can offer a guaranteed position, but not prosperity. Moreover, such income statements do not include the "extras" company supervisors earn as bribes from labor brokers. Although such graft is certainly important, it still does not raise bureaucrats' salaries to the levels found in the private sector, although many try. Furthermore, public companies cannot, or will not, hire enough supervisors, which spreads managerial duties too thinly.

Land reclamation company officials argue that they cannot pay their supervisors competitive salaries—or for that matter compensate their workers with higher wages—because government financial procedures for the public sector severely restrict its operating budgets. The confusion in state policies that at one time or another included state socialism, private ownership, joint ventures, and privatization left public-sector company budgets in an impossible disarray. Until the policy confusion is cleared up, the government remains reluctant to fund land reclamation budgets adequately.

Yet a closer scrutiny reveals that budgets are not so much restricted as they are improperly allocated in the first place. Line items for costly technology, high salaries for upper management, and expenses such as employee housing and transportation receive far greater priority but then unduly limit what can be allocated to other, "less important" areas such as salaries for field supervisors and workers' wages. Frequently, surplus capital is drained off into other failing state businesses. For example, it was clear when I examined the annual financial reports from 1978 to 1980 for the Mariout Reclamation Company that the profits it did earn were used to finance unrelated projects (mostly residential construction), service foreign-currency bank loans, and purchase expensive equipment such as threshing machines, diesel combines, and helicopters for crop spraying.

Worried over growing labor shortages, managers had once hoped to increase productivity and revenues by replacing workers with modern machinery. But Cairo was unwilling to allocate scarce foreign currency for such imports. Instead, the reclamation company borrowed dollars at high commercial rates. It also leased equipment from local subsidiaries of foreign companies in local tender but at exorbitant prices. These arrangements doubled and sometimes tripled operating costs, thereby reducing funds for underpaid supervisors and migrant workers. Frequently, to economize on such high expenses, additional funds that were to have been budgeted for hiring experienced drivers and mechanics and for buying imported spare parts were simply omitted. This led to numerous situations where expensive imported equipment rusted away for want of a skilled operator or a fan belt. Manual laborers were then hired to replace inoperative machinery but at extremely low wages so as to avoid even greater cost.

But wages had not always been low. Earlier, in the mid-1960s, when land reclamation companies cut quotas and work hours in half as a result of labor union pressure, *tarāḥīl* laborers regarded this a victory of sorts as long as wages remained even. But after 1972, this achievement was subverted when state companies essentially cut the daily wage in half—or, in point of fact, failed to raise wages to the high levels reached in the private sector. Workers who were once drawn to public-sector employment because of low quotas and good pay soon began receiving wages below those in the private sector. This guaranteed that the private sector would not be short of able-bodied workers, for the strong and experienced increasingly bypassed the public sector and worked instead in a private sector, where assignments were heavier but where wages better matched the workers' greater effort and consumption needs. Because the labor union never organized private-sector businesses, it never acquired any leverage over lowering their high quotas. (The history of this labor union is described in chapter 6.)

In government land reclamation, low quotas and low wages attracted weaker laborers and became a refuge for those more concerned with fatigue than with income. Then, as the budget for supervisory staff was retrenched both in numbers and in salaries, these muted quotas became even milder. Yet in the end, the low wages public-sector workers earn, regardless of the lower effort they require, drastically limit their effective income and the standard of living it can support. As for the reduced productivity, management once believed that it could compensate by offering extra overtime work that would attract those laborers capable of more effort.

Yet again it became less a situation of unenergetic workers and more the case of underfunded company budgets that limited production. For if overtime stints were a daily practice, then at least some workers, mostly the young, would be active each afternoon. But because public-sector companies do not allocate sufficient funds for overtime, such work is not usually available. A survey I conducted in 1981 over the course of three *tarāḥīl* labor trips revealed that only 50 percent of the possible overtime slots were actually filled. Thus those "idle afternoons"—great for conducting interviews with workers otherwise too tired to speak to an inquisitive foreigner—were the direct result, ostensibly, of "tight" company accounts. Or again, once the nature of budgetary planning is scrutinized more closely, the financial constraints are explained better by recognizing the improper allocation of limited resources for those less productive company projects mentioned above.

Thus reduced incomes and productivity are more the result of fiscal rather than physical restrictions. Yet lower wages and a lower quality of labor become mutually reinforcing. Low earnings attract a less robust workforce that, in turn, is willing to, or has to, forfeit income for more lenient work conditions. But although public-sector quotas are lower than those in the private sector, they nonetheless exhaust a workforce that is even less capable of completing them. Thus workers still have need to adjust company assignments to their own energy potential, and retrenched

8. Migrant workers irrigating a bean field, Mariout Land Reclamation Company, July 1981.

supervision readily permits them the space to do this. Public-sector migrants thus employ a number of practices that take advantage of this lenient supervision to accomplish their tasks by redistributing and rescheduling their burdens.

A common technique used in land reclamation activities is when cooperative foremen pad or inflate the size of their work crews as a means of distributing task assignments to more laborers than management would otherwise wish. Unlike the arbitrary calculations of field supervisors in the private sector, the quotas in government land reclamation projects are fixed by official company manuals. Padding surreptitiously adds more workers to a team's formal composition.

In principle, a task crew is composed of a specific number of workers assigned to a certain area of land, an inversion of the *maqṭūʿiya* published in the labor manuals that designates a fraction of workers to one *faddān* of land. It is clear, though, that half a worker does not toil on one *faddān* in irrigation, for example, as the manual stipulates, nor even, keeping the same ratio, for one laborer to work on two *faddāns*. Instead a larger team of laborers is assigned to complete a day's task for a wide swath of land. The team usually includes a number of "nonworkers" such as foremen, task leaders, and waterboys who carry out service chores but who are still paid like other team members even though they perform no physical labor. Yet when a number of teams are merged together, redundant foremen, task leaders, and service workers are dropped from the combined team but not from its payroll. This also occurs in the private sector, but there the extra wages can go to the laborers, who increase their efforts to compensate for missing team members. In the public sector, the extra wages gained from dropping support personnel can also go to harder-working laborers, but more often they find their way either into the pockets of foremen and supervisors or are spent on adding extra laborers.

The team works on several *faddāns* at a time. Seldom is just one *faddān* dealt with in isolation. The ideal "patch" (*al-qiṭʿa*) of four *faddāns* is the standard unit assigned. But its size can expand or shrink depending on the on-site assessments made by supervisors and foremen and on whether they want to ease the workload and keep laborers or increase their hardship and risk their loss.

Here is how one foreman, Ṣalāh ʿAwad from Kafr Abdū, explained his staffing arrangements:

> At 6:30 in the morning, the twenty-seven men in the gang I supervised left Ṣalāḥ al-Dīn labor camp. Three men went off to the Muṣṭafa Kāmil farm where they irrigated vegetable crops while the remaining twenty-four walked to the Abū Bakr farm where they prepared wheat fields for operating the diesel combine harvester.

Ustādh ("Professor") ʿIzzat, the supervising engineer, later commented that "such work for six men costs £6.00 for a four-*faddān* patch. This works out to one and a half men per *faddān* since each gets paid the regular £1.00 wage." This somewhat resembles the figure of two men per *faddān* stated in the official norms published in the company manual.

> Ṣalāḥ ʿAwad continued:
> Yet in each six-man team, one "worker" was the waterboy and another was the task leader. This reduced the active work team to four. When two such teams were combined, as the other foreman Ḥāmdī Fatūḥ from Manshīat al-Khudra had done the day before, duplicate waterboys, task leaders, and foremen were dropped but their wages were still paid. Yesterday, Ḥāmdī's two (4 + 1 + 1) work crews, after they had been combined, became ($\begin{smallmatrix}4\\+\\4\end{smallmatrix}$ + 1 + 1), for a total of ten, not twelve workers as the official manual specifies. Using this composition, Ḥāmdī received £12.00 in wages for two patches; he paid out £8.50 to nine workers—the wage of the waterboy was just 50 piasters—and kept the remaining £3.50 which included his own wage of £1.00. Thus his own wage increased three and a half times. The other options he

considered included raising the wage for each of his workers while keeping their numbers constant, or else increasing crew size with no subsequent rise in individual pay. However, workers complained that there were not enough men on the job.

So today I decided to add an additional worker to each of the two task crews [thus padding the team size]. This could have resulted later in a loss to my own income—the two extra wages coming out of the money which, yesterday, Ḥāmdī had pocketed himself. But instead of losing money, I asked Ustādh ʿIzzat to please help me out by submitting an overtime pay voucher to the Company [which expanded the total wage bill for this task]. He agreed. So the wage bill did not remain as we originally bargained but actually was adjusted and expanded to include additional workers. Regardless of how many composed the team, each laborer still received his regular £1.00 wage and I received my share and more. I also gave Ustādh ʿIzzat something in appreciation for his cooperation.

Thus I was paid £14 for two (5 + 1 + 1) work teams but when these were combined into a bigger ($\overset{5}{\underset{5}{+}}$ + 1 + 1) crew of twelve men responsible for two patches, redundant workers dropped out but I kept their wages. In addition, twelve more men from another village, Mīt Abū Karim, were formed into a similar task group [totaling twenty-four workers, the original number leaving for Abū Bakr farm that day] headed by its crew leader, Sharīf Fahmī, who, while only supervising and not actually physically working, was still paid like any other worker. Instead he went to al-Ḥūriya [a nearby village] for vittles. I was now in charge of the entire work group and received wages for twenty-eight workers [£28.00] forming four uncombined work teams. I paid out £22.00 in wages for twenty-one men and two boys, and kept the remaining £6.00 which included my own wage of £1.00. Thus my wages increased six-fold.

The men arrived at the job site at 6:45 and began work. The task involved knocking down those irrigation channels used to water wheat but which later impede the smooth movement of the diesel combines through the fields. By 8:30, the four assigned patches were completed. [As it turned out, the patches were far from ideal. Rather than the standard four *faddāns*, each patch was approximately 2.5 *faddāns*. But the official manual quota for the number of workers was followed nonetheless.]

As the regular morning assignment neared completion, workers began slowing down by lengthening the actual time spent in the field and interspersing the morning with numerous tea breaks. Normally, the work day lasts until 2 o'clock. But taking longer reduces the like-

> lihood of supervisors discovering bad unfinished work. And, if the regular [morning] quota was increased, the men would strongly protest and refuse to do it. But if additional patches were assigned as overtime—even before 2 o'clock—and were paid as such, the men would not complain. Since I knew that ʿIzzat wanted extra work done, I paced the men accordingly. These four teams finished in slightly more than an hour and a half, rested for twenty minutes [actually thirty-five minutes], and then began working on additional patches for overtime pay. The men took slightly longer on this new assignment [which was identical in size to the first] and so finished around 10:30. They then took their official half-hour work break [stipulated by the company contract and government labor regulations] even though in principle they were working overtime.
>
> Normally workers who finish by 10:30 would take their break back in the camp or, worried that the company supervisor or engineer would spot their absence, stay in the field but otherwise be unoccupied and just "look busy." Today the men had little trouble finishing either their regularly assigned tasks [by 8:30] or their overtime [by 10:30]. In fact, the padded crew made the work load so light that most men engaged in yet a third quota, a second overtime piece. The effort I saved them by assigning them easier loads and padding the task groups was spent on doing more work. They earned a total of £3.00 today—and I took another £6.00 in this second overtime stint.

Not all team members had worked this third piece, however. Two workers indicated their response for a second overtime request by going over to the shady ground under some trees next to the road and falling asleep while their companions finished the job.

> Those who did the work split the wages of those who were napping. The teams took longer this time and finished between one and two o'clock. Some teams which ended early helped out those that had become understaffed.

Despite the certainty in which the *maqṭūʿiya* is calculated, determining each task's labor quota is far from consistent. It varies according to its source. The official piece rates for government land reclamation activities published in the company manual were determined in 1973 by the agricultural experimental station at Cairo University. More recently, the Food and Agricultural Organization (FAO) conducted an on-site farm survey and recorded the amounts of labor actually used in 1979. The difference be-

Table 4.1. Relative labor allocation index, Mariout Land Reclamation Company, 1981

Crop	Foremen	Engineers	Company Manual	FAO Survey
Wheat	126.34	72.30	112.60	100
Egyptian clover	192.10	71.20	155.40	100
Old alfalfa	111.49	30.16	115.76	100
Seedless grapes	59.10	87.10	92.06	100
Z-maize	92.54	83.40	71.69	100
Sweet sorghum	247.42	185.93	90.50	100
Yellow corn	97.63	88.01	100.00	100
Winter tomatoes	42.06	63.67	84.89	100
Peas	–	60.82	103.66	100
Watermelon	39.45	39.11	82.29	100
Zucchini squash	43.73	57.96	57.24	100
Beans	275.00	175.00	183.33	100
Total	1326.86	1014.66	1249.42	1200
Average	120.62	85.56	104.12	100

tween the two indicates just how much the *tarāḥīl* workforce had declined during the intervening years. Yet neither the high official norms nor the lower amounts recorded by the FAO were those followed by supervisors or foremen.

In the spring of 1981, I collected four different versions of labor quotas that constituted a "fair day's work" for *tarāḥīl* laborers in the Mariout Reclamation Company region. Sources included migrant gang foremen, supervising engineers, the 1973 manual, and the 1979 FAO farm survey. Quotas were recorded for the entire range of farm operations performed on twelve major crops. In order to compute the figures found in table 4.1, I combined the labor requirements for all tasks for each crop and indexed the results to the FAO farm survey since 1979 was not an atypical year. Together and individually, the conflicting results tell a very interesting story.

Divergent figures indicate the degree to which the workers' foremen and company engineers attempted to independently define what work quota should be imposed. The differences resemble the "finger on the tape-measure" mechanism operating in the private sector, where the critical quota measurement was slid back and forth until the point of momentary agreement was reached. Average index figures at the bottom of table 4.1 suggest that in comparison to the more recent norms recorded in the 1979 farm survey (100), foremen who sought to defend workers' interests consistently *overstaffed* or padded their task crews (120.62), assigning more workers than indicated by supervising engineers or the two sets of normative quotas. Engineers, in turn, and despite their access to official standards, invariably *understaffed* work assignments (84.56). They did assign undersized patches of land, but in computing their labor allocations, the differences in area were factored in. The results was a wide discrepancy in the allocation of workers, especially when contrasted to the official figures computed in 1973 or even the prevailing standards recorded just two years earlier.

When asked separately, foremen and engineers both indicated they were aware of the difference between ideal labor allocations and the practices that actually took place. But without reservation, foremen admitted to padding their task groups and engineers conceded to reducing their size. If, when together, they disagreed, as Ṣalāh ʿAwad's account indicated, foremen frequently won. But given the migrant workers' weak formal position in the labor process, how could such labor "victories" have been achieved?

Padding tasks crews does not immediately restrict output so much as it redistributes the burden of completing it. Easier per capita assignments lighten individual loads, reduce fatigue, and lengthen the period in which productive activity can be sustained. But all the same, inflating crew size does expand an already tight wage bill and eats into relatively scarce overtime funds. Moreover, since padded teams contain workers transferred from other crews, fewer remain available to form additional work teams to be assigned other tasks. Ultimately, less gets done at a higher cost. How can this situation continue?

Supervisors answered that they acquiesced to team padding in order to moderate high labor quotas and to keep a critical mass of labor necessary for minimum farm operations. Since field supervisors cannot raise wages, they instead alter quotas in order to retain the necessary workforce so that they can fulfill their own responsibilities and look competent. In the public sector, moribund bureaucracy and government regulations prevent easy wage adjustments. If, given the quota, the public-sector wage is too small and/or the effort expended to earn it is too great, workers may go elsewhere. One way to keep a dwindling workforce, then, is to lower the amount of effort expended by those who are left. Foremen oblige by negotiating with supervisors for more funds and spending this to add extra workers taken from other teams. Then management acquiesces to padding techniques in order to provide a small incentive to those concerned about minimizing physical exertion, although it does not encourage those who want greater compensation and are willing to work harder to earn it. In the end, fewer participate in *tarāḥīl* labor, but the ones who are left are allocated even heavier workloads and lower wages, which, however, the foremen and cooperative supervisors readjust to the workers' benefits so that they can keep enough workers just to complete the assigned tasks.

Workers' Own On-site Actions

The evidence so far indicates that the wage = effort relationship in *tarāḥīl* work camps is, in actuality, determined through intense bilateral negotiations despite the formal asymmetric organization of the labor process. Indeed, in recent years, labor has used a variety of techniques to defy management's official authority and successfully redefine production more to its liking.

However, these negotiations do not actually involve the workers themselves, but rather consist of compromises between company supervisors and the laborers' foremen, who act on their behalf but who may also have different interests of their own. Yet apart from how their foremen intercede, do *tarāḥīl* workers themselves ever show any real opposition to management? Are there ever any tactics of resistance by the workers that pressure both supervisors *and* foremen to concede to their wishes? Moreover, the previous examples of divergences and disagreements do not really take place inside the actual labor process itself. Instead they occur in the domain of "production politics"—the acts Michael Burawoy once identified (1985:8) as involving the maneuverings that occur apart from specific production activities but which instead regulate this toil. Yet are there ever any techniques practiced inside the migrant-labor process itself and consummated right at the work site instead of just those accomplished in the separate arena of production politics?

For if, indeed, the labor process constitutes the very heart of the regime of accumulation that is the motor force of history, then we ought to expect struggles inside production itself and specifically between capitalism's two major antagonists, labor and management. The question then becomes: Do *tarāḥīl* laborers ever initiate any actual job action of their own against management apart from what foremen and supervisors do separately after hours and off the work site?

The answer is yes, but the tactics that are practiced are, indeed, the "weapons of the weak" that James Scott once described (1985:29) as the kind of "everyday forms of . . . resistance . . . the ordinary weapons of relatively powerless groups: foot dragging, dissimulation, false-compliance, pilfering, feigned ignorance, slander, arson, sabotage and so forth." Individually, these acts of *tarāḥīl* resistance may be of little importance; cumulatively, however, they can and do take on substantial proportions.

What turns these "weak" weapons of resistance into strong instruments of opposition is the wholehearted support and the collective solidarity fostered by migrant workers. Group responsibility protects individual perpetrators and only imperfectly compensates for the withdrawal of their labor such that accommodation with management is preserved, but overall productivity is reduced, while exhaustion is curtailed and survival is assured. In the end, workers depart, either permanently or to return again shortly, but the lack of individual accountability means that the company is left with less production and more costs, which eventually accumulate to jeopardize performance and profits.

Labor-gang solidarity is based primarily on kinship and age, a mutuality and comradeship shared among relatives and between generations. Chapter 2 described how these ties of kinship and seniority gave workers the ability to resist management's high work quotas. It is this collective fellowship that protects *tarāḥīl* workers from the divisiveness of the labor process and the exploitation of the piece-rate system, which together threaten group unity.

When workers informally reschedule their activities by taking unannounced rest breaks, stopping to socialize, hiding in the bush or barracks, or constantly switching to crews that are in mid-break, they shrewdly avoid the heavy burdens of hard work assignments. When laborers decrease their production by leaving bulges, carelessly completing quotas, neglecting to finish their assignments, or doing inferior work, they are not only limiting the effort they expend, they are also warning supervisors and foremen alike that their concessions are insufficient. Individual tactics like "soldiering" and "shirking" are single acts of quiet, desperate defiance, but when they are performed on a wide scale, they mount up to significant declines in productivity.

Tarāḥīl workers are more concerned with the actual amount of work than with the time it takes to complete it. The hours in a "day" are somewhat variable, so that a fast-paced task can be slowed down by stretching out the hours and elongating the "day."[2] This does not actually lower daily quotas, only the speed at which they are completed. It does, however, reduce fatigue. Conversely, if regular morning assignments are completed too quickly, then supervisors may be prompted to assign extra tasks, which, without prior arrangements with the foreman, are considered regular work and are not paid overtime. And if the workday is prolonged until after two o'clock, when supervisors stop work for the day, then careless or unfinished work might better go unnoticed and simply be included in the next day's tasks. Thus, to avoid extra, unpaid work or wage penalties, regular

9. New city rising up in the desert, "15 of May" City project, Helwan, April 1982.

quotas ought to be finished no earlier than the time that the workday ends for supervisors.

Thus task groups that finish a piece of work do not necessarily return straightaway to their barracks or tents. Often, after the assigned task is technically completed, laborers linger around the work site, "looking busy" only when under the gaze of approaching supervisors. Back in the clear, they return to their sleeping, tea drinking, gleaning of free provisions such as firewood and food for use back in the camp, and chatting with their companions until time to leave. Labor crews also delay completion by "de-Taylorizing" the work schedule, by "opening pores,"[3] and inserting rest periods into their daily routine. Thus, work time is extended until after two o'clock by punctuating work activities with several informal rests besides the official mid-morning break.

In public-sector construction companies, employment exhibits a repertoire of resistance similar to that practiced in land reclamation projects. Here, too, fiscal constrictions limit wage increases, so workers reduce their exertion when assigned heavy quotas by switching to easier task teams. Thus, in once instance, shortly after construction operations started, I noticed that some task teams began to shrink in size. However, the number of extra members participating in crews assigned lighter jobs increased throughout the workday to the point where per capita effort was reduced to a minimum. When supervisors loomed on the horizon, these extra workers found it easy to switch to yet other task groups and eventually get lost in the organizational shuffle. Here switching teams is relatively easy because adjacent tasks are nearby, unlike in land reclamation where long distances between job sites prevent workers from joining other teams, although laborers in the New Lands were not at all averse to wandering off and hiding in the bush while crop work proceeded without them. Thus, throughout my investigations, *taraḥīl* construction workers were able to get lost in the crowd of laborers, to shift from difficult to easy tasks, and to take advantage of participating in gang labor with its lack of individual accountability in order to momentarily avoid exhausting tasks.

In a private moment, the foreman from Manshīat al-Khudra, Aḥmad Abū Ḥanafī, described where his men were located one day in October 1981 at the planned community of "15 of May" City on the outskirts of Helwan south of Cairo:

> Some men disappeared to get store goods or hunt for provisions. Others appeared momentarily [shell] "shocked" from minor accidents [Aḥmad's voice indicated that this was almost a fabrication]. Yet others took extended breaks. Sometimes the work was interrupted by reasons beyond our control—delays in the arrival of machinery which had to operate before we could begin our jobs, slowdowns by company employees which in turn created bottlenecks in completing our work, or disagreements and mistakes made by engineers and higher management over exactly how work was to proceed. We were always quick to take advantage of this slack.

I also recorded a number of other instances in my field notes:

> A census of task assignments at the road paving company's supply yard, taken informally every half hour, revealed a constantly shifting work force rotating among several different teams.
>
> Elsewhere on the same project, tired or ill workers assigned to surface grading in preparation for laying sidewalk tile rotated among a series of sequential work breaks without much trouble.

When pacing is undertaken by machine or company supervisors, task team size remains more stable. Yet even Abū Ḥanafī chuckled over one fumbled attempt by the company to exert greater control:

> In this case, the work team was delivering curbstone from a flatbed truck. We were under constant observation by the company driver whose truck speed established the rhythm of throwing cinder blocks to the ground. He was in a hurry to finish his work and go home. But

10. Finishing road grading, "15 of May" City project, Helwan, April 1982.

> when he sped up, it curiously resulted in increased breakage as stones rapidly collided with each other. The driver became very angry and shouted for us to be more careful but all the same, he did slow down.

Surely these are all "weak weapons," but they often make the difference between endurance and exhaustion, between acceptable completion and pay deductions for poor performance. Foremen and supervisors clearly recognize such "weapons" and frequently yield to labor's pressure by negotiating workloads, team size, overtime, and wage increments in its favor. No longer in the hands of the authorities outside the production process, this arsenal of weapons is used daily at the job site by the workers themselves so as to ensure that they finish their tasks, receive their pay, and survive to the time when they can leave and go home for a full rest.

Subverted Victories

It seems, then, that during the years of my fieldwork, *tarāḥīl* workers not only used "weapons of the weak" but they also used them effectively. "Haggling," "padding," "rescheduling," and "shirking" were small acts of resistance, perhaps, and deeds of little consequence. But replicated throughout the migrant workforce and duly amplified, they accumulated in the end to reduce productivity, restrict production, raise labor costs, and lower company profits. Lower management even acquiesced to labor's more favorable definition of the effort = wage relation. Supervisors graduated excavation assignments, shortened canal measurements, allowed padded task teams, and allocated undersized land units. They also overlooked negligent work and incomplete assignments and ignored workers stretching out the workday. Their loyalty, too, had its limits, held in check by the low budgets and staff retrenchment that their companies imposed. Workers got lost in the organizational shuffle. Drivers did slow down. It surely looked like labor was beginning to win in its small contests against capital.

Certainly the victories were not all one-sided, but workers still seemed to be getting their way in work site negotiations over the labor process. Foremen interceded on their behalf, and the laborers themselves resisted the demands of both *ru'isā'* and supervisors. Both sides negotiated with all the techniques available to them. Yet what really made the workers' tactics effective, what allowed these triumphs to succeed, was the emergence of new job opportunities that were drawing workers away from *tarāḥīl* labor. When private-sector laborers assumed the quotas of fictitious colleagues and worked that much harder, when padded task teams in the public sector reduced the number of workers available elsewhere, and when labor norms decreased over the years, it was evident that workers were in short supply. Confronted with such shortages, management did what it could just to keep a minimally available workforce.

Those who remained in migrant labor benefited from this threat to withdraw their labor. Yet for it to be effective, workers had to translate this potential into reality by actually leaving. When they did, it was not because *tarāḥīl* employment had become easier, but because migrant labor still remained exhausting and underpaid despite these labor victories in recent years. Too many foremen and supervisors had simply kept the sums intended to pay for extra wages or to add more workers. Yet as rural workers abandoned *tarāḥīl* labor, wages ought to have risen and quotas should have declined. Instead, the reverse seemed to be happening, notwithstanding labor's pressure from below.

In fact these shortages did not generate the response economists would otherwise expect of a free labor market operating on the theory of low supply, high demand, and a subsequent increase in wages. Instead, that free market was upset by corrupt labor brokers and managers who took advantage of labor shortages to increase their own profits and income. For when *muqāwilūn* delivered migrant workers to the job site, they frequently billed companies for a higher number of workers than the amount they recruited. The wages of fictitious workers—the difference between the actual numbers present and the official labor invoice—were illegally appropriated by brokers who used a portion to pay off company officials. Faced then with the options of either keeping the extra wages or else bending to the workers' will, many brokers—far more than met my eye—pocketed these sums, understaffed labor gangs, and forced the existing workforce to toil even harder. Such corruption, I was told, was rampant throughout the brokerage business.

In May 1981 I left Minūfiya to study another *tarāḥīl* labor gang. Before going, the local *muqāwil* told me the total number of workers he had sent the company. But when I arrived, a careful headcount did not match the broker's figure. I asked the foreman, but he equivocated. Yet if I could not verify this simple number, how could I then expect workers to talk honestly about their lives and jobs? Weeks later, the broker disclosed what had really happened: he had sent fifty workers but had listed a hundred laborers on the company invoice and had told me the same. He then divided the wages of those who were absent between himself and the company supervisor. This unsolicited confession resolved several outstanding questions from my fieldwork. It became clear that such fraudulent transactions occurred frequently enough in *tarāḥīl* recruitment that it had serious repercussions for those who remained employed in migrant labor.

For when more workers were reported on official invoices than the few who had arrived, companies still assumed the higher number to be on-site and still demanded that their projects be completed on time. Therefore, those who were actually present had to compensate for their fictitious colleagues by working much harder to make up for the difference. Their income did not increase, however, unless brokers or foremen forfeited their own earnings for the sake of their workers. Extra workloads were partially offset by the workers' own "weapons of the weak" and by cooperative foremen and supervisors. But in the end, *tarāḥīl* employment remained arduous no matter how much foremen haggled and padded, and no matter how often workers shirked or shifted. Such labor victories, then, became small triumphs against the overwhelming labor demands and the exhausting speedups provoked by managerial fraud and corruption. Workers used them to try to reverse quotas that were artificially high to begin with. Overworked and underpaid as a result of this graft, many workers became even more dissatisfied with *tarāḥīl* employment.

The ultimate "weapon" available to these migrants when workloads become too heavy, when supervisors and foremen concede too little, or when their own weapons prove ineffective, is to initiate a movement of their own by "voting with their feet" and leaving *tarāḥīl* work altogether. Many laborers return to farming, while others leave agriculture for more *tarāḥīl* employment. Yet neither pay well, work conditions in both remain harsh, debts mount, and prices continue to rise. Stopping this seemingly endless cycle of shifting back and forth thus becomes a major aspiration for many exhausted and exasperated migrant laborers.

Tarāḥīl workers are employed by different companies, recruited by different brokers, and moved to different job sites. Labor-gang composition is constantly changing. This continuous circulation of people lends itself to profitable manipulation by brokers and employers and reduces the control workers can exert over the labor process. In response, workers seek not so much to eliminate this system of exploitation and subjugation—perhaps more the political goal of middle-class radicals—but instead try to simply rise up within it, to join a more regularized labor force. That is, what they aspire to is to become a true proletariat and thereby achieve greater security, higher income, and better conditions, but not necessarily to abolish capitalism altogether. This became evident when I asked migrants to compare *tarāḥīl* work to other types of employment. Consolidating their various answers reveals a number of job traits that workers felt were important and desirable:

- Permanent urban construction jobs. This continuous employment is high paying enough that few workers would need extra jobs, is lengthy enough that few would have time to do so, and is stable enough that personal familiarity on the job could reduce high labor demands and bad work conditions.

- Skilled agricultural employment like fruit picking or cotton processing. Its greater expertise could provide laborers with better leverage that can secure contracts, high wages, and light workloads.

- Workers recruited directly through companies and government offices and hired under formal agreements. With contracts, workers would benefit from a clear statement of accountability for procuring provisions and implements and for paying work-related expenses. With direct employment, brokerage commissions that reduce wages would be eliminated.

- Local day labor. Its proximity could remove the problems of transportation, food, and shelter from under the control of employers

> and brokers, and would enable workers to press for greater wages either by using threats of withholding their effort or else by switching to other employers.

Permanent, skilled, high wage, noncoercive, local, direct-hire employment—not only does this list summarize what *tarāḥīl* work is not, it also contains the elements of better employment that many migrant workers found appealing and aspired to achieve should personal and economic circumstances become more favorable.

Ironically then, what many *tarāḥīl* workers coveted were jobs in a Fordist economy. Yet in leaving migrant labor, they were becoming the very ones who were preventing its emergence. Those who remained migrant workers somehow understood the sensibility of retaining Taylorist forms of paternalism for it provides a more rewarding and personalized way of regulating their efforts, income, and consumption than does the more rigid, bureaucratic style of Fordist supervision. Those who quit did not necessarily repudiate paternalism. Indeed, it is what they knew best and could manipulate well to their own advantage, and so they never forgot it. But they did want a better life, and they saw the sparkle and shine of Fordism that was looming on the horizon as the most promising way of getting it. That such ambition conflicted with prudence is not unusual; what is peculiar here is the fact that in striving to realize these aspirations, departing workers helped cause it to fade even further from view.

When *tarāḥīl* workers finally leave migrant employment, their intentions are to find a permanent job that can forego the need to fluctuate back and forth between local farming and distant migrant employment. But achieving this goal critically depends on the existence of a more favorable labor market. In the past, when not enough jobs were available, workers were stuck, and employers knew it. Yet since the early 1970s, migrant workers were able to find permanent jobs elsewhere, mostly in the urban construction sector. This permitted those in the rural labor market to try and join the permanent workforce and acquire the stability, higher income, better treatment, and easier work conditions that such employment promised. This also allowed those who remained *tarāḥīl* laborers to use the threat of departure as a lever to gain more concessions. Those who did stay then found it easier to employ techniques such as haggling, padding, shirking, and soldiering to negotiate better—although not necessarily the best—work conditions and wages. Those who left found new ways of regulating their lives.

5

The Stillbirth of Arab Socialism, 1961

Back and forth. Work in the village. Work at distant labor camps. Up until the 1960s, *tarāḥīl* migrant farm workers had few opportunities to alter this movement, although they certainly had the ambition. And not only did they oscillate back and forth like economic pendulums, but at each work site there was a constant tug-of-war between them and those who were nominally in charge—employers, supervisors, brokers, creditors, merchants—with each side using the methods it had available to alter the effort = wage = price formula. Curiously, the state as a major institution in the mode of regulation remained relatively silent.

In the village, employers used seasonality, debt, gender, limited jobs, and property ownership patterns to lower wages and increase effort. Workers resisted by using neighborliness, propinquity, and cooperation—and the option of *tarāḥīl* labor trips—to at least raise incomes. In distant work camps, supervisors took advantage of their formal bureaucracy, but also of informal paternalism, to impose their own definition of the labor process. Workers, for their part, also relied on paternalism as well as "weak weapons," gang solidarity—and the wider, outside labor market—to refashion the labor process more to their liking.

These economic and social institutions were fairly immediate, local, and informal. The state did not loom large before the 1950s except as a distant agent maintaining polarized property relations and overall social stability. It is as if both sides of local capital wanted to keep Cairo at arm's length, at a safe distance, out of harm's way. One could argue that this laissez-faire orientation was merely part and parcel of Taylorism; one could also argue that it simply reflected a weak peripheral state. Such a conclusion differs, however, from Lipietz' characterization of "bloody" Taylorist governments overseeing phases of export promotion. Yet such a presumption may reflect more Lipietz' coloring all noncore states the same shade. Immanuel Wallerstein argued more precisely (1984:80–81) that peripheral, colonized governments remain relatively ineffective in controlling capitalist flows across and even within their borders. It is only when they strive to become semi-peripheral formations that they turn into the strong, even bloated, state apparatuses required to vigorously insert peripheral Fordism into a Taylorist colonial economy. In the late 1950s, an independent Egypt was about to do just that under Jamāl ʿAbd al-Nāṣir and his program of Arab socialism. The state, heretofore silent over the shifts and the struggles of *tarāḥīl* workers, was poised to impose its brand of competitive Fordism and import substitution onto a recalcitrant countryside.

This and the next chapter examine the state's attempt at planned development in the 1960s as it reverberated throughout rural Egypt. Chapters 7 and 8 then investigate Egypt's inability since the early 1970s to achieve the greater international position Cairo aspired to. *Tarāḥīl* migrant farm workers were important agents in producing this history, albeit indirectly, unintentionally, and without much recognition. The present chapter begins acknowledging their agency by exploring the reasons behind the first major impediment to that development—the agricultural crisis of 1961. Because agriculture was and remains so important to Egypt's economy,[1] this crisis had further repercussions that significantly affected the nation's future growth.

Egyptian agriculture is essentially a labor-intensive business. Add labor, and production increases. Remove labor, and production falls unless workers are replaced by substitutes or machines. When men leave, they can be replaced by women and children, but not completely. Equipment proves expensive, and has become widespread only since 1985. Labor-intensive agriculture therefore remains the basis for most of the country's exports and food. Exports crops earn hard currency, and domestic cultivation reduces food imports that deplete foreign currency reserves. Chronic shortfalls in both undermine the state's international transactions. Unless replenished from other sources, these deficits require foreign loans and credits. Larger deficits in food and export production raise the international debt levels, require more borrowing, and prompt banks and credit agencies to attach stringent conditions for further assistance. Agricultural supply problems thus translate into national financial, economic, and political difficulties that seem far removed from those initially responsible for the agricultural failures. Production may not be the only ingredient for national development, but without it, the society grows at the risk of generating even greater problems. The present chapter documents the first of a series of economic difficulties brought about by agricultural production shortages, labor's own self-removal, and its refusal to tolerate the conditions that once held it down.

Rural workers have shifted and struggled, albeit in different ways, ever since Egypt's introduction to the "modern" era in 1798 (the year Napoleon invaded Egypt) and after the countryside's introduction to cotton in the 1820s (thus realizing the country's "natural advantage"). In the late nineteenth century, corvée labor transformed into *tarāḥīl* labor under the dual pressure of Suez canal builders and British colonialists. Earlier in the twentieth century, migrant farm workers responded to economic depression by staying home, and then moving again when new wartime opportunities appeared. Yet even with the new republican government, their lives remained relatively unaffected. The year 1952 proved uneventful as land reform passed them by; the year 1961 serves as a better benchmark, however, for it was not until the beginning of the 1960s that the state began to actively intervene in the lives of rural workers, altering the effort = wage = price formula in ways that continue to change Egypt's history even today.

The year 1961 was a particularly important year for *tarāḥīl* workers and the Egyptian state because it represented the conjuncture of five government policies—High Dam construction, land reclamation, nationalization, farm price controls, and agricultural cooperatives—that began to generate problems in agriculture that were to have a lasting impact on national development. These state programs became new elements in the mode of regulation that critically reshaped the tensions that were rooted in the agricultural labor process. The government formulated policies that unwittingly transformed the regime of rural accumulation, permitting the conflicts between workers and employers, merchants, creditors, and brokers to overflow the narrow boundaries of village fields and affect the entire nation's economy.

In the early 1960s, a substantial number of rural workers began leaving the Egyptian countryside and reducing the ranks of agricultural labor by joining gangs of *tarāḥīl* workers recruited for employment in new and revived government construction projects south in Aswān and north on the edges of the Delta. Although the Aswān High Dam and Taḥrīr land reclamation had been conceived soon after the 1952 revolution, actual implementation remained negligible—the High Dam for want of international funding and a bilateral agreement with Sudan, land reclamation for want of clear-cut, uncorrupted state authority. Once these thorny issues were resolved, however, both projects rapidly expanded their operations in 1960.

Yet by removing large numbers of unskilled male workers and leaving behind an overburdened workforce of women and children, these national projects collided with the intention of village employers to hire cheap workers. Construction jobs disrupted the rural mechanisms that previously had pauperized the rural workforce. Large landowners were no longer able to employ enough low-cost laborers to produce expected yields at acceptable profit levels. Nor were these farmers willing to slow down the flow of farm labor leaving the countryside by offering higher wages. The nationalizing of urban enterprises and country estates that climaxed in July 1961 and the strengthening of state controls over rural production through its agricultural cooperatives threatened to preempt their livelihoods and so were beginning to trigger uncertainty and conservatism in the countryside.

Thus indigent and indignant male workers critically damaged Egypt's agricultural economy by rejecting village farm work in favor of continuous, long-distance *tarāḥīl* labor. Egyptian agriculture was drained both of workers whose intensive labor normally produced indispensable export and food crops, and of capital which normally could reverse the flow by offering better rural incomes. Male workers were not replaced by machines and only imperfectly replaced by women and children. The state's extraction of capital from agriculture impeded the process of mechanization and the rise of a viable home market in the countryside, and instead subsidized state plans for urban economic growth. The ensuing exodus of workers provoked an unexpected agricultural crisis and a damaging currency devaluation. Together with ineffective nationalizations and insufficient foreign aid, these agricultural problems meant that Egypt's government was not able to successfully realize its ambitions for further economic development.

Although many *tarāḥīl* workers did revert back to local farm employment by 1963—and then only temporarily—still, the damage to agriculture and the national economy had already taken place. Later events were to further amplify these difficulties from which Egypt has yet to recover.

Early Rural Labor Movements

Ever since the early nineteenth century, Egypt has promoted the export of raw long-staple cotton as its primary economic resource. This colonial monoculture tied the economy to European textile manufacturing and kept the national labor force overwhelmingly rural. In cotton cultivation, labor constitutes the single most expensive input.[2] Thus, in order to keep export earnings high, labor costs invariably were cut, and a sizeable portion of the rural workforce was compelled to resort to migrant labor in order to earn an adequate income. But here, peripheral Taylorism was not so much enforced by Lipietz' "bloody" acts of repression as it was by the regulation of valorization—reducing crop prices and farm and migrant wages, and raising the cost of consumption and production inputs. This formula guaranteed profits and wealth for the state, private merchants, and large landowners, and ensured low incomes and poverty for workers and their families.

Today's pattern of *tarāḥīl* labor is essentially an outgrowth of nineteenth-century Egyptian feudalism. But such "feudalism" is not so much the unaltered remnant of what existed before 1798 but more the type suggested by Immanuel Wallerstein's concept (1974:90–94) of a second infeudation or "coerced cash-crop labor" system. In Egyptian feudalism, the appropriation of surplus labor occurred by means of rents, taxes, conscription, and corveé labor gangs. The corvée began to disappear in the 1860s when de Lessep's company wanted more dependable and efficient workers in excavating the Suez canal (al-Shināwī 1958). Its death knell came soon after Britain occupied Egypt in 1882 (Brown 1990:73–74). Today, *tarāḥīl* labor is its direct, commodified descendant, although the state no longer monopolizes its recruitment. Over the last hundred years, it has become privatized as a profit-making business. Recently, however, the government has resumed some jurisdiction through its efforts to organize a labor union and to establish local Employment Offices. Thus private and bureaucratic corveé have replaced its pre-capitalist forebear.

In the Great Depression of the 1930s, stagnant commodity markets, depressed crop prices, and high interest rates combined to force many small Egyptian farmers to mortgage or sell their plots so as to avoid complete insolvency. Banks and individual moneylenders frequently seized land and sold it when debts became overdue, dispossessing cultivators of their incomes and livelihoods. Yet neither the countryside nor the city was providing landless and near-landless workers with much nonfarm employment, and not even casual labor was readily available. As employment opportunities in *tarāḥīl* labor proved negligible or, similarly, as wages became worthlessly low, inactive workers had little alternative but to remain unemployed until either new migrant trips were announced or else local agricultural jobs and income increased. Thus in the 1930s, when the national economy came to a standstill, many idle laborers remained in their villages, presenting a static picture of vast numbers of redundant workers.

It was this temporary picture of stagnation that Wendell Cleland first depicted in 1936, as discussed in chapter 3, that then set the tone for future rural labor market analyses. Yet even when the economy reversed itself and grew with the start of World War II, economists continued to blindly calculate the proportion of labor redundancy. Numbers were still simplistically computed as the remainder left over when those engaged in farming were subtracted from the total rural population. However, now that construction projects were again hiring and wages were increasing, rural workers thwarted such arithmetic and went on to undermine the ability of the agricultural sector to continue producing at profitable levels.

In the 1940s, the urban economy began to expand, and migration to the cities siphoned off those who otherwise would have entered *tarāḥīl* labor. During the war, the Anglo-American Middle East Supply Centre organized and expanded industrial production so as to avoid regional shipping and trade difficulties. In Egypt, the Centre created numerous new employment opportunities, and even more workers left their villages to work in manufacturing. The resulting labor shortage provoked a wheat crisis in the spring of 1942 that threatened to cause social unrest just as the German army swept eastward out of Libya. In response, the Centre quickly organized a compulsory grain collection scheme to ensure adequate supplies of bread, a scheme that anticipated Cairo's own control of agriculture twenty years later (Wilmington 1971:chap. 8).

After the war, the subsequent economic slump sent most of these workers back home. Many were absorbed back into migrant labor, yet others who had become more affluent sought to invest their urban earnings into acquiring additional land. As a consequence, farm rents rose to exorbitant levels. Rent inflation and speculation polarized rural communities and further aggravated the gap between prosperity and poverty. The urban lower classes too were caught between an industrial slowdown and a stagnant colonial economy. After mid-century, these problems helped provoke a number of estate takeovers in the countryside and turbulent riots in downtown Cairo (Brown 1990:121; Goldschmidt 1988:87).

By 1952, Egypt's economy was at an impasse. Rural and urban discontent threatened to shatter the frail alliance of political forces keeping the kingdom together. Alarmed that the chaos might spread, a group of ten army officers led by Jamāl ʿAbd al-Nāṣir took over the government on July 23, 1952, in order to reform Egypt's precarious economy. One of their first acts after assuming command was to implement a radical reform of Egypt's agricultural sector.

The agrarian program of September established land ownership ceilings, fixed rent prices, and disenfranchised powerful landlords belonging to the Turkish and Egyptian ruling elites. Family landholdings were not to exceed 200 *faddān*s per holder plus 50 for each of two children. Excess property was confiscated, compensated with interest-bearing state bonds, and distributed in plots ranging from 2 to 5 *faddān*s to small owners with less than 5 *faddān*s, and tenants and sharecroppers who had previously worked the land. Rents were set at very low levels calculated on the basis of low

1949 land tax assessments. Unfortunately, rural workers and *tarāḥīl* laborers gained little from agrarian reform. Until a second land reform in 1961, only 3.6 percent of rural families and 5.0 percent of the cultivated area were affected. The reforms benefited more the farmers who already had land and could therefore take advantage of preliminary distress sales and qualify later for receiving more (adapted from Abdel-Fadil 1975:9, 125).

Thus the 1952 agrarian reform program was more important for landowning farmers than for landless *tarāḥīl* workers. Those laborers from northern Delta provinces (today these include Buḥayra, Kafr al-Shaykh, Daqahliya, and Sharqiya) which contained larger numbers of latifundia estates became more proletarianized than those from southern Delta provinces (Minūfiya, Gharbiya, and Qaliyūbiya), which were characterized more by numerous small family farms. In the northern Delta, land reform broke up the large landholdings and distributed them to farmers who primarily depended on family labor. This reduced local employment opportunities for the landless population, compelling an even larger number to oscillate between earning occasional wages in the village and earning wages as migrants. In the southern Delta, land reform had less an impact on its minifundia regime, which had already become fragmented in the 1930s. Much of the labor released by breaking up the few big estates was absorbed back into existing family enterprises, although many still worked seasonally on *tarāḥīl* labor gangs once their own farm chores were finished (CAPMAS 1978a:133; Toth 1987:210–23).

In the southern Saʿīd, the pattern of *tarāḥīl* employment had been far more severe. Before the introduction of the perennial irrigation and multicropping that once had prevailed only in the Delta, seasonal unemployment in the south was much more pronounced, especially during the summer. Saʿīdī labor gangs had been routinely sent north to work on Delta cotton fields where in turn they bumped out local farm workers who were then forced to engage in *tarāḥīl* labor elsewhere on infrastructural projects (Richards 1982:62–63). Since there were no tangible skills differential between Saʿīdī and Delta workers, this replacement and bumping-out remains inexplicable except as another example of dividing the rural labor force, creating rivalries, and debasing wages in the ensuing competition (much as village employers manipulated the gender division of labor), but now capitalizing on the Saʿīdīs greater need for work and their docility far away from home.

After 1952, government programs of land reform and accelerated agricultural production in the south absorbed any extra Saʿīdī labor and thereby reduced the number of those traveling north. The "privilege of

Table 5.1. Size of the *tarāḥīl* labor force, 1960 (in millions)

A	National population	26.09				
B	National work force	7.73				
C	Rural work force	5.06				
D	Agricultural work force	4.40	4.40			
E	Farm employers		0.43			
F	Self-employed farmers		1.11			
G	Landless laborers		2.86	2.86		
H	Wage workers (53.1% of line G)			1.53		
I	Family labor (46.9% of line G)			1.33		
	Rural work force seeking waged employment:					
J	Landless laborers (100% of line G)				2.86	
K	Self-employed farmers (50% of line F)				0.56	
L	Total				3.42	3.42
M	Day laborers (30% of line L)					1.03
N	*Tarāḥīl* laborers (70% of line L)					2.39
O	Service sector workers					1.37
P	Manufacturing sector workers					0.71
Q	1973 *tarāḥīl* labor force					1.50
R	1980 *tarāḥīl* labor force					0.80

Source: United Arab Republic, *1960 Census of Population*, vol. 2, *General Tables*; Department of Statistics and Census 1963, table iv, xiv; table 4, 16; table 30, 105.

backwardness" was such that these workers took even greater advantage of the ensuing national developments and dropped out altogether from migrant labor much earlier than those in the Delta.

In the 1950s, then, the size of the rural workforce declined in the Saʿīd but increased in the Delta. National programs to develop Egypt's infrastructure—the Aswān High Dam project in the south and the Taḥrīr Province land reclamation scheme in the north—could have employed many of these workers as *tarāḥīl* laborers, but by the middle of the decade, the government had suspended further activity until their financial situations were resolved. Even so, Cairo did initiate some preliminary construction in these two projects that absorbed a modest proportion of rural workers, but the increase in the size of migrant labor force by 1960 was essentially negligible.

In 1960, 4.4 million people over the age of six toiled in agriculture, constituting 57 percent of the national economically active workforce of 7.73 million in a total population of 26.09 million people (see table 5.1). Since 5.06 million active workers were classified as rural residents (comprising 65 percent of the national labor force), these 4.4 million agriculturalists represented the largest single employment sector, 87 percent, found in the countryside. Yet since this sector earned only 56 percent of all rural income,[3] it is clear that nonfarm employment remained much more lucrative.

One-third of these 4.4 million operated their own land either as farm employers (0.43 million) or as self-employed farmers (1.11 million). The remaining two-thirds (2.86 million) were full- or part-time landless laborers who either worked for wages (53.6 percent) or as unpaid members of extended families (46.4 percent).[4] Census figures do not indicate when workers did *both* wage and family labor. However, many of the laborers I interviewed who had land or access to land stated that to work locally for wages was shameful (*'ayb*); they preferred, if they were to work at all, to do so far away from the village and its local employers (Galby et al. 1980). *Tarāḥīl* employment was often a solution to this cultural dilemma.

Certainly this third segment of 2.86 million workers included recruits to *tarāḥīl* work, but was the second group of farm operators completely immune to this sort of employment? The number of Egyptian landholders who had to resort to part-time migrant labor depended very much on the size of their farm plots.

Egypt is a land of small farms, mostly poor family enterprises, where, in 1961,[5] 85 percent of all landholders worked 5 *faddāns* or less. Many of these farmers did not employ workers at all but relied mainly on family labor, and even themselves hired out temporarily to increase total family income. In 1960, the minimum amount of land required to sustain an average family of five members was estimated to be between 2 and 3 *faddāns* (International Labour Office 1969:36; Saab 1967:14). In 1961, 50 percent of all landholders owned and/or rented 2 *faddāns* or less (Abdel-Fadil 1975:14).

Although the nation's 433,535 farm employers did not need to find extra work, many of the farmers who were self-employed required additional income to augment family revenues. Therefore, in addition to the 2.86 million who were working for their family or for agricultural employers, 50 percent of those 1.11 million who were self-employed farmers, or 0.56 million, most likely were also engaging in casual labor as well. This enabled them to earn extra income but to return and work at home when their labor was needed on their own plots. In all, approximately 3.42 million workers out of 4.4 million—or 78 percent of the total rural labor force—were in the critical predicament of making their family income last the entire year. They therefore viewed *tarāḥīl* employment as one way to fulfill their consumption needs.

However, this final figure of 3.42 million involves a dilemma, for not all temporary workers from the countryside went into *tarāḥīl* labor. Some engaged in local day labor, especially those who lived within commuting distance of cities and towns. Day labor is not organized into village gangs, nor is it transported so far from home that food and shelter have to be provided. Workers appear daily at nearby urban locations, mulling around in the early morning hours until brokers appear who first select familiar acquaintances and then later pick unfamiliar strangers. Workers have much greater control over their labor and are much less dependent on a single labor broker. However, the occasional villager who prefers day labor competes with the full-time urban unskilled who often are better known to paternalistic contractors and who are therefore hired more frequently. Nevertheless, day labor and *tarāḥīl* work do not vary in required skills and posted wages, and there is no statistic that distinguishes between the two in the census. A rough estimate of their proportion, based on government *Labor Force Sample Surveys* for the 1970s,[6] suggests that in 1960, 70 percent of the rural casual labor force was engaged in *tarāḥīl* employment and 30 percent found work in day labor.[7] Thus a total of approximately 2.39 million workers—perhaps more—out of the agricultural workforce of 4.4 million engaged in *tarāḥīl* migrant employment in 1960 if they were to remain in agriculture and yet earn a decent, livable income. This constituted 54 percent of the total agricultural workforce, and 31 percent of the entire national labor force of 7.73 million workers.

This made *tarāḥīl* labor the largest single segment of Egypt's working class, especially since the next largest employment sectors were the somewhat ambiguous services sector, which contained 1.37 million workers (17.7 percent of the national workforce) and the manufacturing sector, which included 713,100 laborers (9.2 percent). However, many migrant laborers did not readily acknowledge their membership in this stigmatized category but instead claimed more prestigious occupations, principally in farming but also in services. (Egyptian censuses and labor force surveys remain notorious for ignoring second and third occupations.) This denial made their dismissal an easier task in economic analyses. Nevertheless, by disregarding this self-professed ignominy, we can see clearly that this group, because of its large size, had the potential to critically disrupt agricultural production should they ever withdraw their labor.

Agricultural and National Crises

In November 1961, Egypt suffered a major failure in its cotton crop. Production fell 40 percent despite a record area sown. In addition, a drop in rice production and an increase in domestic consumption created a major shortage in the amount of rice available for export as well (Hansen and Nashashibi 1975:50–51). Yet cotton crises, in and of themselves, were not new in Egypt. Production failures had been recorded as far back as 1909 for reasons related to poor drainage, and again in 1934, 1946, and 1955, years when yields fell by 20 percent. These last three failures were blamed on severe attacks of boll weevils, as was the 1961 crisis as well (Mohie-Eldin 1966:109, 188). But in 1961, such declines in cotton and rice could not have occurred at a worse moment. For the government had just launched its program of Arab Socialism and had just published its first Five-Year Plan. To be successful, Arab Socialism required the equitable distribution of the fruits of state-planned development. At its core, the Five-Year Plan depended on a vast infusion of machinery and equipment to revitalize Egypt's sagging industrial performance and to stimulate economic growth (O'Brien 1966:225, 266).

These capital goods, necessarily imported from abroad, required a major allocation of foreign currency. At the moment, however, Egypt's foreign currency reserves had fallen to their lowest point. The drain on such reserves had begun after 1956, with settlement to Suez Canal stockholders, compensation to foreign banks and firms nationalized since 1957, payment to the Sudanese government for High Dam construction, and declines in foreign aid and investment. Just as the government issued its first Five-Year Plan and launched its program of Arab Socialism, the well of foreign funds had run dry (Hansen and Nashashibi 1975:51, 73; O'Brien 1966:218, 225, 260).

The loss in cotton and rice that year and the subsequent decline in export earnings in foreign currency was the last straw. Coming on the heels of the first Five-Year Plan, with its government programs of nationalization, industrialization, and economic growth, the 1961 agricultural crisis had more than just rural consequences. Foreign exchange earnings plummeted 38 percent, from £E121 million in 1960–61 to £E75 million in 1961–62, forcing the government to curtail its ambitious plans for industrialization (Waterbury 1983:94). In order to obtain £E20 million in foreign currency, it desperately turned to the International Monetary Fund (IMF) for assistance.

In May 1962 Cairo reached the first of many standby agreements with the IMF in exchange for a promise to curb imports, restrain government expenditures, and devalue its currency. Egypt devalued its pound by 24 percent, from 35.2 piasters per $U.S. to 43.5 piasters, in order to receive short-term credit.[8] As a result, prices for imports rose dramatically while the inelastic status of Egypt's exports further deteriorated. Consumer prices increased on average while agricultural revenues and incomes fell, so that the ripple effect of the cotton crisis soon came to engulf most of Egypt's consuming public. Unfortunately, the IMF stabilization program resolved nothing, for within two years, another agriculturally induced financial emergency erupted (Hansen and Nashashibi 1975:90). Meanwhile, the Five-Year Plan verged on collapse.

What was behind this critical crop failure in 1961? The Agriculture Ministry's official response was that pest control efforts had been seriously neglected. First, carelessly planting incompatible crops on adjacent plots had allowed one crop to conceal the infestation of the other. Furthermore, the government had not delivered chemical insecticides in sufficient quantities at the appropriate time. For this negligence, the government blamed the Agriculture Minister and director of the 1952 land reform program, Sayyid Marʿī, and forced him to resign (Springborg 1982:155–57). Consequently, the Ministry under ʿAbd al-Muḥsin Abū al-Nūr began to accelerate its program of establishing Agricultural Cooperative Associations (ACAs) in order to complete them in two years instead of the ten-year schedule planned originally. It was to be the network of ACAs that henceforth would consolidate and rationalize crop rotation schemes and organize and supervise village insecticide spraying activities (el-Togby 1976:56).

Yet if the disorganized and wasteful cropping decisions of Egyptian farmers were the actual root of the problem, then in earlier years, without such state guidance, many more failures from cotton worms ought to have been recorded. Although the Ministry sought to blame the "ignorant peasantry," it appears that the fault lay somewhere else instead.

In May 1961, at the height of the boll weevil infestation, the Agricultural Committee of Parliament issued a decree requesting the urgent allocation of £E1 million not only for purchasing chemicals but also to subvene the wage costs of a multitude of "emergency" seasonal workers to fight the plague of cotton worms (Government of Egypt 1961:715). But such pests are not just a technical matter of chemical spraying. A former undersecretary of the Agriculture Ministry, Hassan el-Togby, argued (1976:74–83) that too early a spraying eliminates the natural enemies of boll weevils and thus spraying should remain the last possible step applied at the last possible moment. Instead, the overall process, particularly in its earlier stages, requires countless numbers of hands deftly passing over the maturing cotton leaves looking for worms, intensely scouring the ground looking for their burrowings. Thus, what was missing in 1961 was not so much preliminary crop coordination or terminal insecticide spraying so much as the huge numbers of local workers who, at the intermediate stages, pick the cotton worms off the leaves and scoop them out of the ground. If, as the Parliamentary committee reported, more workers had to be hired for these emergency operations, then the countryside's normal labor force must have been experiencing some unusual shortages.

In fact, correcting dubious cropping errors or dispatching embezzled bags of pesticide would have made little difference. The Ministry's opportune response of organizing ACAs merely sought to entrench its own domination over the countryside instead of realistically confronting the actual problem. Sayyid Marʿī may well have been a sacrificial victim pilloried for his conservative policies and arrogation of power elsewhere in the bureaucratic halls of Cairo, because the responsibility for this crisis can be laid instead at the feet of labor—or more accurately, the feet of numerous men leaving agriculture when wages rose in *tarāḥīl* migrant labor, which then left the feet of the fewer women and children who replaced them overburdened in their absence.

What had prompted such a large movement of workers was a major change in the rural mode of regulation and a wholesale shift in the technical division of rural labor. For, as chapter 3 suggested, many village males, otherwise afflicted by seasonal unemployment and chronic debt, can readily find jobs with landowners during the cotton season but are unwilling to stay when they are paid women's wages or replaced by women themselves. Instead, they leave on migrant labor trips if these are available and pay better wages. Without the option of *tarāḥīl* labor, most male workers would ultimately concede to the labor process defined by large village farm employers. Now, however, the state—previously a silent institution in the mode of regulation—began formulating new projects, programs, and policies that were to significantly alter the core struggle taking place in the village over effort, wages, and prices.

Labor discontent in the village, pervasive but formerly subdued, soon turned into determined action instead, propelling the struggle in the village workplace to overflow the bounds of local crop cultivation and, in turn, to impede agricultural production. This movement was the unanticipated consequences of new state programs in infrastructural development and restrictive state policies in agriculture. It occurred at a time when many investigators even thought the country's inflated workforce could stand a reduction.[9] Yet, as we shall now see, both building a High Dam at Aswān and reclaiming the deserts in Taḥrīr province provoked an extraordinary rise in the demand for unskilled male workers. Then when the state announced its property confiscations, when government agricultural cooperatives encroached on farmers' livelihoods, and when its crop price controls restricted their revenues, rural employers were reluctant to raise wages that otherwise could have reversed the rapid movement of workers out of farming.

Building the Aswān High Dam

In January 1960, after a five-year delay, full-scale work finally began on building a century dam at Aswān. In tandem, the government's land reclamation program, moribund since the mid-1950s, received a financial transfusion to ensure that its infrastructure would be completed at the same time as the High Dam, so that the new land could optimally benefit from the dam's improved hydraulic management.

Both projects sought to expand agricultural production: the High Dam by supplying more water, desert reclamation by supplying more land. They reflected the growing demand of rural producers for more resources, of urban consumers for more food, and of state planners for more exports, hard currency, investment capital, industrialization, and job generation. Thus, these projects were initiated to develop and strengthen potentially troublesome sectors of the national economy: rural farmers, domestic consumers, urban laborers, and state managers. Yet in its attempt to satisfy these demands, the government unwittingly aroused the simmering discontent of what still remained, after all, the largest segment of Egypt's working classes.

Both projects had been approved soon after the July revolution and had received high priority as early as the spring of 1953. Yet by mid-decade both undertakings encountered difficulties and slowed down until the early 1960s when, revitalized, they then combined with other government policies to unwittingly generate a crisis in agricultural production.

The High Dam at Aswān was one of the first major development projects the new Revolutionary Command Council (RCC) considered. It sought a spectacular project that would be a striking illustration of its commitment to improve the lives of all Egyptians, an undertaking that could strengthen the agriculture sector, reclaim desert land, increase Egypt's sparse cultivatable territory by a third, and satisfy the energy needs of its ambitious industrialization drive. By 1955, Cairo had the blueprints and was ready to begin building the High Dam. All that remained was to reach an agreement with Sudan over water allocation, and to arrange for foreign credit (Waterbury 1979:102).

Negotiations with Sudan had been launched in the fall of 1954, but the talks remained inconclusive until after Sudan declared its independence on January 1, 1956. Yet by then, Cairo's own efforts to complete the complex financial arrangements had collapsed, and further negotiations with Sudan seemed pointless until the project received adequate foreign financing. What was to eventually employ thousands of Egyptian workers soon became embroiled in a web of international diplomacy and war.

As early as January 1953, Egypt had approached the World Bank for $1.3 billion in High Dam funding, but the Bank stalled until after the Anglo-Egyptian treaty of October 1954 and only if Cairo would accept the Bank's stringent fiscal restrictions on its national budget and future foreign credit. In December 1955, the Bank, the United States, and Britain agreed to finance but the first stage of the project (Waterbury 1979:103–5). Yet ʿAbd al-Nāṣir hesitated to accept for fear that such restrictions would be used to force major changes in Egypt's foreign and domestic policies. Shortly thereafter, negotiations began to unravel. Egypt's weak economic position gave Cairo limited flexibility: either submit to the Bank's demands, forfeit its plans for the dam, or seek other sources of credit.

On July 23, 1956, after the Western powers had withdrawn their support for High Dam funding, ʿAbd al-Nāṣir announced the complete nationalization of the Anglo-French Suez Canal Company. Its revenues, he proclaimed, would henceforth provide the hard currency necessary to build the Aswān High Dam. Britain and France condemned the act and joined together with Israel to reverse the expropriation by attacking Egypt on October 29. Egypt survived—indeed, ʿAbd al-Nāṣir was hailed at home and throughout the Arab world as the hero of Suez. But although Cairo's portion of the Suez Canal's transit revenues grew enormously, jumping from the £E2.3 million earned in 1955 to £E42 million in 1958, it still proved insufficient to finance the Aswān High Dam (Waterbury 1983:68).

By the summer of 1957, the Soviet Union, already a supporter during the Suez conflict, began to increase its assistance to Egypt. In October 1958, Moscow offered to underwrite the High Dam's foreign finances. By December, final arrangements were concluded to provide Egypt with 400 million rubles (approximately $100 million) for the first stage (Waterbury 1979:108–9).

Already construction work had begun on a small scale at the dam site six kilometers south of Aswān city. As early as 1955, teams of workers had moved south to start building support facilities. When the World Bank arrangements collapsed, the pace slowed considerably. Yet in the summer of 1957, gambling on its ability to complete satisfactory financial arrangements, Cairo allocated £E2.75 million for preliminary site preparation. This remained limited primarily to constructing asphalt supply roads and building a power station at the existing Aswān Dam. Projects for railroads and buildings were planned as well. Because Egyptian officials remained cautious about investing local currency before the foreign funding could be raised, much of these early operations involved capital-scarce, labor-intensive activities, especially since the imported equipment and machinery that foreign currency would later procure were not yet available. Initially then, raw labor was the chief ingredient in the Dam's preliminary stages. At first the catchment area for labor recruitment consisted of just the adjacent provinces in southern Egypt. But soon it expanded to include the entire length of the country. Already at this early date, drawing upon supplies of unskilled rural labor had begun reducing the number of *tarāḥīl* work gangs that routinely traveled from the Saʿīd to the Delta. Once the Soviet agreement was signed, Egypt allocated an additional £E700,000 in 1959 for further construction work (Little 1965:56, 58, 88, 91).

In November 1958, the pro-Egyptian commander of the Sudanese army seized government authority. A year later, Cairo and Khartoum concluded an agreement to apportion the Nile waters and to indemnify Sudan for the Nubians displaced from Wadī Ḥalfa. With international funding guaranteed and a bilateral agreement with Sudan secured, Cairo was now ready to begin building the Aswān High Dam, and officials immediately issued orders to begin work (Little 1965:64–65).

On January 9, 1960, President ʿAbd al-Nāṣir personally inaugurated the High Dam project. Project engineers targeted July 1964 as the date for completing the first stage of construction. Planners were very aware of the importance of keeping to a tight timetable, for construction had to be completed before the mid-summer Nile flood reached Aswān, which would destroy any unfinished work.[10] This urgency meant in many instances throwing huge numbers of workers at tasks that could otherwise have been undertaken better by machines, but until such equipment arrived on-site, this work required the immediate efforts of multitudes of manual laborers in order to meet the strict deadline requirements.

After the January inauguration, construction activity accelerated rapidly, and the demand for more workers, both unskilled and skilled, rose sharply. "Laborers had to be summoned," Tom Little reported (1965:87), "from the length and breadth of Egypt" as supplies and equipment were shipped in slowly from Cairo, Alexandria, and abroad. Yet despite the presidential ceremony, delays in delivering heavy machinery impeded a full-scale attack on excavating the initial diversionary channel, which would then permit building the actual dam in the dry riverbed.

Government officials grew increasingly anxious as these slowdowns threatened to upset the project even before the first bulldozers had started operating. Efforts, therefore, were directed toward completing auxiliary projects, including constructing and paving a 30-mile ring road, laying down a 10-mile rail transport, installing electrical transformers in the old Aswān Dam and setting up the area's power supply, building a new river harbor at Khur Kundī for delivering equipment and supplies, and erecting water towers, utility buildings, machine workshops, and housing for foreign and local workers. Within a few months, a new, somewhat ramshackle pioneer community began to rise in the desert outside Aswān (Little 1965:88–90).

Egyptian machine operators, mechanics, and technicians were scarce and difficult to find. Many had been local foreigners who had left the country following the Suez war and the foreign nationalizations, and the Egyptian government was slow to train more. Yet even the recruitment of manual laborers became difficult because workloads were so enormous and wages were so low. By the summer of 1960, just six months into the project, labor shortages at all levels had become so acute that the entire operation threatened to come to a standstill (Little 1965:90–94, 99).

In August, project managers decided to award contracts to local Egyptian companies instead of dealing exclusively with foreign firms. One of the first agreements was with a growing construction company headed by Uthmān Aḥmad Uthmān and his brother Muḥammad. After May 1961, the two began opening offices throughout Egypt to hire skilled and unskilled laborers. By the summer of 1962, their company was employing tens of thousands of workers for the diversionary channel site alone, not to mention the numerous auxiliary projects adjacent to the principal work site. It also subcontracted with many smaller firms, which also recruited large numbers of workers for employment on and around the High Dam (Little 1965:101–2).

By January 1962, when High Dam officials celebrated their second anniversary, delays had diminished considerably. Bottlenecks had been cleared, technicians trained, engineering problems solved, and supplies and equipment delivered. The main task then, as Tom Little recounted (1965:93), was simply to "dig and dump." Laborers worked around the clock in three shifts. Only during the summer months were afternoon hours curtailed so as to avoid the extreme Aswān heat. Wages for unskilled laborers approached £E10.00 a month, or 42 piasters daily, which, while low, nevertheless exceeded the 13 piasters a day they received in agriculture (Little 1965:117).[11] Others earned less for working on subcontracted projects but with paychecks that still surpassed the wages paid for unskilled labor elsewhere. The logistics of the Dam were enormous and extended well beyond the thousands who toiled just on the Dam itself. Buildings were going up everywhere. Aswān was assuming the appearance of a frontier town, and Egyptians swarmed to it in large numbers in order to take advantage of the greater opportunities—and wages—such employment offered.

When ʿAbd al-Nāṣir visited Aswān in January 1963, he commented that the workers he saw throughout the region living in tents and makeshift shelters were *tarāḥīl* migrants who suffered from extreme deprivation and heat in order to build Egypt's future (1964:18; *al-Ahrām*, January 12, 1963). But the president was not the only one to notice the workers' hardship. As early as the spring of 1962, the workers' discontent with their desolate working and living conditions had already provoked "sporadic disorders and strikes" that required military intervention in order to prevent further disruptions from slowing down the frenzied pace of work. Exhausted and underpaid workers threatened to halt many of the High Dam's operations. Project officials agreed to change management so they could resolve these problems and end the disagreement among local and foreign engineers. By July 1962, the directors had been replaced in order to streamline the project's administration (Little 1965:109).

By the end of 1962, work in Aswān was operating at a very accelerated tempo, yet it still continued to attract untold[12] numbers of laborers. For even after the delivery of heavy machinery, much of the activity remained labor-intensive, which required hundreds of thousands of *tarāḥīl* laborers to complete. Rarely was there enough equipment, especially for the multitude of small jobs that machines could not perform. Equipment had replaced workers in many instances, but did not sufficiently curtail the High Dam's thirst for labor. As wages rose, as work conditions improved, and as management became more efficient, the demand for additional workers exceeded the ability of Egypt's construction labor force to satisfy its requirements.

Although by 1962, farm labor shortages had already damaged the agricultural sector, still more rural male workers continued to find good employment in and around Aswān. To this was added the opportunities offered in the New Lands that the High Dam water would reclaim and irrigate. Together, this rapidly expanding labor market for unskilled rural workers was critically reshaping the village struggle over the agricultural production process.

Making the Desert Bloom

Reclaiming and cultivating Egypt's deserts was another thrust the new administration chose in order to modernize the nation. Sequestering land from large landowners and distributing it under the agrarian reform program proved insufficient. By expanding the total cultivatable area, the state sought to create new economic opportunities for Egypt's farmers and rural workers. Over the next three decades, much of the desert land that came under production was reclaimed by the efforts of *tarāḥīl* workers.

In April 1953, the acclaimed Taḥrīr ("Liberation") Province project was launched as the government's showcase experiment in land reclamation. Located on a swath of desert stretching from Minūfiya in the south to the shores of Lake Mariout, sandwiched between the western branch of the Nile and the Cairo-Alexandria desert road, Taḥrīr Province soon became "the symbol of the economic and social efforts of the Revolution. It was envisaged as more than an agricultural project . . . but as an entire social experiment, the nucleus and vanguard of Egypt's new rural society. . . . Plans were grandiose, implementation was enthusiastic, in a pioneering effort to conquer the elements and create a new province in the desert" (Voll 1979:1–2).

Initially Taḥrīr sought to create a vast number of small private family farmers, but its designers soon rejected this plan and instead advocated retaining reclaimed land in one integrated unit and fashioning it into expansive collective state farms (Springborg 1979:54). By the mid-1950s, these two rival designs provoked a heated policy debate over the final status of reclaimed land. Sayyid Marʿī, the Minister of Agriculture and Agrarian Reform, promoted the smallholder model, reflecting a more conservative, propertied approach to family land ownership and settlement. He was opposed by Majdī Ḥasanayn, a flamboyant army major who as a member of the RCC had personally received ʿAbd al-Nāṣir's approval to initiate the more liberal model of collectivized agriculture at Taḥrīr. The controversy matched a market capitalist against a Fabian socialist.

The first approach proposed turning productive land over to those who had worked on it, to farmers in need, to army veterans, to large rural families, and to *tarāḥīl* workers. Yet this plan more easily strengthened the status quo in the Old Lands since in practice it preserved the existing class structure found in rural Egypt. The second strategy advocated large consolidated state farms. These would be the key to successful land reclamation that would supply the nation with foodstuffs otherwise not cultivated on those Old Lands earmarked for growing industrial crops like cotton. Their economies of scale could more efficiently provide food crops and thereby improve the nation's foreign currency reserves and balance of payments. The first model promoted a new agricultural yeomanry but one transplanted layer by layer from the Old Lands. The second pattern resembled bureaucratic plantations, which favored waged manual workers and salaried company employees.

Tarāḥīl workers benefited both ways. Since many were still land-poor farmers or related to them, they wanted to receive land so as to expand their family's holdings. And because many were also wage laborers, they wanted to find jobs in land reclamation that supplemented their income from home. Large state farms could employ more workers than the number who could gain from the distribution of 5 *faddān* plots of land, but they could also discourage those who were determined to revitalize their fading profession. In the late 1950s, few regarded themselves strictly as workers, for it was not until the 1960s when land reclamation accelerated the demand for raw labor that *tarāḥīl* workers began viewing their position to be that of unadorned laborers and not as part-time farmers. And in either case, migrant farm workers benefited greatly when, in the preliminary stages, reclamation companies employed tens of thousands of them to improve the quality of desert land before government policy determined its final status. But until the Marʿī-Hasanayn debate settled, desert reclamation activities were to proceed relatively slowly.

By 1955, the collision between these two competing visions of Egypt's agricultural future had sharpened and soon became embroiled in charges and countercharges of misappropriations and embezzlement. In March, in front of Marʿī's High Committee for Agrarian Reform, Ḥasanayn was instructed to adopt the small family plot model. Ḥasanayn reluctantly agreed, but still sought to preserve most of the Taḥrīr project as one consolidated state farm. Shortly thereafter, rumors surfaced of embezzled agrarian reform funds in Marʿī's committee. As a result, ʿAbd al-Nāṣir placed it under tighter fiscal scrutiny in June 1956 so as to preclude any possibility of corruption (Springborg 1982:149–50). Ḥasanayn, meanwhile, continued his prodigal expenditures of funds to pursue his ambitious project in the desert.

Then in January 1957 Parliament heard accusations that Taḥrīr was experiencing cost overruns, financial irregularities, and poor planning and implementation. Ḥasanayn came under heavy attack for mismanagement and a committee was appointed to investigate charges of embezzlement and corruption. He was soon dismissed, and the following November, the Taḥrīr Province operations were transferred to the Ministry of Agrarian Reform. Quickly Marʿī began to reverse Ḥasanayn's grandiose scheme of collective farming.

By 1957, negotiations over High Dam financing had stalled and the prospects of irrigating desert land through its improved hydraulics dimmed. Attention turned instead to reclaiming land that relied on non-Nile water sources. A major reclamation project was started in the New Valley, a string of desert oases paralleling the Nile halfway to the Libyan border. A smaller scheme of reclaiming marshland in the northeast Delta was begun in 1958. Other projects were initiated along the western edge of the Nile valley in al-Minyā Province, along the northwest Mediterranean coast, and in the Sinai. Yet despite high government expectations, the overall results by the end of the decade were fairly disappointing (Voll 1979:4).

High-level distractions, policy changes, mismanagement, corruption, and budget cuts caused a slowdown in land reclamation activities. A substantial amount of work still remained in raising desert land to the suitable production levels required for either state farm operations or family-owned cultivation. However, the construction of irrigation channels, drains, roads, windbreaks, buildings, and other infrastructure was suspended until these policy and administrative problems were cleared up.

Marʿī's opponents soon began to challenge the conservative yeoman model of land reclamation, concerned over its diseconomies of scale, the dismantling of bureaucratic fiefdoms, and the unbridled authority of the Agrarian Reform minister. After Egypt secured Soviet financing for the High Dam in October 1958, criticism began to surface over exactly how much land reclamation could realistically be expanded to match the potential increase in water the Dam would supply. Those on the political left reckoned that five times Marʿī's estimates could be reclaimed. The minister, it seemed, was loathe to cultivate the desert and divert funds away from the Old Lands (Springborg 1979:55).

Uneradicated boll weevils finally undid Marʿī. The cotton crisis of November 1961, discussed earlier, deposed him. In his place, ʿAbd al-Nāṣir appointed Abū al-Nūr, a staunch advocate of the state-farm model who removed all impediments to a full-scale attack on reclaiming the desert. In 1962 he reorganized Taḥrīr Province as an independent authority outside the Agrarian Reform Ministry and gave it a larger budget. Operations now concentrated exclusively on upgrading the land, and auxiliary projects in food processing and community development were abandoned. Other reclamation projects throughout the Delta and in the New Valley received similar reinforcement. New funds and a new vitality were poured into the New Lands in order to accelerate their development and coordinate their expansion with the building activities in Aswān.

Abū al-Nūr "took on reclamation like a military campaign" (Waterbury 1983:298). And in military fashion, reclamation projects now assumed economies of scale and remained together as single consolidated estates under direct government control. For the moment, the policy of extensive state farms prevailed over the rival approach of distributing fragmented plots to small farmers, although this outcome remained controversial and was never finally resolved. Still, going into the 1960s, land reclamation remained one of the government's principal development projects that required substantial numbers of unskilled workers.

However, after 1967, these activities suffered major setbacks. After the Israeli attack, Egypt's ruined economy could no longer support the luxury of a large desert reclamation program. In 1968, ʿAbd al-Nāṣir reappointed Marʿī head of a combined Agriculture, Agrarian Reform, and Land Reclamation Ministry and began advocating for a more flexible mix of state ownership and private enterprise. In 1972, land reclamation budgets were cut sharply. Operations slowed considerably and focused exclusively on cultivating what had been already rehabilitated rather than bringing new soil up to productive capacity. The New Lands were to cultivate only export crops in order to improve Egypt's foreign currency deficits and balance of payments difficulties. After 1976, many reclamation companies sought new capital by forming joint ventures with foreign investors, yet few prospects were forthcoming (Springborg 1979:61–63; Waterbury 1983:299–300). Subsequently, numerous reorganizations were implemented without sufficient financing, and company budgets became seriously misallocated as a result.

Yet earlier, back in the heady days of the early 1960s, land reclamation began absorbing the laboring efforts of tens of thousands of unskilled *tarāḥīl* migrant workers organized into labor gangs and rotated in and out of projects according to season, debt levels, gender segmentation by village employers, and the demands of reclamation companies. Mechanization accounted for only a small portion of the work done in reclaiming and cultivating desert land, if for no other reason than that the state treasury's meager foreign currency reserves were already earmarked for purchasing foreign equipment for Aswān. It was *tarāḥīl* migrant workers who tenaciously made the desert bloom; machinery and equipment were shipped down south instead.

The heated rivalry between Majdī Ḥasanayn and Sayyid Marʿī had slowed down project activities in the late 1950s. But once their differences were settled, rejuvenated operations needed large quantities of raw labor to again begin preparing and rehabilitating the land. Marʿī's dismissal and Abū al-Nūr's campaign accelerated reclamation activities even further. This coincided with the high labor requirements needed by construction companies contracted to work on the High Dam at Aswān. Together, these two ambitious projects raised the demand for *tarāḥīl* workers and substantially depleted the rural labor market at the same time that the government was demanding an increase in export crop production in the Old Lands so that it could earn foreign currency at the same high rate that it was spending it. Illusions of vast hordes of unemployed unskilled rural workers blinded officials to the agricultural problems these construction projects were generating.

The State Control of Agricultural Wages

Village farmers wish to keep a large surplus workforce that can swamp the local labor market and keep farm wages low so as to maintain high profits from crop production. Yet as more workers joined *tarāḥīl* labor gangs and drained the labor pool, employers were unwilling to raise wages to keep them at home. Accusations of personal stinginess or avarice become irrelevant, for now even the most benign and generous were constrained from increasing wages by the expansion of direct state intervention in agricultural production.

For in 1961, farm wages could not rise high enough to reverse the growing shortage of workers attracted by jobs in constructing the Aswān High Dam and reclaiming Taḥrīr Province. Since wages, like other production costs, are deducted from farmers' harvest sales, better wages for workers would have meant lower incomes for their employers unless crop prices increased. But instead, most market prices were down. Because farm revenues remained stagnant, rural employers were not earning enough income which would permit them to grant higher wages, small self-employed farmers could not make enough money from crop sales alone, and village workers who depended entirely on local piece-rate wages were unable to earn enough just from farm employment. And even if incomes were constant, consumer prices continued to rise, inflated by the increase in import prices after the government devalued the national currency.

The ever-increasing demand for higher wages from agricultural workers was a common complaint I heard often from the farmers I talked to in Minūfiya. "First it's £1 a day, then £1 and cigarettes and tea—they won't work if they don't get their cigarettes and tea in the field—and then it becomes £1.20." Yet workers everywhere demand higher wages (at the very least), so it is not surprising to have heard the cry in Egypt too. But in Egypt, price ceilings on crops prevent farm employers from conceding to these demands, for their own income is limited enough that they are unsympathetic about the income of others. The more they pay workers, the less they retain for themselves and their families, for their own consumption, savings, equipment, and investment. Raising crop prices and reducing production input costs could leave more for wages, but it would mean reversing policies and favoring farmers instead. However, the trend in Egypt for agricultural prices has consistently gone against the welfare of its small farmers and rural workers.

Yet price and wage limitations are not just natural features of a so-called free market in agricultural commerce. Instead they are the results of an explicit state plan of farm price controls implemented through a program of government Agricultural Cooperative Associations. Although in 1961 these two policies remained in rudimentary form, the mere revelation that the government intended to interfere with agriculture prices and production proved unsettling.

Signs of greater government involvement were already appearing. Reports in early 1961 of more land sequestrations, lower ownership ceilings, more stringent market controls, and a greater erosion of local village authority by national officials upset those in the countryside who bought labor, sold crops, and profited as much as possible from the price difference between the two. Both the nationalizations that culminated in July 1961 and new land reform laws that ordered more confiscations provided strong evidence that state action was intent on limiting the size of private property and the income it generated. The extension of a national network of state cooperatives to implement a policy of agricultural price controls indicated that the government not only wished to replace landlords and displace their supplementary sources of income, it also wanted to appropriate their capital for its own purposes. Apprehensive employers, distressed by the anticipation of these limitations on their prosperity, avoided taking any economic risks that might result in personal misfortune. Few rural employers therefore were willing to pay workers higher wages despite the growing shortage of labor.

As early as 1957, the Egyptian state had emerged as the major institution in planning and controlling the national economy. In January, Parliament nationalized French and British financial and commercial establishments in order to avoid foreign retaliation after the Suez war. Cairo soon began adopting a state socialism modeled after Yugoslavia and the Soviet Union and started moving in the direction of a centralized economy. By 1960, the government had expanded the public sector to include sixty-four companies (Waterbury 1983:68–71).

But the lackluster performance of the private sector was impeding the rate of capital investment needed to maintain economic growth, or, more concretely, as Claus Offe might argue (1975), to expand the employment and incomes that were necessary in order to maintain social stability. During the first year of the state's new comprehensive Five-Year Plan of 1960–65, private-sector investment fell even further below what government planners had expected, and its cooperation was far from forthcoming (O'Brien 1966:137). New and dramatic initiatives had to be adopted if national development was to keep pace with employment and consumer demands. The nationalization policy begun in 1957 against foreign companies was therefore expanded in the 1960s to include domestic firms as well. Profits from urban capitalists, and later from rural landlords, would thereafter finance the government's grandiose plans for economic progress.

In 1960, a number of important Egyptian businesses were nationalized, including banking, newspaper, bus, transportation, pharmaceutical, and beverage companies. Farmers became even more troubled when the entire cotton sector passed over to government control. In June 1961, the state suddenly closed the Alexandria futures market because of cotton speculation. A month later, it nationalized firms that handled cotton storage, baling, ginning, and export operations and later still nationalized most of the domestic cotton trade in order to continue repaying Soviet loans. In July, the government legislated a second land reform law that lowered ownership limits from 200 to 100 *faddāns* and promised to redistribute excess land at half its assessed value (O'Brien 1966:chap. 6; Abdel-Fadil 1975:chap. 1). It seemed evident that the state was intent on controlling agriculture much like it planned to dominate the rest of the economy.

On July 23, in the middle of the 1961 cotton season, ʿAbd al-Nāṣir commemorated the ninth anniversary of the 1952 revolution by announcing even more property confiscations, expropriations, and sequestrations. Within three years, the state acquired complete control over banking and insurance, foreign trade, major textile firms, sugar-refining and food processing, maritime and air transport, public utilities and mass transit, major department stores, hotels, cinemas and theaters, newspapers and publishing houses, most major construction companies, and all ports and port facilities, and partial control of the urban retail trade (Waterbury 1983:73–76). The enormous magnitude of these nationalizations shocked employers and property owners throughout the entire country.

Creating an immense public sector in industry and commerce was soon matched by strengthening state policies in agriculture. Rural cooperative associations and their agricultural price controls became much more widespread during Egypt's first Five-Year Plan as the state further consolidated its domination over the economy. The ACAs were to operate in each village and assume the economic position previously reserved for local landlords. Once large landowners were marginalized, government price controls could then be imposed and capital transfers realized without much resistance.

Privately organized agricultural cooperatives in Egypt began as early as 1907. The first attempt at state involvement occurred in 1931, when the royal government established a national agricultural credit bank, and once again in 1948, but its services were available for landowners only. In its 1952 land reform program, the RCC required all beneficiaries to join newly formed state cooperative associations. These were not merely secondary moneylenders, however. Instead, they became the sole source of farm inputs and credit and the exclusive outlet for marketing crops for its members (O'Brien 1966:49–50, 173). By assuming the auxiliary functions of village landlords as local merchants and moneylenders, the ACAs became the new institutional means for direct state intervention in agricultural valorization.

In 1957, stagnant farm production, dampened High Dam prospects, and land reclamation mismanagement shifted the government's gaze back to the Old Lands. Marʿī reorganized the national cooperative program to include both reform and private ACAs. Government registration and audits of all cooperatives were to ensure greater supervision. State-appointed engineers were to override locally elected ACA officials in deciding crop rotation, land consolidation, cultivation techniques, and financial operations. The state-owned Agricultural Credit and Cooperative Bank (ACCB) was given the responsibility for providing cooperative members with cheap, subsidized loans for seed, fertilizer, and equipment.

In December 1960, reports of financial improprieties in Marʿī's ACA program prompted the government to establish a General Organization for Cooperatives in order to reorganize and more closely supervise public and private associations. In August, following the July 23 nationalizations, the government declared all ACCB loans interest free and gave state ACAs a monopoly on distributing seeds and fertilizers.

Although further state intervention did not emerge full-blown until after the 1961 cotton crisis, these institutional changes in marketing and credit still proved disconcerting. Such state interference generated confusion and enmity in the countryside, although many landowners evaded the enforcement of the new agrarian laws, as the High Committee to Liquidate Feudalism discovered later in 1966 when it investigated the Kamshīsh affair (Ansari 1986:chap. 4). Still, until this turmoil cleared up, large farmers remained uncertain of how far their fortunes would decline. Prices, costs, and wage levels all remained fairly unpredictable.

In 1962, Abū al-Nūr began merging public and private ACAs, making cooperative membership compulsory, and strengthening its control over production (O'Brien 1966:120–21, 139–40; Sadowski 1989:64–65). Landlords who had once augmented their farm revenues with trade in input supplies, farm equipment, and credit perceived that not only were their supplementary livelihoods disappearing with the rise of state institutions, but that even their direct authority over agricultural production was vanishing.

Government officials now concluded that revitalizing agriculture—so essential after the disastrous cotton and rice failures of 1961—was not possible without greater state supervision. Higher crop production demanded better crop rotation, greater land consolidation, and more modern cultivation techniques. To achieve these required stronger institutional controls (O'Brien 1966:141). The state thus resolved to expand and enhance its network of ACAs.

The state implemented three key policies through its expanded network of ACAs. First, it controlled crop production by limiting prices and areal allotments. Initially only export crops such as cotton, rice, onions, potatoes, and peanuts were included in order to reduce the nation's balance of payments, but later wheat, already procured through state agencies since the 1940s, came under ACA auspices as well. Prices were set through either explicit price directives or indirect market restrictions. The state enforced its policy through ACA managers, market police, and monopolizing forward processing linkages, such as operating cotton gins and sugar cane presses. The state also limited supply through controlling imports. During the 1960s, wheat shipments under the U.S. PL-480 assistance program, for example, allowed the government to maintain low grain prices by inundating the domestic market with imported wheat (Hansen and Nashashibi 1975:166).

Second, the state secured the mandatory consignment of food crops by requiring compulsory deliveries so as to ensure a steady supply of farm products. Delivery quotas were determined according to export, industrial, or consumer demands. Third, it furnished most agricultural inputs by making the ACAs the exclusive distributor for pesticides, fertilizers, seed, and machinery and designating the Agricultural Credit and Cooperative Bank the sole institution for credit (Abdel-Fadil 1975:82–89).

Controlling agricultural prices had a detrimental effect on farm income. It could be argued that the capital generated from price controls came instead from merchants and processors, since before 1961 these intermediaries had appropriated 50 percent of the difference between the Alexandria price quotations and actual farm prices (Abdel-Fadil 1975:106). Nevertheless, even though the state replaced these middlemen, growers were still denied reasonable and flexible farm gate prices for their products. Monopolistic government officials proved far less accessible and responsive than did private, competitive wholesalers.

The state devised two formulas to determine rural prices and incomes (Cuddihy 1980:28, 77). First, the farmer received, for each *faddān* of average yield, the cost of inputs, labor and a net profit equal to twice the rental price for that *faddān*. Tenants paid half this net profit for rent and kept the remaining portion. Owners retained the entire amount. But since rents under the 1952 land reform law were fixed at low levels, net profits remained low as well.

Second, all input and output prices were equalized across the various crop rotation schemes. A year's income, derived from selling many different crops, was basically the same per *faddān* for each farmer. Thus the farmer's price responsiveness was curtailed since growing one controlled crop was essentially the same as growing another (except for those without price ceilings and mandatory quotas and deliveries). Incomes remained flat regardless of the crop grown. Cuddihy thus concluded that under these two policies: "[T]he mechanism for farm price setting allow[ed] only for cost of production and consumption. Nothing [was] considered for savings and investment, seen as a state prerogative. Growth and development [were] not expected to come from farmer decisions" (1980: 29).

These limitations were not applied equally. Those who grew standard crops—wheat, cotton, corn—tended to be small farmers who forfeited more as a portion of their potential unrestricted income than those who were financially able to shift into uncontrolled commercial crops like vegetables, fruit, and meat. Large owners were also able to evade state supervision by paying ACA engineers to ignore violations of the crop rotation scheme. Small farmers, meanwhile, were unable to avoid fines for improper planting and incurred even more liabilities (Cuddihy 1980:114). Thus small producers experienced greater income limitations than large employers, which forced many of them to resort to wage labor in order to supplement state-restricted revenues.

The ACAs enabled the government to transfer capital from agriculture to finance its plans for promoting industrialization first and then later for subsidizing consumer purchases. But the fixed prices, mandatory quotas, and compulsory deliveries of inputs and harvests prevented many farmers and workers from otherwise earning adequate revenues or wages since capital was appropriated by the ACAs and consigned, instead, to government budgets. Farmers were caught in a difficult situation as the state gained greater control over agricultural trade. Higher wages would have had to come directly from the profits realized after crops were sold and production inputs were purchased. Restricting profits thus meant limiting income and wages.

Thus, by maintaining firm control over prices, the state left farmers little if any extra income. Although such savings simply might have been consumed—thereby creating a lively home market—they could also have been invested in machinery, buildings, infrastructure, education and training, and local services. They also could have been used to pay higher labor costs. Although such outlays did occur in rural Egypt, they were of such limited size that their local effects proved negligible. Prosperous farmers, when they did invest, instead bought urban real estate. Yet very much because the government designated itself the exclusive investor, most farmers were unable to accumulate extra capital and make their own financial decisions. Thus state officials effectively formulated a policy of total or partial monopoly, market restrictions, and import regulations that gave farmers little room to save, invest, or—important for this study—pay higher wages. Rural poverty became a condition explicitly engineered by state policy—farmers were kept poor—rather than being a case of bad luck, ignorance, unresponsiveness, or culture.

Yet if the degree of government control in Egypt seems excessive, it is necessary to point out that state intervention in agriculture, while perhaps unusual here in its extent and rigidity, is nonetheless common for Fordist economies. The issue is more a political one of whether or not to subsidize farm incomes or to tax them, leaving to the neoclassicist ideologues the question of doing neither and thus realizing the so-called "free market" more typical of Taylorism.

In the United States, for example, the policy is to subsidize farmers. Programs of price parity, acreage allotments, storage facilities, hydraulic development, and rural electrification all increase farm incomes, an important benefit for an important segment of the U.S. electorate. Farm prices are kept high, with the burden assumed by taxpayers who contribute to federal and state budgets and by consumers who pay relatively high food prices. Both are possible because historically wage-earners have demanded—and received—high incomes through concerted job action and labor negotiations. Many U.S. companies can afford to pay higher wages because a significant portion of their corporate earnings comes from outside the U.S. economy, from just those peripheral economies like Egypt's where the ability to earn greater profits thus becomes circumscribed. U.S. taxpayers and consumers are burdened to the benefit of U.S. farmers but can afford it—or if not, can vigorously demand the ability to do so—and are sustained by resilient businesses able to respond positively in return for labor's cooperation.

In Egypt, the policy is to tax farmers. This is achieved indirectly through the government's price control program. Farmers are taxed when sale prices are lower than their market value, and the state profits when it then sells such products locally or abroad at higher prices. At first this state revenue was intended to finance Egypt's industrialization efforts. But most went instead into funding unproductive urban consumer subsidies while only 15 percent remained for capital investment (Cuddihy 1980:iv, 114, 116). Yet food subsidies merely underwrite capital's predilection for paying low wages. Depressed wages cannot purchase relatively expensive food, so food prices are kept down and low incomes remain adequate. But this requires the state to set even lower prices for the crops it purchases. Reduced revenues act to the disadvantage of farmers, who therefore suffer from poor incomes, inadequate consumption, and stagnant economic growth due to the lack of private rural investment. Urban consumers benefit, but then so too do their employers.

Egyptian companies cannot pay higher wages, even though it could create a viable home market, because their profits are limited by high costs, supply shortages, government taxes, international competition, and the ability of foreign capital (at first banks, and now, more recently, multinational corporations) to repatriate their profits outside of Egypt. Yet even if local businesses qualified financially, the ability of Egyptian workers to legally press for wage increases is substantially limited.

Thus the state's revenues from agricultural price controls not only subsidizes urban consumers, it also moderates labor's demands for higher income and subsidizes the labor costs of their employers. Controlling the wage = price formula in the cities helps ensure greater social stability and attracts investors seeking an inexpensive workforce. Should workers still insist on higher incomes, government laws prohibit labor strikes and demonstrations.

So, in the United States, highly paid workers can afford high priced food, and U.S. farmers benefit. In Egypt, poorly paid consumers must be subsidized, and Egyptian food producers end up paying the bill. This complementary asymmetry precisely reflects the basic operating principles of international capitalism. In Egypt, agriculture became an easy sector for state planners to tax once recalcitrant landlords were displaced. Because of the lack of clear-cut procedures for less influential villagers to modify national policy, there were few impediments left to prevent government intervention.

During the first half of the 1960s, the effect of price controls was somewhat benign, although such hindsight obscures the uncertainty and distrust Egyptian farmers initially felt toward increased government intervention. Export crops, which the state had placed firmly under its supervision, were taxed 30 percent, and local food crops were subsidized by distributing chemical fertilizers at 30 percent reduced prices. In all, farmers lost an equivalent of 10 to 11 percent of their overall incomes (Abdel-Fadil 1975:101–6).

Yet, in the 1960s, world food prices remained relatively low and stable. It was only after the 1973 oil crisis that international prices increased substantially. What began in the 1960s as a mild 10 to 11 percent tax escalated sharply after 1973. Export crops were particularly hard hit. In the 1960s, farmers had been taxed 30 percent of their income from these crops; in the 1970s, the tax increased to 60 percent for cotton, 80 percent for rice, and 50 percent for onions. Wheat and sugar production, which had been subsidized in the 1960s, were taxed 30 and 75 percent respectively by 1975. Meanwhile, meat production enjoyed a producer subsidy of over 100 percent, due primarily to the free-floating price of animal fodder (Cuddihy 1980:114). Although agricultural inputs were still subsidized by the state, these outlays were more than compensated by the profits the government earned from keeping crop prices low.

> [In] the state budget . . . the cost of all direct and indirect producer subsidies between 1973 and 1976 [was] . . . £E602 million. This includes all explicit subsidies on all crops, the current expenditure of both the Ministry of Agriculture and of Irrigation to provide water and ser-

> vices, plus all state investment in the sector. The direct state revenue net of payment to growers from cotton sales alone was £E892 million from use of the discriminatory overvalued exchange rate and from price differentials in terms of local currency. In other words, state revenues from cotton alone more than paid for all state expenditure in the sector (Cuddihy 1980:iv).

And the government earned still more from the control of wheat, rice, and sugar prices. Such heavy tax burdens and large capital transfers served to limit the growth of income, wages, and, in general, the rural standard of living. By using price controls, the state through its ACAs continued to impoverish rural Egyptians for the next three decades.

This domination over the rural regime of accumulation discouraged full-time work in agriculture and increased the pressure for small farmers and village workers to seek other employment. Unable to satisfactorily redefine the wage = price formula in the village, many found it necessary to leave. This was especially the case once the state realized the extent of a second agricultural crisis that appeared in 1964–65, then when the Six-Day war intensified Egypt's economic difficulties, and yet later when world commodity prices increased after 1973. At first, the exodus was only temporary, involving *tarāḥīl* labor gangs traveling to Aswān, Taḥrīr, and related infrastructural sites. From 1967 to 1974, however, many of these workers stayed home despite the pressure since there was less outside employment in migrant labor or any other occupation. But then later, after 1973, as urban opportunities expanded, rural workers left the countryside permanently and migrated to towns and cities to find employment. For its part, the state remained excessively rigid in recomputing its pricing structure. This permitted it to make windfall profits and to engineer poverty at the expense of its small agricultural producers and rural labor force.

Therefore the likelihood of farm employers conceding to the wage demands of its rural workers or of local merchants yielding to the price bids of its small farmers has remained low—kept intentionally low by state agricultural policies. Although these were still embryonic in 1961, their outline was clear to many in the countryside. The nationalization and land reform laws of July 1961 demonstrated that the state intended to take firm command of both the urban and rural economies. The network of agricultural cooperatives that the government sought to expand was to be the vehicle for its intervention in agricultural prices and production.

The potential for additional income restrictions made otherwise uncertain landlords even more wary of raising wages to reverse the flow of workers traveling to Aswān or Taḥrīr. Labor's discontent with unemployment, debt, and gender discrimination back home was vented by leaving the village for better employment elsewhere. The government's policies of nationalizations, cooperatives, and price controls reshaped the mode of regulation that previously had contained the local struggle of rural workers to realize better wages, incomes, and standards of living. Constricted by the new policies of Arab Socialism, agricultural employers were in too tight a position to stop the exodus.

This labor shortage drained the countryside of male workers into *tarāḥīl* employment and left those women and children who remained too overburdened to adequately satisfy the labor demands in farming, although their lower wages did somewhat compensate their employers for the limitations on crop prices. But men who otherwise might have pitched in and helped women—perhaps at their wage level, perhaps somewhat higher—instead left in large numbers for work in Aswān and Taḥrīr. This shortage generated failures in the 1961 cotton and rice harvests, two export crops that significantly contributed to the foreign currency reserves that Egypt desperately needed in order to sustain economic development.

These agricultural failures forced the government to resort to the IMF, which then required Cairo to devalue its currency. As a result, consumer prices rose while incomes declined. Yet despite international credit, nationalizations, and capital transfers, the government needed to amass even more investment capital if it was to realize its plans to revitalize industrial and agricultural production and achieve greater economic growth. Egypt's rising demand for more employment and higher incomes, if not satisfied, could break out into urban unrest and rural disorder reminiscent of the years leading up to the 1952 revolution. The state's inability to generate this development and satisfy such demands proved fatal, for it significantly undermined the credibility of both the government's Five-Year Plan and ʿAbd al-Nāṣir's Arab Socialism.

In 1962 and 1963, agricultural production in the Old Lands increased, but just temporarily. Within a year, low farm prices and poor wages returned again to afflict agriculture. U.S. wheat sales to Egypt, previously accepting payment in local soft currency under the PL-480 program, now began requiring hard currency transactions instead. This placed even greater production and financial burdens on Egyptian farmers. Rural workers once again were in a dilemma, but increasingly, the option of *tarāḥīl* labor was blocked. The obstruction was not so much the lack of nonfarm employment—indeed, it was fairly abundant—or even low official wages—for they well exceeded those in agriculture—as it was the corruption of labor contractors and the adversity of working conditions. Much of the wage increase in migrant labor was finding its way into the pockets of dishonest brokers. Work conditions continued to be harsh. As a result, outbreaks of labor discontent, like that which erupted in Aswān in the spring of 1962, threatened the completion of the government's spectacular showcase projects located at either end of the Nile valley.

6

Groundwork for the Six-Day Disaster, 1964

Until 1967, the government remained determined to employ large numbers of *tarāḥīl* migrants for its projects of national development, as Arthur Lewis–like visions of vast quantities of surplus rural labor clouded its policy decisions. The countryside seemed a bottomless reservoir of workers and capital. But not only was the government unaware of the problems it was generating in the agricultural sector by encouraging labor to leave, it even sought in 1964 to preserve the changes it had wrought by further ensuring that those who left would not return. Worried that labor shortages and unrest could sabotage Egypt's showcase reclamation project at Taḥrīr as it had threatened High Dam construction at Aswān, the government intentionally created a national labor union for migrant and agricultural workers to promote the interests of *tarāḥīl* laborers. In the process, it attracted even more rural workers away from agriculture in order to implement its New Lands reclamation schemes.

The campaign to employ and protect *tarāḥīl* workers had begun at a provincial level even before the 1961 agricultural crisis. During the next three years, it continued to make headlines, exposing the hopeless conditions of migrant labor and encouraging workers to seek employment in land reclamation rather than in village farming.

Yet it was the national union, with its elections in the summer of 1964, that really raised the hopes and aspirations of rural workers. For in spite of its fraud and corruption, *tarāḥīl* workers believed the union would give them the greater control they wanted over the jobs so as to obtain higher incomes, more benefits, and better working conditions. And, for a while, it did. Although eventually it became moribund and unresponsive, the union nevertheless initially carved out space in which workers and their sympathetic allies could force companies and the state to yield to these demands. Its organization achieved enough tangible improvements that it drew even more rural laborers into migrant employment.

The union succeeded because of labor's critical potential to obstruct the state's development plans even if the workers themselves did not fully realize it. But then it failed when its Fordist, bureaucratic management of the labor process ultimately netted laborers fewer advantages than old-fashioned Taylorist paternalism. Improvements in control, income, benefits, and work conditions proved temporary, and once the economy deteriorated, they vanished.

But before they disappeared, these gains prompted even more rural workers to leave village farming. These departures contributed to further agricultural shortages, more national financial problems, and ultimately an international political catastrophe.

In 1965–66, Egypt's economy went into recession. Declines in export-crop and food production translated once more into foreign exchange difficulties that then required still more international credit. Chronic hard-currency deficits meant that in allocating scarce foreign funds, state officials often economized, as land reclamation companies did in chapter 4, by omitting budget outlays for expensive imported machinery and spare parts. This time, it affected the military's ability to repair its aging armament factories and damaged battle equipment. Such difficulties made Egypt even less prepared to engage in war such that in June 1967, the government was unable to back up its bellicose rhetoric with strong combat action.

This chapter chronicles the untold story of this union organizing campaign, which not only mobilized Egypt's largest working population but also energized substantial numbers of middle-class activists as well. For a brief moment, it captured the imagination of the entire nation. It constructed a new mode of regulation—although not necessarily the calm, moderate one state officials intended—that favorably redefined the regime of accumulation by opening up more nonfarm employment opportunities, increasing *tarāḥīl* wages, and reducing labor quotas. It deliberately improved production and consumption in the New Lands, but it also unwittingly disrupted valorization in the Old Lands.

And before this campaign died, it not only succeeded in giving new ambitions to migrant farm workers, it also demonstrated their critical capacity to affect Egypt's national development. Ironically, this ability was realized by "negation": by their departure and absence from agriculture, which generated more production shortages and contributed to limiting national growth and Egypt's combat effectiveness. This happened as much because of what took place outside the union as it did because of the organization itself.

No matter how remarkable were the initial victories, in the end rural workers spurned the union the state created for them. Yet without understanding the informal relationships of paternalism that give *tarāḥīl* laborers better control over their efforts, wages, and consumption, a formal institutional study of labor organizations cannot explain why these workers eventually rejected the union's concern for their welfare and returned instead to private labor brokers. And without realizing the benefits that laborers receive from retaining inside contracting and its formal subsumption of labor, it cannot clarify why migrant workers ultimately opposed the union's bureaucratic procedures and its real subordination of labor. For, despite its early triumphs, the union could not overcome its defects and retain the support of *tarāḥīl* laborers.

Organizing Migrant Farm Workers

In the early 1960s, the conspicuous poverty and harsh working conditions of *tarāḥīl* workers distressed many reformers—chief among them ʿAbd al-Nāṣir—who saw them as the forgotten segment of Egypt's rural workforce. Improving their conditions would symbolize the nation's humanitarian commitment. Moreover, the land reclamation companies under Abū al-Nūr were demanding ever greater numbers of manual laborers. Since workers suffering from high labor quotas, unpaid wages, insufficient food and shelter, and inadequate medical treatment were less productive, companies would benefit by exchanging social justice for higher productivity. So, in response to these ethical and economical dilemmas, government officials established a labor union in 1964 to champion full wages and better working conditions.

Despite national legislation dating back to 1942 legalizing the formation of trade unions, rural workers still remained excluded. Even with new legislation in 1959, eligible agricultural "workers" were still limited just to employees in government offices—namely, the supervisors, engineers, and bureaucrats in the Ministries of Agriculture and Agrarian Reform, Irrigation, and Land Reclamation. Because union representatives were not yet permitted into rural communities to organize and register manual laborers, such legislation was merely anticipatory. It required five more years of lobbying Parliament before the General Union of Agricultural and Migrant Workers (GUAMW) was legally permitted inside the thousands of sovereign Egyptian villages. In the absence of national legislation, however, provincial efforts were partially able to override this prohibition (Rishād 1968:13–14).

.. لابد لوسائل الاعلام بما فيها الصحافة أن تعبر عن الشعب فعلاً عن حياته وعن قيمه وعن تطلعاته المشروعة؟

جمال عبد الناصر

المساء ملحق الأسبوعي

كل أحد العمال والفلاحين

العدد ١١٣ — الأحد ١٤ فبراير ١٩٦٥ — السنة الثالثة

وضع خطة جديدة للعمل في لجان الاتحاد الاشتراكي بمحافظة الاسماعيلية — ص ٣

١٠٧ أسرة بمحافظة بني سويف اشتركت في تنفيذ مشروع الأسر المنتجة — ص ٤

تنظيم تشغيل عمال التراحيل

تشكيل لجان بالمحافظات للاشراف على سير العمل وتشغيل العمال

إنشاء ١٠ وحدات تلحق بالمكاتب المركزية للقوى العاملة و٣٢ وحدة بمكاتب العمل

كلمة

رسالتنا..

خبر

تشكيلان نقابيان فقط

طلبات العمل

مؤسسة مصر الجديدة

من كل بلد

فرص العمل

احمد فهيم

اجتماعات عامة للنقابات

لبحث دور العمال والتشكيلات النقابية في المرحلة القادمة

المجلس التنفيذي للاتحاد العام يجتمع لتنظيم اجتماعات النقابات العامة

دفعة ثانية من عمال البناء يتم إعدادها للسفر إلى ألمانيا

مركز الجيزة للثقافة العمالية يحتفل بتخريج الدورة ١٦ من العمال الدارسين بالمركز

مجلس ادارة

11. Headline from the newspaper *al-Masā'*, February 14, 1965, proclaims "Organizing the employment of *tarāḥīl* workers."

Large landlords and their representatives in Parliament strongly opposed such legislation. Having successfully blocked it since 1942, they delayed further debate until early 1964, when ʿAbd al-Nāṣir personally intervened. By then, however, their domination of local government had been eroded by estate confiscations, price controls, and the ACAs. Moreover, government administration at the provincial, district and village levels had been reorganized in 1960. As a result, landlords were no longer so influential that they could prevent new officials and bureaucrats from implementing migrant labor reforms.

Throughout the period of the first Five-Year plan, Egyptian newspapers and magazines carried story after story headlining the most important labor organizing campaign of the decade: establishing a labor union for the "more than 3 million" agricultural and migrant workers[1] who continued to endure high piece rates, low wages, and dismal working conditions. Flying the banner of social justice and national dignity, this campaign called for creating a national union in order to raise these laborers out of their poverty and to provide them with human dignity, new pride, and a better standard of living. The efforts that sought to improve the lives of *tarāḥīl* laborers first began in 1961 in three rural regions and climaxed in 1964 with nationwide union elections. However, they deteriorated after the 1967 war with Israel, yet resurfaced in 1971, although more as empty political rhetoric than as a substantive campaign.

Yet the severe cotton and rice crisis of 1961 had illustrated the folly of employing large numbers of unskilled rural workers on infrastructural projects while still demanding substantial agricultural production. The lack of labor-market coordination proved unfortunate once again. For a too-successful union movement meant even further reductions in the local agricultural workforce.

It might be argued, then, that the first *tarāḥīl* labor programs started by the provincial governments in Daqahliya and Buḥayra were intended to employ migrant workers *inside* the Old Lands and keep them away from higher-paying employment with land reclamation companies.[2] However, this does not seem to have been the case. At best, these reform programs served merely to adjust the flow of manual laborers, yet they always seemed to tilt in favor of reclamation activities before satisfying local demand.

The key to resolving this paradox, many believed, was to eliminate exploitative and dishonest private *muqāwilīn,* who were thought to impede the free flow of migrant labor. Seldom did *tarāḥīl* workers receive their complete wages; once labor brokers deducted for debts, transportation, food, shelter, free days, and extra brokerage commissions, the small remainder discouraged would-be migrants. Frequently brokers fraudulently reported the number of workers they delivered, kept the wages of fictitious laborers, and forced those actually present to work much harder to compensate. Thus reforms proposed to replace private brokers by a government-organized union. Once full wages were achieved and labor quotas were reduced, the migrant labor market would become unblocked and there would be enough workers to satisfy employers in both the Old and the New Lands. In place of the *muqāwil,* each village would instead form a local union committee (*al-lajna* [plural: *al-lijān*] *al-niqābiya*), which would become—once the appropriate national legislation was passed—the foundation of still higher levels of GUAMW organization located in district towns, provincial capitals, and in Cairo. It would be the GUAMW that henceforth would handle *tarāḥīl* labor employment and services.

Yet the government miscalculated the willingness of migrant workers to abandon their time-honored ties of paternalism and replace them with impersonal bureaucratic relations. Workers eventually realized that paternalistic control of the labor process gave them greater leverage than they had with underfunded bureaucratic unions and government employment agencies. The state also underestimated the willingness of labor brokers to withdraw amicably and to simply allow the union and other offices to replace them. Labor recruitment was too lucrative a business to abandon. Brokers soon discovered that it was easier just to infiltrate these agencies, to act through them and use them as façades, in order to preserve their brokerage activities.

The impetus for the GUAMW did not arise from the workers' personal actions but instead from the state's own concerns, which did not really favor a genuine worker-operated union. Laborers were seldom authorized to manage their own recruitment and welfare programs, but instead were made to depend on nonmigrants—clerks and bureaucrats—to supervise these operations. Workers' demands rarely originated from the rank-and-file but were instead formulated by the authorities above, although it was not very difficult to recognize what *tarāḥīl* laborers wanted. Still, workers benefited more from what was done to them than by what they did themselves. Only in one instance did migrants actually gain control over their union, in a radical offshoot in Daqahliya Province that broke away from the national organization and, for a while, established its own labor program, which workers themselves operated together with sympathetic labor organizers.

Yet any instance of itinerant unskilled rural workers coming together—or being brought together—into a trade-union organization normally reserved for permanent, skilled urban industrial laborers is extremely rare in any part of the world, and even more so in a developing country like Egypt. Jeffery Paige once remarked (1978:68) that "the migratory laborer seems an unlikely recruit for radical political action." John Dunlop, the eminent labor economist, concurred. "Migratory labor," he concluded (1949:184), "has been notoriously difficult to form into permanent organizations."

In *tarāḥīl* employment, the turnover of labor-gang members, the change in work sites and employers, and the circulation among different brokerage and employment agencies prevent the formation of a strong worker organization. Workers' group identity is weak, organizing efforts outside the village are dispersed, and important social relations are constructed as much vertically with patrons as they are horizontally with coworkers. Thus the possibility of a formal worker's organization appears limited. Any union, then, and the gains it could win, no matter how ephemeral, were still clearly to the workers' advantage as long as they outweiged the drawbacks.

The drive to recruit and protect *tarāḥīl* workers thus began strictly as a government initiative. Yet workers were in what Dunlop called (1949:179–80) a "strategic," or "critical market," position. That is, migrant workers were in a position, whether they knew it or not, to shut down, interrupt, or slow down land reclamation operations. Such strategic leverage gave workers an aggregate strength by virtue of their position in the labor process. The state was aware of this leverage and became very sensitive to the dangers of potential bottlenecks. It therefore resolved to deliver sufficient amounts of labor to employers by providing workers with greater justice—in the form of allocating them reclaimed land, paying workers their full wages, building better labor-camp accommodations, and offering them nonwage benefits—all in an attempt to induce more rural workers to join *tarāḥīl* labor trips and unblock any bottlenecks.

The first two provinces to initiate *tarāḥīl* reforms were those that had once exhibited the greatest degree of rural proletarianization and the greatest proportion of latifundia. Daqahliya and Buḥayra both had the largest amount of land expropriated under the 1952 agrarian reform program, a measure of the extent to which their territories had been organized into the kind of expansive estates conducive to large-scale cotton and grain production. They also contained a large, propertyless workforce more dependent on wage employment. On the other hand, provinces to the south such as Minūfiya, Qaliyūbiya, and southern Gharbiya were characterized more by

إحتفالات الدقهلية بالعيد القومي تعتمد على الإمكانيات المحلية

عمال التراحيل في مرحلة الانطلاق

تمليكهم الأراضي لاستصلاحها.. واستثمار مدخراتهم لزيادة دخلهم

الأخبار

عدد خاص عن محافظة الدقهلية

آخر خبر

بيوت للطلبة والطالبات تزيد عن حاجة الكليات والمعاهد العليا بالدقهلية

تمليك الأراضي البور لعمال التراحيل

إنشاء المرافق العامة قبل عمليات الاستصلاح

جوائز للجان التي تؤدي عملها بامتياز

مشروعات هامة بمجلس مدينة المنصورة

المنصورة الأسبوعية

مع الباعة في كل مكان

12. Headline from the newspaper *al-Akhbār*, May 8, 1964, proclaims "*Tarāḥīl* Workers in the Take-off Stage."

small family farms where land fragmentation had well preceded the agrarian reforms. Here workers were less proletarianized since they remained tied to minifundia through family and community relations.

During the winter following the 1961 crop failures, both Daqahliya and Buḥayra established provincial programs to provide employment and welfare services to *tarāḥīl* workers. Reform efforts in Daqahliya were initiated as early as that summer, just as the cotton crisis was unfolding. Isma'īl Farīd, an army officer who was strongly inspired by the new progressive doctrines of Arab Socialism, and who had been appointed governor a year earlier, ordered the formation of 222 new village union committees in the district of Mīt Ghamr in order to bypass older committees established since 1959 that had become heavily infiltrated by entrenched labor brokers. In February 1962, Daqahliya's provincial legislature prohibited the hiring of migrants through private brokers except where union committees did not exist (*al-Akhbār,* July 24, 1962; *al-Masā',* May 29, 1964).

Farīd organized a transportation headquarters and a training center at Mīt Ghamr, a food distribution center in the town of Balqās, a provincial credit program for workers, and an accident and life insurance plan. He persuaded the land reclamation companies to provide social security and medical care. He publicly claimed to be negotiating lower production quotas and shorter workdays, but migrants reported that instead Farīd was actually tolerating work speedups in order to silence company complaints over higher labor costs (*al-Akhbār,* July 23, 1962). Still, wages did rise, advances became regularized, and free days were eliminated. Farīd sought to use the lucrative brokerage commissions previously taken by *muqāwilīn* to finance workers' medical and pension benefits, purchase safe transport vehicles, and build low-cost public housing at home. At work sites in the New Lands, laborers were provided food from the World Food Programme of the United Nations and were sheltered in new permanent cement barracks. Many received free clothing and some participated in literacy lessons. Laborers were promised that they would be included among the first to receive title to the land they were reclaiming (*al-Ahrām,* January 20, 1964; *al-Akhbār,* May 8, 1964; *al-Masā',* November 15, 1964).

The Daqahliya project was the first of its kind in Egypt, and the press enthusiastically praised it as the dawn of Egypt's new progressive society. At every opportunity, and with great fanfare, Farīd announced remarkable new achievements that were to enhance the lives and work conditions of these laborers. Farīd could not altogether eliminate *muqāwilīn,* but he could restrict their operations. He established government employment agencies in six out Daqahliya's eight districts,[3] which were to operate on behalf of their constituent, village-level union committees in order to displace exploitative brokers. Yet his most prominent accomplishment was the organization of the village *lijān niqābiya* that he championed. These were to deliver the full wages, shorter hours, and unrestricted credit that he had promised workers. Income, health, transport, safety, shelter, land, clothing, education, honor, dignity—all these and more would improve as a result of these village union committees. For all these efforts, Farīd was proclaimed the "spiritual father" of *tarāḥīl* workers (*al-Akhbār*, July 24, 1962).

Yet more quietly, the governor also began forming separate village supervisory committees to oversee the union locals and administer their affairs. Each supervisory committee was to include three village officials—the mayor, the local committee secretary from the Arab Socialist Union (ASU), and the ACA supervisor—and a knowledgeable labor broker of "good character." Even though he was careful to avoid including "exploitative" brokers, Farīd's intent still was to rely on village elites whose interests were opposed to those of migrant workers and who frequently were related to *muqāwilīn* through kinship and marriage ties.

For despite all the media attention over creating local union committees, it was the village supervisory committees that were to wield real authority. The village union committees were charged with enumerating and registering local workers who wished to become eligible for government services and assistance, and with receiving labor requests from the reclamation companies relayed down through government employment agencies established at the provincial and district levels. The supervisory committees, on the other hand, were responsible for collecting and dispersing brokerage commissions and program funds. Their payments of high administrative overhead to village, district, and provincial officials appropriated a large proportion of the commissions that many *tarāḥīl* workers considered a rightful part of their full wage (*al-Akhbār*, July 24, 1962).

Nevertheless, the national publicity for the workers' union organization provided its village committees with many opportunities in which to challenge elite agendas. Government domination was never a foregone conclusion, and enough pressure emanated from below that occasionally these union committees developed a strong rural vitality. In several instances, supervisory committee members, caught up in the crusade to organize *tarāḥīl* workers, genuinely cooperated with village locals. This provided an important arena where migrants and their middle-class supporters worked together to exert leverage and to resolve labor issues.

In the mid-1960s the Daqahliya program was proclaimed the most successful model since it supposedly exhibited the viable village union committee structure commensurate with the prevailing rhetoric of progressive Arab Socialism. Yet in practice, it was actually the program in neighboring Buḥayra Province, with its more top-down approach and the absence of any real or even feigned worker participation, that eventually became the prototype adopted later for the larger national undertaking.

Unlike Farīd, Wajīh Abāzha, Buḥayra's more aristocratic and conservative governor, offered only superficial support for migrant labor reforms, a not-so-thin disguise for relying principally on rural notables who earlier had filled the ranks of labor brokers or who were related to them through kinship. In practice, he dispensed with union committees altogether, citing their radical and communist tendencies as grounds for dismissing their grassroots activities.[4] Instead, he simply deputized those brokers who operated in the two border towns of Kūm Hamāda and Abū Maṭāmīr adjacent to Taḥrīr Province to henceforth employ *tarāḥīl* workers and to turn over a portion of their commissions to the provincial treasury.

Labor brokers were less entrenched in Buḥayra than in Daqahliya since the accelerated operations to the west in Taḥrīr Province had only recently demanded, and rewarded, sizeable brokerage activities. Thus not as much time had elapsed to create divisions within the local upper class like those in Daqahliya, which could weaken its ability to collectively resist provincial pressures for migrant labor reforms. In Buḥayra, landlords were more united. They were more entrepreneurial, more accustomed to a fast-paced wage-labor market, and more enthusiastic about investing their profits in urban enterprises in nearby Alexandria. Unlike Daqahliya, where local government bureaucrats frequently opposed the interests of atavistic landlords, in Buḥayra administrators were much more in harmony with the landed gentry. In addition, those activists in Buḥayra who advocated forming a workers' union were less radical and received less support from ASU pa[illegible] dres. In brief, the outcry for reforms in Buḥayra was milder, the opposition more consolidated, and provincial cooperation less accommodating. Perhaps too, these differences explain why tepid provincial government programs eventually succeeded in Buḥayra, whereas the strident GUAMW initiatives in Daqahliya failed. In Daqahliya, the initial discord between conservative landlords and liberal officials deceived many union organizers into declaring their campaign a success. Yet in the end, they were isolated and crushed when elite interests united and reasserted themselves.

The reform movement in Buḥayra began shortly after the *tarāḥīl* worker program had started in Daqahliya. Earlier, institutional recruitment activities had operated strictly through the ACAs (Harik 1974:252–257; *al-Ahrām*,

August 26, 1961). But in February 1962, Aḥmad Yūnis, the village mayor of Najīla in Kūm Hamāda District, petitioned Abāzha to open a migrant Employment Office. Opposition from the district president and more than 300 labor brokers in Kūm Hamāda forced the provincial government to choose Abū Maṭāmīr as the first site. Nevertheless, pressure built, resistance was somehow overcome, and a second office opened in Kūm Hamāda the following month. Both offices assumed the organizational shape that in Daqahliya constituted district-level government employment agencies, which, together with their constituent village supervisory committees, oversaw local union activities. In Buḥayra, however, village supervisory committees were omitted, and village union committees were much weaker since they were not established immediately and never to the extent observed in Daqahliya. Moreover, the two district offices contained so many private labor brokers that one journalist half-seriously suggested that these *muqāwilūn* ought to just hang signs on their door saying "Employment Office" in order to avoid government censure (*Akhir Sāʿa*, September 7, 1966).

Buḥayra's Employment Offices viewed themselves strictly as commercial bureaus that supplied employers with as many workers as possible, with little if any attempt to provide laborers with benefits and assistance. They recruited workers from as far away as the Saʿīd in order to fulfill company contracts. Yet not only did they neglect to displace private brokers, they instead actively resorted to their "marketing expertise" when they were unable to recruit sufficient numbers of local migrants. Still, because the two district offices rationalized and expanded employment operations, wages rose from 6 to 10 piasters to 18 to 22 piasters,[5] and brokerage commissions declined from the 15 percent charged in Daqahliya to 5 percent. Work conditions improved with the construction of permanent labor camps in the New Lands, where workers received adequate shelter, nourishment, and medical attention from the Health Ministry. As a result, large numbers of enthusiastic workers turned away from agriculture and engaged in *tarāḥīl* labor instead.

When later in 1964 the Labor Ministry designed its own migrant labor program, it replicated the Buḥayra Employment Office project instead of the more popular union program operating next door in Daqahliya (Baradāʿī 1972:24). Even though both programs offered basically the same material improvements—for Daqahlawis, mostly in their village; for Buḥayris, primarily at their work site—the Daqahliya program offered something extra: the opportunity for workers to achieve greater control over their labor so that they could ensure that these improvements would continue and even possibly get better. The Buḥayra program had essentially omitted the progressive discourse, the slogans, and even the pretense of advancing workers' concerns in its effort to recruit as many migrants as possible. Economic incentives were furnished only when they helped to attract workers. The province encouraged the construction of permanent labor camps, for example, but it also charged fees of 1 piaster a day for its services and 5 piasters a day for food, which in Daqahliya were both free. It is not surprising then that later, when Egypt experienced a deep economic recession after 1965 and officials in the provinces and in Cairo were no longer able to sustain what few material benefits these Employment Offices provided, workers forthrightly abandoned them. Unlike the union programs in provinces like Daqahliya, here there were far fewer opportunities for workers to seek redress and gain greater control over their labor.

Besides the migrant employment projects in Daqahliya and Buḥayra, a third *tarāḥīl* labor program was established in Wādī Natrūn, an oasis located on the desert road halfway between Cairo and Alexandria. As early as the summer of 1961, the Youth Ministry had offered its international summer youth camp facilities for use during the winter as an experiment to increase the workers' productivity. The first camp began in December with migrants recruited from Daqahliya, but it ended abruptly when labor brokers from that province came and attacked the workers. Tents were set on fire and workers fled home (*al-Akhbār,* March 17, April 13, 1964). A year later, in December 1962, a second attempt was made. This time the Youth Ministry was more cautious and recruited workers from Buḥayra instead. Together with the Ministries of Labor, Culture, Health, and National Guidance, a model labor camp was erected to provide such basics as shelters, meals, beds, and latrines, but it also added such luxuries as medical examinations, rest days and vacations, radios, televisions, weekly movies, lectures, sports, and social and religious festivities. Wages rose significantly, and camp accommodations greatly improved the living conditions of *tarāḥīl* employment.

When this second labor camp ended in June 1963, the organizers proclaimed it a major success, announcing that productivity had increased at an average rate of 71.6 percent (Rishād 1968:37).[6] Two years later, Aḥmad Yūnis, now a member of Parliament, initiated a third workers' camp at Wādī Natrūn. As a result of these efforts, the Labor Ministry constructed two permanent labor camps in North Taḥrīr based on the costly prototype established at Wādī Natrūn. Even though after 1967, these and other New Lands labor camps fell into disrepair as many of the accommodations deteriorated or disappeared, many of the favorable work rules and practices first adopted at Wādī Natrūn continued to be enforced in later years and significantly improved *tarāḥīl* work conditions throughout the land reclamation areas. Migrants had received better treatment, and the increased quality and quantity of work proved that there was a tangible connection between humanistic reforms and economic results (Baradāʿī 1972:37).

From a national perspective, all of these early reform programs remained decentralized and uncoordinated. Yet by 1964, pressure to do more had grown, especially from ʿAbd al-Nāṣir, who felt that the plight of *tarāḥīl* workers represented a stain on the national character of Egypt. On March 26, the president addressed Parliament and spoke of the national shame of three million neglected agricultural and *tarāḥīl* workers (*al-Akhbār,* April 13, 1964). Two weeks later he personally ordered the Labor Minister, Anwār Salāma, to establish a national union for rural workers. The Ministry then submitted legislation to Parliament that revised the 1959 labor laws so as to permit the formation of village union committees throughout the entire Egyptian countryside.

Within weeks, an outburst of union activity erupted as the excitement of forming new local committees infected workers, officials, and ASU activists. Between April and July, branch unions in each of Egypt's twenty-seven provinces and 4,000 *lajna niqābiya* were established, if not concretely, then at least on paper. Local village elections were held to select union committee officers and to prepare for the national elections, which were scheduled for July 12, 1964, along with other labor unions (*al-Akhbār,* May 19, 1964; *Majallāt al-Thaqāfa al-ʿUmmāliya,* June 1964).

In the months immediately before the elections, the Labor Ministry consolidated a number of unrelated occupations together into the GUAMW in order to ease the burden of supervising all the different separate elections. Imprudently, *tarāḥīl* workers were mixed in with sponge divers, fishermen, chicken raisers, animal breeders, straw mat producers, and cotton seed cleaners—an odd assortment that diluted their unique individual situations in a bureaucratic clutter of colliding demands and contradictory interests (*Majallāt al-Thaqāfa al-ʿUmmāliya,* June 1964; *Majalāt al-ʿAmal,* September 1964).

From the beginning, Labor Ministry directives defining exactly who was eligible for union membership were never straightforward. This ambiguity allowed many labor brokers to infiltrate village union committees. Since the ranks of *tarāḥīl* workers included both poor farmers as well as propertyless workers, land ownership could not be strictly enforced as a criteria to disqualify participants. Labor brokers, like other wealthy landlords, had parceled out their property among relatives in order to evade the agrarian reform laws. Once officially registered as small farmers, they could then legally take part in union activities. Such subversion clearly undermined GUAMW operations, and in many cases, the government actively cooperated when it ratified fraudulent election results. For the next several years, opponents soundly criticized the GUAMW for these irregularities. Muḥammad Zaīdān, a writer for the weekly magazine *Rūz al-Yūsif*, described (September 28, 1964) the atmosphere he found in one village in Buḥayra, where workers were systematically excluded from participating in union committee elections but where local elites were not. It is worthwhile citing portions of his article at length:[7]

> When election day came, the laborers from the village of Kafr Salmūn in Buḥayra Province were far away at work sites in the new reclamation lands in Taḥrīr Province, Wādī Natrūn, and the Qaṭṭara Depression. They had been informed that the election was the next day but how were they suppose to return to vote? The next day when officials gathered to hold the election, a worker arrived delivering a letter signed by the Taḥrīr Province director and the district law enforcement official requesting that the union election be postponed because the migrants at Taḥrīr were required to continue working and could not return to vote. "The election took place," Zaīdān acknowledged, "but many who won had never worked a day in their life."
>
> The workers felt that this was their election and that it was impossible for any landlord or outsider to influence it or penetrate it. But it happened. The landlords made every effort to stop this last hope of the workers for an impartial election. "What happened was a mistake," said the president of Kūm Hamāda district. "Real workers were not represented in any of the village elections."
>
> This district official[8] had received numerous complaints about voting irregularities but had simply passed them along to the Labor Ministry's district Labor Office. Yet the Labor Office was already far too busy since it had to complete all village elections in just 10 days, which meant holding as many as three village elections per day. The Labor Ministry in Cairo had provided only one independent labor inspector for each district. Moreover, it had already been negligent in forming union committees and had not registered all the village workers. "The response was that the Labor Office only wanted thirty workers in each village, and thirty workers only,"[9] the inspector recalled. In other provinces, labor inspectors were also faulted for merely recording thirty names of workers without informing them about what a

union committee meant or encouraging greater participation. With limited time and limited manpower, but many villages and many more workers to cover, inspectors faced pressures for which they were not completely responsible [see also *al-Ahrām*, November 16, 1964]. In Buḥayra, over 4,000 workers were unable to vote.

Despite official orders not to talk to the press, the district labor inspector conceded to Zaīdān that he had not received adequate cooperation from his headquarters. The district Labor Office had only one motorcycle for transportation. Nor was the inspector allowed to rent a car or spend any funds without permission from the provincial Labor Region office in Damanhūr, the provincial capital. Permission, however, was not forthcoming. Without a vehicle, the inspector was left to depend on what favors he could curry, with the result that he relied primarily on brokers, landlords, and reclamation company officials to drive him to the different villages. On election day in Kafr Salmūn, the inspector arrived in the car of a local landlord. To workers, this clearly signaled that the labor inspector would discourage the votes of real workers while encouraging those who were loyal to his automobile companion.

In despair, the labor inspector tried instead to enlist the services of local ASU committees, village council presidents, mayors, and councilmen to help solve these problems [frequently the same persons, or their kinsmen, who opposed the interests of *tarāḥīl* workers]. In the end, the labor inspector failed to hold sound and impartial elections, and local administrators, loyal to local elites, were not willing to correct these problems.

Nevertheless, and despite numerous instances of fraud, corruption, and conflicting interests, elections were held for village union committees. Then, in July 1964, over 300 district delegates chosen by these local committees met in Cairo to elect national officers. Harry Hopkins, a member of the British Labor Party, was on hand (1969:314–16) to witness the first GUAMW national election. Again it is valuable to quote his personal recollections at length:

> [T]hat first meeting of the new union [was] held one hot July night in an empty school in a shabby Cairo side-street [Bāb al-Lūq] that was clamorous with the sounds of men and boys beating out crumpled cars. It was a remarkable occasion. Three hundred delegates from every part of Egypt jammed the stairs on their way to the lecture room where the election of the executive was to be held. There were statu-

esque giants from Upper Egypt, Nubians from the New Nubia, a Bedouin or two from Borg el Arab, wiry fellows from the labour gangs of Liberation Province and the reclamation projects on Lakes Borollos and Manzalah in the far north. What they had in common was their poverty. An old man in a white turban, from Minya, told me that, with five children in his family, his pay was twenty-five piastres a day. Work was still hard to find for two months in the winter; but before the revolution, he said, his pay had been eight piasters.

The delegates squeezed on to the tiered benches of the lecture room and sat there reading the new statutes of the union which they were being invited to pass. Lips moved painstakingly. It had not been possible to insist on the usual literacy requirements. To organise agriculture workers anywhere is difficult: to organise *tarahiel* labourers in a country like Egypt verges on the heroic. Several earlier attempts had failed, or resulted in little more than a union of Ministry of Agriculture employees. This time, 4,000 committees had been formed covering all Egypt and it was these which had now sent forward their delegates.

As is the practice in Egypt, several Ministry of Labour Trade Union Department officials were present to supervise the election and see that legal requirements were met.

"Sometimes they are suspicious of each other," their chief explained. "With us here, they feel safe."

But not, it appeared, quite safe enough—for within five minutes a faction fight had broken out which kept the room in an uproar for upwards of an hour. The volume of sound was truly formidable. Men climbed on tables, and chairs piled on tables, to gain a better vantage point for verbal fire. Accusing arms stabbed the air. After vainly pounding the table for ten minutes, the Ministry of Labour chief gave it up and walked out. "They are *simplistes*," he explained, tolerantly. "They are ignorant. They like to make a noise." They were insisting, it seemed, on voting immediately; they suspected that someone was trying to put something over on them.

The pandemonium subsided as swiftly as it had begun. The voting started. When a delegate was illiterate, a Ministry of Labour official sat beside him on the bench and quietly read down the list of seventy-one candidates (for twenty-one seats on the executive). As the voice read a favoured name, the man made his mark. They made their choice with great deliberation and earnestness. An Egyptian reporter asked me what I thought about it and I said it was a very moving sight, and I meant it.

> And now, eight months later, the Land Workers' Union was an accomplished fact, an affiliate of the Trade Union Confederation of Egypt, and, with its three million members, by far the biggest trade union in the land. It was true that of this number, only half a million—the regular, year-round employees—could as yet afford to pay even the smallest subscription. But the casual and the *tarahiel* workers were registered and organised in the union's 4,000 branches [*sic*],[10] with their elected committees. For the first time it had become possible to plumb these lower depths—and not only plumb them, but build some sort of floor beneath. The union, for a start, was demanding proper tented camps and medical attention for the *tarahiel* workers; private contractors were to be abolished in favour of contracts negotiated through local union committees, backed by a special section of the Ministry of Labour, and plans were mooted for training centres to equip at least some "surplus" labourers for jobs in industry or elsewhere.

Immediately there were voting complications. A dissident group appeared to express its dissatisfaction with the newly elected president. In response, another contingent complained that a number of agricultural employees had been excluded and that additional union committees still needed to be created in the Ministries of Agriculture and Agrarian Reform, Land Reclamation, and Irrigation. Field workers reacted by defending the existing regulations, opposing new elections, and declaring that they would not have *affandiya* (white-collar employees) in the union to crowd them out. The inclusion of *affandiya*, they argued, violated the spirit of the revolution and defamed the meaning of the word worker. Many complained that the union was better off for having held the elections the way they were. However, the next day, the Labor Ministry annulled the elections. New union committees were quickly formed, and new elections were held a week later. The outcome was the same as the week before (*al-Akhbār*, July 13, 20, 1964).

Two serious flaws afflicted the formation of the GUAMW: the infiltration by labor brokers and the inclusion of white-collar employees. Several of the new union leaders were either already secretly labor brokers who had intimidated voters into electing them, or else, later, as commission revenues rose and village union committees failed, were to slip quietly into private brokerage activities. The degree to which brokers infiltrated the union was never fully revealed, but it occurred frequently enough that union activities often became mere façades for their uninterrupted operations. Different employment agencies frequently accused their rivals—not without evidence—of resorting to "hidden" brokers in order to discredit their competitor's operations and advance their own contested authority.

The GUAMW also included white-collar employees from government ministries and public-sector companies. Indeed, the July voting elected more white-collar employees into leadership positions than manual laborers. And even the label "manual worker" becomes suspect, since many of these executives were literate enough to assume the duties of their new posts and thus were not working with their hands at all. Among the ten officers, seven were nonworkers, and of the ten board members, six were listed as employees and not laborers (*al-Akhbār,* July 12, 13, 1964).[11] This distinction between white collar and "no collar"—for the standard peasant tunic lacks this piece of fabric—but their consolidation within one single union, enabled educated, middle-class supervisors to dominate the union and to dilute the demands of less articulate and more dispersed manual laborers.

Ṣalāḥ Abū al-Majd was elected the union's first president. He had been a salaried supervisor from the Wādī Kūm Umbū Agricultural Company in Aswān, a sugar manufacturer. Since 1959 employees working in several agricultural companies had been permitted to form local union committees to negotiate directly with company executives. As their chief representative, Abū al-Majd had gained valuable experience, which enabled him to win the election (*al-Ahrām,* November 1, 1969). And even though ordinary candidates from Daqahliya had won more posts than those from any other province—reflecting the union's greater strength there after three years of continuous activity—many rank-and-file workers still complained that Abū al-Majd and other white-collar bureaucrats had stolen the election.

Four distinct political tendencies soon emerged within the GUAMW. First there were the radicals, principally clustered in Daqahliya, but also sprinkled throughout other provinces. This pocket of authentic organizing advocated absolute workers' control of union activities, which, as they argued, should focus primarily on labor recruitment. They urged the national union to pressure Parliament to outlaw private brokers. Other demands included full and higher wages, improved working conditions, workers' pensions, health and medical care, leadership training, job-site recreation, and workers' participation on company productivity councils. Radicals did receive support from outside sympathizers in the ASU and from individuals from the Labor Ministry's General Administration of Unions and the

Workers' Culture Organization, but despite these influential allies, their perspective became increasingly marginalized.

The remaining three tendencies all reflected the perspective of employers and the state. They proposed, with varying degrees of distrust and disdain, dependence on outside nonlabor agencies to conduct migrant labor programs. The first approach displayed a liberal outlook. It considered labor recruitment an essential union activity but sought to rely on a variety of government agencies to perform this service. The second position exhibited a moderate approach. It insisted that the union should not be involved with employment whatsoever, but instead should stress classroom courses for workers' literacy and (re)training, relying in Arthur Lewis–fashion on the eventual dissipation of the *tarāḥīl* workforce and its absorption into industrial jobs to finally resolve their difficulties through attrition. A third perspective presented a conservative view. It argued that the union should altogether ignore the majority of its members who were manual laborers and instead concentrate exclusively on the issues of white-collar employees, who after all were the only dues-paying members. Although poor migrant workers had been excused from paying dues, the high brokerage commissions their employment earned still constituted the largest contribution to the union's treasury. Nevertheless, the conservatives disregarded this, and many even advocated forming an entirely separate agricultural employees' union.

One of the major difficulties of organizing unskilled workers was that the uneducated rank-and-file by and large lacked sufficient political clout to challenge any of these last three perspectives. And even the radical position required workers to rely on educated allies who, however, were not entirely insincere and could still be counted on to sympathize and understand the root problems that ordinary workers encountered. Nevertheless, even the radicals did not promote united job actions such as organized strikes, slowdowns, or mass resignations. Informal job tactics did exist in *tarāḥīl* work, as chapter 4 demonstrated, but they were never organized at higher levels and remained weak weapons practiced by individual laborers or individual *tarāḥīl* labor gangs. Yet even though the radicals championed a rather mild set of legitimate demands, they still became isolated and their influence waned. This left workers' programs and union affairs squarely in the hands of those advocating more white-collar-oriented agendas.

Was the GUAMW then, with its nonworker leadership, simply another example of the corporatist labor organization supposedly found elsewhere in Egypt (Bianchi 1989:chap. 5)? Was this state-organized union merely what June Nash once labeled (1985:153) a "labor control mechanism?" In fact, the new union was not entirely a government artifact. Despite its white-collar leadership, it still became a significant arena for struggle over the control of labor, income, benefits, and work conditions. Although it ultimately failed to permanently enhance the quality of migrant lives and work, it nevertheless won a number of momentary victories—raising wages, improving work-site conditions, and attracting national attention—which lured large numbers of agricultural workers to register with the GUAMW, or enlist with rival government agencies, or even return to working for private brokers of "good character."

After the elections in the summer of 1964, the national union set about doing what most labor organizations do: mobilizing its members and holding mass meetings. The first two meetings proceeded in a calm, corporatist fashion indicative of the new leadership style (*al-Jumhūriya,* August 19, 1964; *al-Akhbār,* November 17, 1964). But a third gathering, scheduled later that fall, came during the lull that follows cotton harvest and wheat preparation, when more rural workers were free to attend. At this meeting, held on November 9 in Ajā, Daqahliya, the illusion of a government-dominated workers' organization disappeared.

The official agenda was suddenly disrupted when "thousands of workers," as *al-Masā'* newspaper reported (November 15, 1964), confronted union officers over the real purpose of village union committees. Rank-and-file members from Daqahliya, together with supporters from local ASU party committees, Labor Ministry bureaus, and village and district government offices insisted that the GUAMW should directly handle all employment operations.

To calm the confusion, Daqahliya's crusading governor, Isma'īl Farīd, offered to help. "If the union is able to set up the hiring of workers now," he declared, "we are ready to deliver [our] project to it." Farīd naively proposed to hand over the province's entire recruitment project to placate those in insurrection, intending, it seemed, that the local provincial government would assist the union committees but come to dominate them in the process. Instead, the offer was interpreted as a complete takeover by the union committees of his entire three-year undertaking. Suddenly, as the *al-Masā'* journalist recounted, "many members of the General Union announced moving their offices from Cairo to al-Mansūra," Daqahliya's capital. The provincial union committees threatened to secede completely from the national headquarters in Cairo. Eventually a compromise was reached by calling the new organization a "branch" union, still nominally attached to the national union. But despite this cosmetic reconciliation, the GUAMW became deeply split between real workers and their supporters on the one hand, and those in white-collar positions on the other.

The branch union emerged as an important organization for satisfying labor's demands, particularly in the Daqahliya districts of Ajā and al-Sinbalāwīn. Elsewhere in the province, and in neighboring Sharqiya and Kafr al-Shaykh Provinces, local union committees became radical strongholds. Together as a "branch," they began in December 1964 to directly contract with land reclamation companies to supply *tarāḥīl* laborers in return for gains that would actually reach their members. These agreements continued until 1971, when a combination of reclamation company and Labor Ministry maneuvers undermined this branch union's employment and welfare activities.

Reclamation companies frequently requested more workers than the branch union could recruit. Such deficits would result in speedups and higher quotas for those who actually arrived on-site unless the branch turned to local private brokers to hire more workers. Furthermore, any shortfalls in labor were immediately exploited by rival government agencies, which offered to provide the workers that the branch could not supply. Yet even when shortages approached 60 percent, the Daqahliya branch still refused to resort to *muqāwilīn*. In response, the public-sector companies evoked penalty clauses and assessed fines that amounted to as much as £E78,000 (Baradāʿī 1972:42).

Comparing this predicament with the generous arrangements concluded with the provincial Employment Office in al-Minyā reveals the companies' animosity toward the Daqahliya branch union. Al-Minyā's contract with the Mariout Reclamation Company agreed to provide even fewer workers, yet at a higher commission, than Daqahliya's—a much more expensive contract from a company perspective. Yet when shortages in al-Minyā rose to levels of 50 percent, Mariout still did not impose any costly delay penalties (Ḥussaīn 1971:26–29). And although the national union in Cairo offered to pay the fines for the Daqahliya branch, the Labor Ministry that supervised union finances refused permission (Aḥmad al-Rifāʿī, personal communication, 1992). Moreover, land reclamation companies like Mariout frequently delayed final wage payments to the branch, forcing it to draw upon its capital reserves and borrow from banks in order to pay workers on time. *Tarāḥīl* workers on tight family budgets were not pleased. Many rejected the branch and turned instead to government agencies or private brokers, which were more accommodating (*Akhir Sāʿa*,

September 9, 1966). These financial problems continued to plague branch union operations, which were finally suspended in 1971.

For at the same time the Labor Ministry had submitted legislation and was prodding Parliament to create an independent workers' union, it also began to implement a separate but parallel plan for creating regional Employment Offices that would fall under its own authority rather than become attached to provincial and district governments. Paradoxically, by providing the same services the union offered, these ministerial Employment Offices directly competed with the GUAMW. The Labor Ministry's activities proved inconsistent, for although it was mandated to form a workers' union, it also acted to retain its own bureaucratic control over labor as well. Yet the Ministry denied that the national union constituted its main rival. Instead it launched an attack against the "corruption" of provincial government Employment Offices such as those in Buḥayra. Eventually, government Employment Offices were established in Sharqiya, Daqahliya, Buḥayra, Kafr al-Shaykh, Minūfiya, Gharbiya, al-Minyā, Assiyūṭ, and Sūḥāj, although their central administration shifted back and forth between the Labor Ministry and provincial governments.

State agencies attached to the Labor Ministry or to provincial offices vigorously competed with each other as well as with independent union committees and private labor brokers for exclusive authority to oversee *tarāḥīl* labor employment. Yet the question arises as to why they were all so intent on such authority? Certainly justice and national dignity were at stake, but these ethical issues in of themselves could not sustain such strong competition. A glance, however, at the finances of *tarāḥīl* brokerage commissions suggests another good reason.

Years later, in 1975, the Agriculture College at the University of Assiyūṭ was publicly chided in the press for using an exploitative labor broker (*al-Akhbār,* January 11, 1975). The article cited financial figures to support its position. Each month the broker hired 22,000 workers for the college. For each worker's 15 piaster daily wage, the broker pocketed a shilling—5 piasters—for his commission. Each day, then, the broker took in £E1,100; each month brought him £E33,000. At the existing exchange rate, the labor broker received $500 a day, $15,000 a month, and an annual income, even if he was busy just half the year, of $88,000. Little wonder, then, that private brokers, various state offices, and the national union all were eager to employ *tarāḥīl* workers and collect such lucrative commissions.

Control over the expenditure of these funds constituted a major source of influence. The GUAMW wanted this money spent on various benefits and programs for its workers, although unsympathetic union officials who insisted it find outside partners meant allocating these commissions instead to agencies staffed by white-collar employees. Local provincial officials wanted to disburse these funds at home for projects involving housing, road paving, and construction—just the sort of local activities that could employ seasonal, unskilled manual workers who would therefore stay in the vicinity and remain more easily accessible to local agricultural employers. The Labor Ministry recommended investing these commissions in perquisites for migrant workers—clothes, pensions, medical services—and in funding labor camps in the land reclamation areas that would thereby draw workers away from the Old Lands and keep them employed and contented in the New Lands.

Plainly, these employment agencies were delighted with such revenues, but their expenditure plans also contained a more fundamental agenda: who would control where *tarāḥīl* workers moved? Provincial authorities answered to local village elites who wanted rural workers to stay nearby. The Labor Ministry cooperated with the land reclamation companies, which wanted migrant laborers to leave their villages and commit themselves to hard work at Taḥrīr. Officially the GUAMW wanted only to obtain workers benefits, but in practice it sought to spread costly payments around to include white-collar bureaucrats as well. For their part, private labor brokers simply wanted to remain rich and powerful. *Tarāḥīl* workers, on the other hand, distrusted all of these ulterior motives and preferred to have commissions reduced drastically and to use the extra money to increase their own incomes and consumption. However, without a genuine union, their political weakness and isolation meant that this labor reform movement would prove insignificant.

By the end of 1964, the two provincial experiments operating in Daqahliya and Buḥayra and the labor camp prototype established at Wādī Natrūn had been elevated to national prominence. The GUAMW had been established under direct pressure from President ʿAbd al-Nāṣir. Then, throughout the next seven years, the GUAMW, the Labor Ministry, local provincial governments, and private labor brokers all competed intensely for the exclusive authority to employ and assist *tarāḥīl* workers, mixing together altruistic intentions of resolving labor problems with pecuniary goals of accumulating profitable employment commissions. For the moment, workers did benefit from the ensuing rivalry, as the price for their participation and commitment rose. But gradually, once these agencies had carved out their own exclusive territories, the rigid rules and procedures that their administrators adopted served to prevent any real services and benefits from reaching workers.

The ultimate failure of the GUAMW was not unexpected. Radicals who had once advocated control by and for *tarāḥīl* workers were soon isolated from the national organization. The GUAMW president Abū al-Majd had become the organization's leading liberal advocate of transferring the union's hiring functions over to government employment agencies.

The radicals' last hurrah took place in March 1966. Again they disrupted a national conference, this time held in the less congenial environs of Cairo. They demanded that the GUAMW become the sole employment agent and completely displace private brokers and government agencies. The radicals' ultimatum for a totally worker-operated organization clashed directly with the corporatist approaches of white-collar officials. Yet despite help from ASU party radicals, pro-worker elements were unable to change the direction the meeting took. When final recommendations were voted on, dissident voices were drowned in a sea of various innocuous suggestions and proposals (*al-Ahrām,* March 5, March 8, 1966; *al-Akhbār,* March 7, 1966).

White-collar members soon managed to limit the radical threat. By the end of 1966, this leftist tendency was dead for all intents and purposes.[12] Egypt soon had new worries—the economic recession of 1965–66 and the political crisis generated by the Israeli defeat—so that the humanitarian cause célèbre of organizing *tarāḥīl* workers began fading into the background. Abū al-Majd and collaborating officers and board members had successfully delivered the union into the hands of those indifferent to real migrant labor concerns. Workers saw their last real opportunity disappear with the end of radicalism within the union and the organization's decline toward an elitist position. It had been their one opportunity to gain direct and immediate control over their wages, benefits, and work conditions.

The competition between central ministries and provincial bureaucracies, and between them and the GUAMW, did not permanently improve the conditions of *tarāḥīl* laborers, who consequently returned to their poverty and quiet discontent much as before. The stalemate among rivals, coupled later with a financially stagnant economy unable to support further government and union activities, eventually brought a halt to any additional migrant programs.

Workers hesitated to permanently break paternalistic ties with brokers in order to participate in the bureaucratic confusion of new and possibly temporary state-sponsored union committees or government Employment Offices. Workers did gain benefits by remaining with a single labor broker.

Loyalty had its rewards. Despite the disguised exploitation found in patron-client relationships, workers were frequently able to manipulate these ties to their advantage. Labor quotas were far more negotiable under the paternalism of inside contracting than they were when imposed impersonally by company supervisors with union endorsement. Workers were more able to use "weak weapons" under lenient supervisors than was possible under the diligent management of bureaucratic authorities. They were also able to receive loans since they were personally known to labor brokers and foremen, although repaying their debts often required more than they bargained for. But under the more impartial style of union and company management, workers were seldom, if ever, extended credit except at the village level, and then from the supervisory committee, not the union local. Easier daily work quotas, down-time for illness, loans for consumption, nonwork service assignments, and even foreman or task-leader duties came through an informal system of seniority and long attachment to one broker. In general, *tarāḥīl* workers were in a much better position to alter the effort = wage = price formula under Taylorist paternalism than they were when they were brought into Fordist forms of bureaucracy. Thus workers were not so eager to give up such personalized relations for the sake of participating in increasingly empty and uncertain programs. The state had become too distant and indifferent a broker.

Once the spotlight of the national crusade had dimmed, and despite the sympathetic support of radical allies, it was, in the end, *tarāḥīl* workers who alone faced the consequences of the failures that the GUAMW and government programs experienced. When by 1966, these new agencies had failed to keep their promises, workers returned to what they knew well. They rejected the union and state efforts and moved back instead to private *muqāwilīn*.

Still, back in the beginning, the separate provincial efforts in Daqahliya and Buḥayra after 1962, the model labor camps at Wādī Natrūn, the first national union elections held in the summer of 1964, and the turbulent mass meetings convened later that fall were exciting and inspiring. The extent to which these initial victories enticed rural workers into *tarāḥīl* employment and drew them away from farming is not easily measured. A number of Minūfī foremen I met in 1981 in the New Lands did start their careers as *tarāḥīl* workers in the mid-1960s because of the attractive benefits they received. Moreover, Egypt continued to experience tight labor supplies in agriculture. Although from the government's perspective the union movement was essentially an opportunity to secure labor, from the workers' viewpoint it provided them new arenas in which to gain greater control over their own labor so that they could then demand better incomes, benefits, and work conditions. Already, one government bureaucrat employed on a Delta reclamation project had complained as early as July 1963 that "the worker began to increase his demands and later he felt that there was someone concerned with his affairs and to protect his interests. I believe that it is necessary for the worker to be satisfied with what the province achieved" (*al-Akhbār,* July 23, 1963).

This indicates that workers were beginning to use the provincial program to go beyond its mild reforms. Just the year before, laborers at Aswān had struck for better working and living conditions. Now workers in the Delta were no longer prepared to accept the multiple corruptions of migrant labor. As "some person"—the bureaucrat was referring to ʿAbd al-Nāṣir—or the union he championed took up their cause, rural workers began to insist on receiving their full entitlements. Workers were no longer content simply to exchange reduced incomes earned in the village for the hardships encountered in migrant work. Many left agriculture and went to work through government-sponsored *tarāḥīl* programs in order to improve their incomes and their standard of living. Yet these programs had the unintended consequences of being too successful, and once again by increasing the number of *tarāḥīl* migrant workers left too few farm laborers back in the countryside.

Dire Consequences

In village agriculture, male labor shortages persisted, women and children remained overworked and underpaid, and production problems in cotton, rice, and (in 1964) wheat continued to create problems for the national economy. Not only were foreign currency reserves depressed, but now the United States was demanding hard dollars for its grain. Revoking financial credits for U.S. PL-480 wheat sales would have been inconsequential if sufficient quantities of wheat had been grown domestically. Production shortfalls in cotton decreased the accumulation of hard currency; deficits in cereal yields meant importing foreign wheat to pacify urban consumers. In order to pay for imported grain, Egypt had to dip into its foreign currency reserves, already low because export cotton production had declined.

After 1971, the rural workers' union curtailed most of its activities because of corruption. Yet as early as 1966, the damage it had done to the national economy by successfully organizing migrant farm laborers had already taken place. Ironically, the government had carelessly scheduled its projects and policies. First back in 1961 it initiated infrastructural construction at Aswān and on the fringes of the Nile Valley. Then it formulated policies of confiscating property, expanding agricultural cooperatives, and imposing price controls. Finally, in 1964 it organized a momentarily effective workers' union. In all instances, these policies encouraged more rural workers who were dissatisfied with village agriculture to shift into distant *tarāḥīl* migrant labor. Government planners deluded themselves into thinking that the countryside contained unlimited numbers of surplus workers that could satisfy the demand for unskilled labor throughout Egypt. In reality, such numbers were critically missing. Instead, village women and children replaced departing men in farming, however imperfectly, but became so much in demand that not enough nonmale workers were able to produce the food and export crops Egypt needed to advance its economy.

Just as in 1961, problems in agriculture again engendered a crisis in national finance and economic growth. Failures in crop production once more affected Cairo's plans to use its hard-earned foreign currency reserves for worthwhile projects in national development instead of avoiding default and falling hopelessly behind. From 1964 to 1966, cotton production declined 20 percent. To compensate for the subsequent imbalance of trade, Egypt resorted to deficit financing, borrowing an average of £E60 million annually up to 1966. Soon a second foreign exchange emergency shook Egypt. Hansen and Nashashibi concluded (1975:108–11) that "[t]he exchange crisis reached such proportions in 1965 and 1966 that Egypt was unable to fulfill contractual debt service obligations, got involved in short-term financing through European (particularly Italian) commercial banks at interest rates that even the Khedive Ismail would have found immodest, and had to ask for moratoria from both West and East."

This forced Egypt to restrict wheat grain imports and to draw on its foreign exchange reserves to pay for what was already traded. This contributed to food shortages that raised retail food prices by 11.5 percent and added to the overall price inflation that gripped the country. The value of imported wheat and wheat flour in 1965–66 (£E55 million) exceeded the value of all Egyptian exports to Western markets (£E52 million). In meeting its import demands, Egypt fell into arrears in servicing its external commercial debt (Waterbury 1983:95–96, 98).

During the period between 1960 and 1964, Egypt's GNP had expanded by 5 percent per year. But in the two years preceding the war with Israel, GNP grew at a rate of just 0.3 percent annually. Thus, on the eve of the 1967 debacle, Egypt was in a serious economic crisis.

Again, this downturn could not have taken place at a worse possible moment. The rise of pan-Arab nationalism under ʿAbd al-Nāṣir and the belligerent position he assumed against Israel were certainly not coordinated with Egypt's financial capacity to wage war. The 1965–66 recession that struck Egypt made it frightfully ill-prepared for an outbreak of fighting. By 1967 Egypt had so depleted its foreign exchange reserves that it was no longer able to purchase parts and equipment from abroad. Thus the historian Arthur Goldschmidt (1988:125) concluded, "Economically, neither Egypt nor Israel could afford a war. Egypt had exhausted its hard-currency reserves and could no longer buy spare parts to run some of its factories or to fly its United Arab Airlines passenger jets."

In the early morning of June 5, Israel attacked Egypt. Within three hours, Israeli planes bombed 80 percent of its air force. Even those aircraft that were salvageable could not be repaired. Shortly thereafter, Israeli troops invaded the Sinai and in three days reached the Suez Canal. Without air cover or serviceable equipment, Egyptian troops were unable to withstand the assault. Twenty thousand soldiers died, as much from exposure and thirst as from battle injuries. On June 8, Egypt accepted a UN Security Council cease-fire (Goldschmidt 1988:127; Nutting 1978:417). Despite the familiar label "Six-Day" war, the defeat actually took place in just seventy-two hours.

The June war demonstrated that the manufacture of essential military armament and munitions, which relied on imported machinery, had been starved of foreign currency. Parts for repairing damaged battle equipment were not in stock. The dissipation of hard-currency reserves had further reduced Egypt's ability to successfully engage in combat. The foreign currency earned by insufficient cotton exports was not even enough to pay for the imported wheat that compensated for shortfalls in domestic grain production, much less to pay for foreign components and spare parts. Thus a labor-induced agricultural crisis helped contribute to Egypt's humiliating military defeat by reducing the nation's foreign currency reserves. Such failure in agriculture was the outcome of attracting large numbers of *tarāḥīl* workers to work first in Aswān and later in Taḥrīr, handicapping village employers by controlling agricultural prices, and then further encouraging the exodus by establishing a momentarily effective union for migrant laborers.

Once again government policy had inadvertently supported the movement of migrant farm workers out of agriculture into land reclamation. As the Labor Ministry organized the GUAMW and then together with provincial governments established a number of rival employment agencies, even more *tarāḥīl* workers left their villages for better employment. Viewed from the vantage point of rural unskilled labor, the momentary benefits gained from these competing efforts were very inviting.

Some *tarāḥīl* laborers still considered receiving land grants appealing, for it allowed them to continue working as farmers. They were disappointed therefore when in 1962, the New Lands policy under Abū al-Nūr had reverted back to focusing exclusively on state farms. Yet increasingly, many more migrants had begun viewing themselves more as workers rather than as farmers, more interested in raising incomes than in raising crops. Thus they sought more employment, not more land. With the growth of state intervention in agriculture, owning or renting farm plots had become a losing proposition. And although *tarāḥīl* labor still constituted transitional employment between farm work and urban jobs, clearly enough had begun seeing themselves as full-time, permanent migrants that the idea of a workers' union seemed intriguing.

Although the government created the GUAMW in order to meet its own strategic labor needs, workers joined it because now they viewed themselves more as permanent *tarāḥīl* laborers than as part-time farmers and therefore found its goals and opportunities worthwhile. But when the union movement failed, it was not because the state had finally satisfied its own labor demands, but because these workers had become disenchanted with its empty promises. Instead they turned back to private brokers, seeing that their paternalistic control of labor offered them relatively more advantages than the impersonal exploitation of an unwieldy, remote bureaucracy.

Rival viewpoints had collided over the central issues of who would run the new union and who would profit from its commissions. The state had viewed the union as a source of lucrative revenues and bureaucratic influence. Workers, on the other hand, had seen it as a means for taking over employment activities and increasing their income by appropriating the brokerage fees they considered part of their income. The government and white-collar agencies had hoped to use the union as a labor-control mechanism. Workers and their allies had struggled instead to improve what was becoming a permanent way of life.

But the June war destroyed any possibility that the government could continue its crusade to help and hire *tarāḥīl* workers. It also dealt a major blow to Cairo's efforts at becoming a semi-peripheral state and introducing peripheral Fordism. Subsequently, the government enacted severe austerity measures: consumption costs climbed, incomes stagnated or fell, and forced capital transfers expanded. Government budgets were cut, except for defense expenditures. The result was what Waterbury called (1983:112) a period of "seven lean years" stretching from 1967 to 1974: "[T]he enormous military expenditures needed to avoid capitulation to Israel [meant] [e]verything else in the realm of social and economic policy was held in suspended animation; the apparatus of the public sector, the programs of the welfare state, as well as the country's infrastructure, were barely maintained, and . . . production levels and the quantity and quality of services began to deteriorate."

Not until 1973, when a regional oil boom ignited a new expansion, did the economic retrenchment subside. Skilled construction workers emigrated abroad to take advantage of new foreign opportunities and left numerous job openings at home, which offered *tarāḥīl* workers new opportunities for domestic employment. Migrants benefited from the chain reaction of filling positions emptied by those more skilled laborers who left. Thereafter, the smoldering discontent of rural workers over the transient character of both *tarāḥīl* and agricultural employment fueled a new mass exodus, this time out of the countryside altogether.

When workers once again began "voting with their feet," this time they walked away from the GUAMW, from Employment Offices attached to the Labor Ministry or to provincial governments, and from *muqāwilīn al-anfār*. Instead they found more rewarding full-time employment in places like Cairo, Alexandria, and al-Minyā. As for the union they abandoned, there were increasingly fewer migrants left to actually mobilize. The fate of Egypt's once-inspiring experiment for employing and protecting *tarāḥīl* workers, now essentially moribund and ineffectual, was finally sealed as laborers left migrant work and left the GUAMW to its own corruption and fraud.

7

Sowing the Seeds of Urban Discontent, 1977

Throughout the first half of the 1960s, rural workers dissatisfied with low wages and harsh treatment in agriculture had switched to higher wages and better working conditions in *tarāḥīl* labor. But after the 1965–66 recession, they were no more content with migrant-labor jobs than they were back home in farming. From 1967 to 1974, struggles within both labor processes were thwarted by the "seven lean years" of economic retrenchment. Afterwards, however, new global conditions expanded the unskilled labor market, which provided a resolution that once again seemed to benefit rural workers.

Upon the death of ʿAbd al-Nāṣir in 1970, Egypt changed presidents. Anwār al-Sadāt adopted his predecessor's post-1967 shift to the right, but soon added his own distinctive policy orientation (Hirst and Beeson 1981:104–5). Al-Sadāt's popular support remained weak. To help strengthen his legitimacy, the president resurrected the plight of *tarāḥīl* workers as a reliable crusade that would demonstrate the government's concern for the downtrodden while distracting attention from the more distressing implications of the Corrective Revolution of May 15, 1971.

Numerous Parliamentary hearings that summer vacillated over which ministry would be awarded authority over *tarāḥīl* worker employment and welfare. The new GUAMW president, Aḥmad al-Rifāʿī, had suspended the union's programs with migrant laborers because of internal corruption and so the GUAMW was out of the picture. The ensuing rivalries between the Labor Ministry and the newly consolidated Local Government Ministry, and between these two and private *muqāwilīn*, were by no means empty victories for government bureaucrats. Yet they were not very important to a *tarāḥīl* workforce that was rapidly shrinking in size.

Even for the few who did remain, government efforts proved ineffectual. *Tarāḥīl* labor shortages aggravated the existing corruption when either bureaucratic or private labor brokers delivered fewer workers than requested, and pocketed the difference in wage payments between high official invoices and actual labor rosters. To conceal these deficits, underpaid company supervisors were bought off. Those migrants left were forced to work even harder in compensation and to use whatever techniques possible to renegotiate hard assignments and low wages. But these "weapons" could succeed only if outside employment offered a way to alter the migrants' regime of accumulation. Yet in the late 1960s, economic retrenchment kept the effort = wage = price equation tilted to the workers' disadvantage. Only after 1973, when new employment opportunities opened up in towns and cities, were they able to reject *tarāḥīl* labor. Ostensibly, the event that so transformed the unskilled labor market was the outbreak of war against Israel in October 1973, the three- to fourfold increase in world petroleum prices that it generated, and the emigration of skilled workers to the newly enriched oil-exporting countries.

When veteran construction workers left Egypt for work in Libya, Iraq, or the Gulf, ex-*tarāḥīl* workers filled their domestic vacancies. *Tarāḥīl* employment served as an occupational "bridge" between rural agriculture and urban employment. Migrant workers had already learned nonfarm skills and established outside social networks that enabled them to switch easily from cultivation to construction. But then the critical complementarity between migrant labor and agriculture began to take effect. For once lost to migrant employment, workers also became lost to agriculture, its complement in the rural division of labor. As the *tarāḥīl* workforce shrank, it ceased to be a labor reserve for village agriculture. With the cost of farm machinery still prohibitive, Egypt's agriculture remained labor-intensive. So as the rural labor force declined, so did farm output. Now rural workers left both *tarāḥīl* labor *and* agricultural employment, and, in the process, disrupted agriculture, crop exports, food self-sufficiency, and the nation's finances, thereby reducing Cairo's ability to sustain long-term economic growth.

The problems of shortfalls in agricultural exports and food crops, and balance of trade deficits, which rural labor had caused in the early 1960s, had never really disappeared even after workers had returned back to the village following the 1965–66 recession. Throughout the 1970s, agricultural price controls tightened, food imports increased, cotton exports stagnated, balance of payments difficulties deepened, and the national debt grew. By the end of the decade, Egypt was importing almost 50 percent of its wheat, for example, at a time when high international commodity prices and low export performance placed even more burdens on its already depleted hard-currency reserves. This generated still larger trade deficits, foreign debt, and inflation. Subsequently, higher prices without attendant income adjustments were guaranteed to outrage consumers and lead to social unrest.

One possible solution might have been to raise both consumer prices and incomes together. Yet only price increases were ever considered, thereby preventing the growth of a viable home market. Even so, the rise in food prices and the reduction in state consumer subsidies could have been passed on to farmers in the form of higher crop prices. Moreover, the profits the government earned from buying low-priced produce discussed at the end of chapter 5 could also have been reduced, and the proceeds passed along to farmers as well. These higher market prices could then have stimulated domestic agricultural production and raised crop yields that then would have offset imports and expanded exports. Since labor still represented the largest single production input, its share could have risen as long as other costs remained stable. In other words, higher food prices could have given farmers greater sales revenues and higher incomes, and could have enabled them, when pressed, to pay better wages.

On the other hand, the government funds resulting from lowering consumer subsidies and maintaining state crop sales could also be used to reduce budget deficits and to service the country's external debt without any income benefits for farmers and rural workers. Farm prices would then remain low or fall even further, depending on how much pressure the state encountered for raising capital and repaying its foreign loans. Given the urgency of Cairo's mounting credit problems, it would not be surprising that in order to accommodate the International Monetary Fund, these resources would go instead toward deficit reduction and debt servicing.

In January 1977, the government abruptly doubled bread prices by reducing subsidies of basic consumer commodities. What extra funds that might have gone to boost agricultural production, incomes, and wages, to limit urban migration, and to stimulate domestic commerce went instead to comply with IMF requirements. The public's immediate response was a spontaneous riot in Cairo that demonstrated the folly of ever stimulating the agricultural sector. When low prices were reinstated, it meant further stagnation for the countryside. The zero-sum game of keeping food prices low, urban consumers satisfied, and businesses profitable while reducing crop prices, limiting farm production, and pauperizing rural workers seemed to be the preferred choice for state policy makers.

As rural workers abandoned the countryside, they generated production problems in agriculture and land reclamation. Then, once in the urban informal sector, they began to provoke social disorder as well. Their exodus also severely reduced the number of workers this study had intended to analyze. When I returned to Minūfiya for a visit in 1985, most of the *tarāḥīl* workers I had traveled with just four years earlier had found other employment unrelated to farming or migrant labor. This change in occupation and location, then, could seemingly bring the study of Egyptian migrant farm workers to an end. However, while working in al-Minyā province south of Cairo, I found that many of those Saʿīdīs targeted for assistance by community development projects had previously been *tarāḥīl* laborers who had moved to the city. Ironically, and despite their aspirations for better employment, their town lives were not much different from what they had left behind in the countryside. Higher wages (but higher costs), full-time work (but still interrupted by periods of inactivity), and direct supervision (yet still regulated by paternalism) made the urban regime of accumulation just as precarious as the rural one.

Yet now there was something more. Their style of politics had changed. The quiet resentment and resolve that had first brought them to the city turned into direct protest and confrontation with state officials, reflecting their new circumstances. Migration and flight had once been an unsophisticated but nevertheless a practical political response to unsatisfactory conditions. Now, however, there were no more places they could move to, especially when emigration declined after 1985. Stuck in an increasingly inhospitable city, their political tactics shifted as a result.

These new practices likewise reflected their rural origins. The January 1977 riots erupted in ways reminiscent of what Nathan Brown referred to (1990:chap. 5) as the "spontaneous communal action" of peasants collectively reacting to immediate outside threats. The Islamic militancy since the mid-1980s has organized itself in ways that recall Eric Hobsbawm's example (1959:chap. 2) of Italian secret societies that defended the rural populace "against threats to its traditional way of life." These political practices had first been learned through controlling wages, effort, and prices on farms and in labor camps. Then, once rural workers moved to the city, these tactics were used to advocate partisan issues of equity, justice, and piety as well.

Since increasing rural-to-urban migration meant that there were many fewer migrant farm workers to research, this and the next chapter deliberately change the perspective of this study away from agricultural villages and distant *tarāḥīl* labor camps and follow these rural laborers as they permanently moved into the shantytowns and the informal sector of Egypt's cities and towns. Here we can begin to appreciate just how much their rural experiences subsequently came to influence their urban lives and to impact on government plans for national development.

In 1970s, the state still proved to be the most dominant institution in regulating the conflict between labor and capital. Its policies and programs were just as potent for ex-*tarāḥīl* workers in the city as they had once been for migrant farm laborers in the countryside. Cairo refused to be the silent night watchman it had been before the 1960s in spite of the setbacks it had suffered in achieving semi-peripheral status and in initiating competitive Fordism. The three state policies of emigration, construction, and investment examined in this chapter proved particularly important for ex-rural labor.

After the October war of 1973, the government reluctantly changed its restrictive emigration laws in response to pressure from skilled construction workers. Their movement abroad opened up new job opportunities in the cities and towns, attracting vast numbers of *tarāḥīl* laborers. New arrivals were easily absorbed into the large number of small subcontractors, allowing the unwieldy public-sector construction companies to respond more flexibly to the increased number of building projects financed by state funding and private remittances.

Labor's attitude toward relocation was contradictory: workers were certainly eager to find better employment and enjoy a better life, but they were also reluctant to abandon their village with its familiar rhythms, respites, and relations. After overcoming this hesitation and moving to the cities, they tried hard to get the permanent, skilled, high-wage, noncoercive, local, direct-hire employment they had once told me they coveted, as described in chapter 4.

Soon, however, these aspirations faded, and the bright city lights dimmed when, despite the paternalism they used to control the immediate effort = wage = price formula, jobs became erratic, incomes fell, and consumption prices rose. Then, when ex-rural workers, their colleagues, and their families began insisting on more employment, higher wages, and lower costs, the state was unable to secure the additional investment capital necessary to create or expand the productive activities that could satisfy their demands. Inflation, social polarization, and uncertainty further fueled labor's resentment. Additional financial restriction from the IMF ensured that both the countryside and the city would remain poor and discontented.

Workers' anger grew stronger. Unable to contest government policies through legitimate political channels, these ex-rural workers instead resorted to the political techniques they had once learned in the countryside:

first by spontaneous mob action to indicate their dissatisfaction and then later, as chapter 8 shows, by more deliberate, organized forms of opposition.

Emigration Abroad

Even before the massive rise in international petroleum prices, Egyptians had been traveling abroad for work throughout the Arab world. Prior to 1967, this flow had consisted principally of lower-middle-class schoolteachers unable domestically to realize their aspirations for upward mobility.[1] After the June war, they were joined by large numbers of highly educated but disenchanted upper-middle-class professionals who vacated jobs in medicine and engineering and moved to the United States, Canada, and Australia (Hansen and Radwan 1982:83–84). The difficulties caused by the emigration of this specialized labor force prompted the state to reassess its emigration policy and restrict which occupations could leave.

Soon, however, the flow of Egyptians changed into an exodus of skilled craft workers. Since 1968, new investment capital had begun financing economic growth throughout the periphery. Plant and infrastructural construction required skilled and unskilled workers even before Organization of Petroleum Exporting Countries (OPEC) boosted its prices to record levels. High rates of emigration for construction workers had already appeared two years earlier in 1971 (Choucri et al. 1978:63). In that year, professionals pressed the state to guarantee their right to leave Egypt through constitutional fiat. In May, the Corrective Revolution warned workers of al-Sadāt's impending turn to the right. Rather than see the collapse of sympathetic labor policies, laborers sought employment abroad. Many had grown disenchanted with Egypt's retrenchment such that the flow of skilled workers had already reached impressive proportions even before petroleum price hikes triggered a far greater exodus.

The 1973 price increases, which were sparked by and were in support of Egypt's October war, greatly accelerated labor emigration. By 1976, as much as 60 percent of Egypt's labor force in the construction sector was employed abroad. In 1978 this proportion may have risen to as high as 80 percent (Hansen and Radwan 1982:89; Choucri 1980:83). "There is little doubt," two veteran economists concluded, "that emigration is now dominated by construction workers, unskilled workers, and farmers, and represents a much broader sample of the Egyptian labour force" (Hansen and Radwan 1982:89). This sector displayed such an appetite for manual workers that subsequent domestic vacancies were promptly filled by dissatisfied male workers moving out of *tarāḥīl* and agriculture employment. No longer tolerating the low wages, heavy assignments, and inadequate consumption found in this dual employment, they wanted instead permanent, full-time, high-wage, contractual jobs in urban construction.

But this enormous drain of labor from the countryside was not merely an automatic response to the impersonal forces of supply and demand that supposedly operate across international borders. Instead, it was the outcome of a deliberate government policy, which, however, was formulated not in a disinterested fashion but rather was adopted under intense pressure from numerous workers demanding higher incomes and a better standard of living. Just as *tarāḥīl* labor benefits like lower quotas, higher wages, and better accommodations had once resulted from persistent pressure from workers, so too was Egypt's emigration policy eventually an outcome of increased labor agitation. Rather than being the result of the impartial "referee's decision" found in the theories of political pluralism, this policy was instead an outcome of increased demands coming from skilled workers in the construction trades.

By 1974, two policy perspectives on emigration had emerged. One viewed emigration as a useful means for removing dissent. Workers grumbling over low local wages and bad working conditions could turn into a potential source of trouble:

> [T]he migration of construction workers is depriving the political system of a potential source of political opposition and of dissatisfaction with economic conditions. Migration opportunities are serving as absorbers of social unrest . . . and protect some sectors of the labor force against the effects of inflation. . . . By leaving the country, the potential constituents for a stronger labor organization are withdrawing from effective participation in a class-based movement. This will reinforce the fragmentation of Egyptian labor and reduce the potential for political organization. (Choucri et al. 1978:137)

However, a second view worried that emigration would "sap the society's strength and its most productive elements" (Dessouki 1978:5). A labor drain could lower the surplus numbers of workers who, in previously swamping the labor market—according to the questionable theory of surplus labor—had kept wages low. The threat of labor shortages among skilled workers was particularly disturbing. Production bottlenecks and wage inflation could raise construction costs and add to the price of doing business in Egypt.

Under pressure from construction companies, the government initially responded by adopting this second view. The state, confronted with the large emigration of workers, hastily prohibited all skilled craftsmen from leaving the country. In July 1974, just nine months after OPEC raised its prices, the government announced travel restrictions for all craft trades. The Housing and Labor Ministries ordered travel bans and decreed that all workers must carry identity cards and legal documents clearly stamped with their occupation and travel authorization.[2] Passports, visas, and military and security clearance documents became obstacles used to prevent emigration (Dessouki 1978:22).

Yet workers did not accept such restrictions calmly. They bribed government officials to overlook identity card stamps, paid others to have their card altered, and many gave false occupations when renewing "lost" cards. Once their status was "revised" to a more harmless category, craft workers left Egypt in unprecedented numbers and sought and accepted foreign employment.

Challenged by the unauthorized departure of such large numbers of workers, the government finally capitulated in the fall of 1974 and abandoned its adamant opposition. As Parliament demanded changes in ministerial regulations, the only viable option left was to permit open travel. "When export of the labor force became an officially recognized policy objective," Suzanne Messiha reported (1980:12), "migration restrictions were lifted, conscription restrictions eased, bureaucratic procedures for migration were decentralized, exit visas were abolished and replaced by a travel permit obtainable from one's place of work, and passports were issued from police stations." Thus, documenting departures was simplified, which encouraged many who did not actually hold contracts to leave and find employers once they were outside the country.

As the Egyptian government saw the fiscal advantages of migration and remittances, its initial hesitation gave way to support. State officials soon began "to encourage emigration as a means of alleviating the foreign exchange shortage and of providing an outlet for Egyptians to improve their conditions which the domestic economy was unable to supply" (Hansen and Radwan 1982:84). In 1975, Parliament ratified a number of formal treaties governing the movement of laborers in Iraq, Libya, Qaṭar, and Saudi Arabia, not only to protect them against exploitation and bad working conditions, but also to stop the flow of unregistered workers.

Labor emigration exhibited four distinct phases (Assaad 1991:152). In the beginning, during the first half of the 1970s, workers went to Libya where overland travel reduced transportation costs and thus attracted those who were less prosperous and were not yet so well funded. By the second half of the decade, workers' remittances began underwriting the more expensive movement to the Gulf countries. Emigrants were predominately skilled and urban, but many who had earlier moved from the village to replace their urban counterparts had acquired enough skills and connections that they, too, could travel abroad. Then in the early 1980s, the outbreak of war between Iraq and Iran raised the demand for unskilled emigrants to replace those drafted into the Iraqi army. This third phase saw an increase in the flow of workers moving directly out of the countryside. Until the mid-1980s, the average duration abroad was one and a half years (Hansen and Radwan 1982:86).

However, in 1985, when world oil prices began to decline, workers' duration abroad began to fall and fewer workers were actually able to find jobs outside Egypt. Many returned to Egypt to stay, although they still continued to work in urban construction. Occasionally, returning expatriates did replace and bump out their less qualified and less connected colleagues, but a reverse chain reaction did not send workers back to the countryside to expand the ranks of the agricultural and *tarāḥīl* labor force. Instead, when workers did leave construction, many shifted into full-time employment in the informal manufacturing, transportation, and service sectors (Assaad 1991:149–50). At first this meant urban residence but increasingly, small informal businesses started to appear in the countryside as well. Yet regardless of locale, few workers returned permanently to farming, or to its counterpart, *tarāḥīl* labor.

Arriving at accurate numbers for Egyptian emigration is a difficult task. No single government bureau has maintained adequate records; the actual figures are scattered throughout a number of offices in Cairo and conflict with each other. The absence of good records, and the disagreement among those that do exist, led Robert LaTowsky to conclude (1984:12) that emigration is a "politically sensitive issue in Egypt, which explains the administration's continued reticence on the subject."

Nevertheless, a number of sources agree on the following figures. From 1968 to 1972, the annual migration rate numbered between 50,00 and 80,000 individuals. By 1973 this had risen to 157,000. Estimates for 1975 vary from 375,000 to 600,000 to 1 million. In 1980 anywhere from 500,000 to 1 million laborers worked abroad. By 1982, 2 million Egyptians were abroad, and by 1985, 3 million (Hansen and Radwan 1982:86–87; Halliday 1984:8; *al-Ahrām*, November 3, 1985). The overall labor force in 1980 was approximately 12 million workers.

The employers and state officials who had once warned that emigration would generate labor shortages and higher wage rates seemed to have had their worst fears realized. Between 1974 and 1978, construction wages increased three- to fivefold and, in the same years, grew to levels three times higher than those in agriculture (Hansen and Radwan 1982:74–75). By 1973, over 1.5 million unskilled rural workers (out of an agricultural labor force of 4 million) were still moving back and forth between farming and *tarāḥīl* labor.[3] But as the expanding labor market called for more construction workers, first for petroleum exporting nations, and then later for their domestic replacements, local companies increasingly recruited those with lesser skills from the ranks of farm laborers and *tarāḥīl* workers, and drew ever larger numbers of workers permanently away from casual infrastructural projects, land reclamation, and, finally, from agriculture. Because of such rapid turnover, building jobs were eventually filled by less qualified replacements who then erected more substandard and less durable structures.[4] Yet even as buildings began to crumble because of shoddy construction, and as agricultural production declined because of understaffing, the state never realized that replacing a skilled urban labor force with less experienced workers from the countryside, and depleting the agricultural workforce by permanently employing migrant farm laborers in construction could generate harmful economic consequences for the nation.

Could machines have replaced departing rural workers and thereby averted greater agricultural problems? In a thorough study on the impact of agricultural mechanization, Nicholas Hopkins was unable to conclude whether purchasing machines actually displaced rural workers, with no adverse effect to production, or else merely replaced them, albeit imperfectly, *after* their departure: "Meanwhile, the kind of landless person or smallholder who would have been a good candidate for casual wage labor in earlier days is more and more finding a way to escape that niche, principally through a combination of education and migration. Thus while machinery slightly reduces the overall demand for labor, and requires larger labor gangs, the labor pool is diminished: parallel processes, but it is hard to say which is the cause of the other" (Hopkins 1987:132; see also Weyland 1993:96).

Mechanization did not entirely reverse production shortfalls due to labor shortages, although it certainly saved the agrarian economy from even worse declines. When machines were introduced, they substituted first for animals before replacing workers since the lucrative market for livestock products placed a premium on raising inactive, stall-fed animals. Even so, tractors and pumps—the two machines of choice—were not always available by rental because of the coincidence of demand, nor were they procurable even with multiple partnerships because of their high cost. Such acquisitions gradually took place in the late 1970s only as educated members of middle-class farm families, having diversified out of agriculture, began remitting their foreign salaries back to the village. Until then, mechanization was unable to sufficiently replace the rural workers leaving for urban employment. It was only after the mid-1980s that the increased use of equipment and fertilizers finally began to compensate for shortages in labor and deficits in exports and food crops. By then, however, the damage to the national economy had already taken place.

Yet it must be clearly pointed out that poor, illiterate *tarāḥīl* workers were *not* the ones to travel abroad and earn such generous incomes. They merely replaced those who did. Nor did they remit funds back home since they rarely earned enough even to support their own families. Yet if emigration abroad did not immediately and directly affect migrant farm laborers, then we must turn and examine what it was about the domestic construction sector itself that did attract so many village workers apart from their persistent dissatisfaction with the harshness and exploitation of their rural occupations. The state had altered the unskilled labor market, but unless rural workers found these new opportunities familiar, their reluctance would have generated far fewer departures.

Fortuitously, the skills and leverage *tarāḥīl* workers had once learned in the villages and labor camps appropriately prepared them for an informal sector whose organizational similarities allowed them to slip easily into such positions. The wide variety of urban construction jobs spanned a continuum from consecutive *tarāḥīl* trips, to roving, acephalous teams of independent workers, to foreman- or contractor-led gangs, to permanently employed crews moving from one site to the next for the same employer. Ex-rural workers considered the move from temporary, "casual" labor to these full-time situations more satisfactory, for they established strong social bonds, high wages, and congenial work conditions not found in migrant labor or seasonal farm work. The greater demand for their labor, the steady employment it initially generated, and the fixed composition of work groups made urban construction jobs a much better occupation. Moreover, the paternalism of these small construction operations enabled workers to keep their position long after the time when building activity and investments declined.

In the decade before al-Sadāt became president, rural to urban migration to Cairo alone involved over 700,000 people. During the following ten years, that level rose to over a million. By the end of the 1980s, the figure had more than doubled to include 1,430,000 migrants (Ibrahim 1996:100).[5] Not all migrants, of course, were ex-rural workers, for many farm family members diversified out of agriculture into skilled labor and professional employment. Yet of those who were laborers, no matter whether they were inter- or intra-provincial migrants or village-based commuters, their departure from farming constituted a major problem for agricultural production, and their arrival in cities and towns represented a significant increase in the demand for urban employment, higher incomes, and lower consumption costs.

The Construction Sector in Egypt

Since the 1970s, Egypt's construction sector has contained three types of enterprises:

- A small number of very large public sector companies nationalized after 1961 that operate in Egypt and throughout the Arab world.[6]
- A larger number of small domestic private firms that operate both independently and as subcontractors to the larger companies.
- A much larger number of informal builders and individual subcontractors who supply local specialty craft and labor-only services.[7]

The relationship between public-sector companies, private firms, and independent subcontractors involves contracts and agreements to supply products and services, supervision and labor, and finance and credit. Public-sector companies clearly dominate the sector, but are very often too large and unwieldy to be efficient. Their management involves large administrative bureaucracies that are constrained by government regulations that reduce their versatility, particularly in the areas of financial control and manpower staffing.

Subcontracting, however, gives these companies a flexibility that is essential if they are to adjust to sharply fluctuating demands. The steady increase in subcontracting after 1972 shifted the economic burden of this adjustment onto the shoulders of small private firms and informal businesses. Subcontracting permits large numbers of workers to be quickly employed and easily dismissed by relying on less capitalized companies and labor-only subcontractors from provincial, district, and village locations that provide higher-level operations with workers and supplies.[8]

Here management involves a single family or just one man. The same staff is used at the job site as well as in the home office, so little is spent on administration. Frequently these firms perform double duty, operating as subcontractors to large public enterprises during the day and working independently as main contractors to smaller private jobs in the afternoon (General Organization for Housing 1981, 2:120, 3:G. 4–6, 34).

The proliferation of these smaller firms is the result of monetary ceilings the government imposed in 1961 that limit the size of subcontracts tendered by public-sector companies in order to reduce favoritism and corruption. But since then, many private firms have expanded their operations instead by establishing related sister businesses that specialize in different complementary activities—labor, skilled crafts, building materials, finance, design. This enables a number of related, but technically independent firms to win contracts that, were they combined, would exceed the legal limit (Koch et al. 1978:5).

Both public and private construction companies rely heavily on labor subcontractors to provide them with workers despite the presence of their own small but ordinarily specialized work teams. Such subcontractors specialize in recruiting and supervising both skilled craft specialists and unskilled manual laborers, and on occasion provide them with tools and equipment. Although their number is large, their capital assets are negligible and their monetary contribution to total production is small, consisting mostly of wages. Even though most business relations in construction involve formal legal contracts, labor subcontractors usually operate with personal, verbal agreements. Because they mostly work for just one or a few main contractors, effective business depends on mutual familiarity, trust, and dependability (General Organization for Housing 1981, 3:G. 18–19). They constitute another example of what Buttrick called "inside contracting."

Specialized laborers are hired at village gathering places, urban coffee shops, and familiar street intersections. So too are unskilled workers who are also recruited initially through *tarāḥīl* employment, but who rarely return to their village even when short-term assignments are finished. Instead workers either (1) remain attached to individual brokers who contract them out to large companies that switch job sites on a continuous basis; (2) stay together as independent but acephalous labor teams that go on to new employers according to prior arrangements; or (3) if disbanded, use collegial networks to attach themselves to new brokers or join new labor gangs (Koch et al. 1978:42).

In 1987, nearly 65 percent of Egypt's domestic construction workforce was not permanently employed. Ninety percent (both permanent and temporary) lacked formal contractual arrangements, relying instead on personal patron-client ties to contractors. Egyptian labor law protects permanent workers from arbitrary dismissal and entitles them to benefits like retirement pensions. Laborers with permanent or even temporary contracts are entitled to paid vacations, sick leave, and disability compensation. But the vast majority of workers are employed by small private firms that, as part of the informal sector, ignore contract agreements, official registration, labor and social insurance laws, and tax requirements. This informality allows them to quickly adjust to rapid changes in demand, wages, locations, and contractors (Assaad 1991:137). And although it reduces high permanent labor costs for prime contractors, it also reduces job security and employment stability for workers.

While small firms and individual subcontractors depend heavily on public-sector companies for credit, funds, and subsidized building materials, this relationship is extremely erratic. Many find it difficult to get paid. Bills can be as much as three years in arrears and are frequently five to six months late. Some firms carry unpaid government debts for years. Technically public-sector companies can allocate 30 percent of their project funds to advance to subcontractors. But because of bureaucracy, insufficient budget allocations elsewhere, and cash flow problems, such funds are seldom passed along. Intermediate payments and final settlements are frequently delayed as well.

Yet, at the same time, subcontractors are required to pay cash for building materials and advance payments and disbursement of workers' wages. Prices are determined when agreements are first negotiated, but since labor and materials procured later usually involve higher costs, subcontractors have to absorb any losses unless they receive credit. Labor costs are particularly vexing, with huge differences arising between the original and later wage bills. When prime contractors delay paying advances and later, in settling intermediate and final charges, subcontractors have to either borrow or else slow down or even halt work activities. Resuming work once laborers have left to go home or have gone on to new jobs adds additional expense to project costs. Retaining an available but inactive workforce can resolve this dilemma and can prevent paying penalty fees, but at the risk of further depleting scarce capital. Delays in delivering materials often force contractors into the black market where they pay higher prices in order to ensure speedier consignment so as to adhere better to fixed completion dates.

This squeeze between immediate payment for labor and materials, and delayed reimbursement by clients or prime contractors is critical. It makes working capital and cash flow a major constraint in construction operations. Frequently subcontractors initiate a large number of contracts simultaneously so that the many advance payments provide them with enough operating capital to execute just a single project. Meanwhile, other contracts, although formally begun and partially paid for, are delayed while other clients settled their accounts. In turn, subcontractors withhold making payments to their own suppliers and workers when possible in order to keep their existing operations running (Koch et al. 1978:38, 46, 51).

Contractors are thus inclined to accept as many jobs as possible in order to accelerate their cash flow, yet they have little incentive to finish the work underway since to do so means settling their own outstanding debts. Contracts are therefore constantly juggled, and actual work proceeds slowly as startups and slowdowns postpone job completion. This seriously disrupts continuous activity, with work teams frequently shifted to different sites and alternatively experiencing vigorous speedups and idle unemployment. But it also raises the overall numbers employed or available in order to have a potential workforce that can start or resume work quickly when financial bottlenecks clear up. Paternalism keeps numerous workers attached to specific subcontractors when the latter are unwilling to pay wages in periods of unemployment or are unable to pay them at moments of financial constriction, but are still able to promise jobs and perquisites to loyal and familiar workers once operations and cash flows start up again.

This pattern of finance and labor control generated a momentum that throughout the 1970s and 1980s maintained abundant work activity long after actual investments declined. Construction remained an active employment sector because it was buoyed up by government plans (1) to build apartments and subsidize the costs of a financially pressed urban labor force searching for limited (and therefore expensive) housing; and (2) to erect facilities and infrastructure in preparation for as yet unrealized promises from international investors to relocate their operations if such state subsidies were forthcoming. This assured constructions workers that high levels of employment and wages would continue even as real investment growth began to decline after 1981–82.

Multiple startups, a myriad of subcontracting agreements with several large companies, complex credit and cash flow arrangements, and effective patron-client ties kept the sector very active. Because of this vitality, the inflated size of the workforce, the intermittent nature of construction work, and the paternalistic ties to employers, laborers who became momentarily unemployed still waited in anticipation of further work instead of returning to the countryside. But even after 1985, when the construction sector began to slow down, many deactivated workers found urban jobs in informal workshops or services, averse to ever going back to alternating between farming and *tarāḥīl* labor.

Yet in the long run, whether ex-migrant farm workers remained potentially available or actively employed critically depended on whether private and public investments continued to ensure a viable urban labor market. The rate of future job generation and income growth clearly hinged, therefore, on the state maintaining adequate investment levels. These, in turn, depended heavily on the design of effective government financial and investment policies.

Building an Open-Door Policy

Following Egypt's victory in the October 1973 war, the government formulated a pro-Western open-door investment policy that aimed to capitalize on the new petroleum wealth. Cairo maintained that the combination of Egyptian labor, Arab capital, and western technology was the solution to the nation's economic ills. Henceforth Egypt would open its door to trade, investment, and technology from the core, reorient its economy away from the barter commerce with the Soviet Union and Eastern Europe, and align it instead with trade from the United States, Western Europe, and the noncommunist community. Cooperative, not competitive, Fordism would now govern both its production and international diplomatic relations. Such a policy had been under discussion since 1971, but it was the October war that made it not only politically feasible but also economically imperative. In June 1974, Parliament endorsed the open-door policy by passing Law 43, which made foreign investment more attractive and more profitable.

This policy encouraged investment by authorizing joint ventures between foreign capital and local private- and public-sector firms. Exchange rates that had benefited state transactions became graduated in order to facilitate capital transfers from abroad. The government legalized private bank operations, foreign land ownership, lower personal and business taxes, and higher land ownership ceilings. Although Law 43 did not explicitly call for dismantling the public sector, it was clear that, in time, targeted sectors such as industry, mining, energy, tourism, transportation, land reclamation, housing, insurance, and banking would be disassembled and sold to private investors, local or otherwise. The new foreign and mixed sectors, together with a reinvigorated private sector, would compete with what remained of the public sector, resulting in either its greater efficiency or its bankruptcy (Waterbury 1978:206–223).

Many joint-venture projects were proposed and approved, but few were actually completed. By the end of 1976, only sixty-six projects valued at £E36 million and 3,450 employees had actually begun operations, although projects totaling twenty times that capital amount had been approved. Serious entrepreneurs were stymied by complicated authorization procedures, inadequate review personnel and frequent staff changes, and the open hostility of public-sector officials. This allowed well-placed expediters to profit from lucrative payoffs and kickbacks paid to facilitate project approvals.

Even al-Sadāt became impatient with the slowness of the response to Law 43. In June 1977, Parliament modified Law 43 with Law 32 to make currency transactions, tax abatements, and investments even easier. New enterprises were also exempted from the existing labor laws. In anticipation, the state authority accelerated its project review process, approving over a hundred applications in just a single day. By the end of 1978, 134 projects worth £E440 million were underway, although this represented only a quarter of the £E1.66 billion initially committed. Most Law 43 projects were in investment companies, banks, tourism, and luxury housing. Yet other than banking and hotels, their efforts were not very noticeable. Few invested in productive enterprises. What the government needed were big joint ventures in manufacturing with well-known multinational corporations (Waterbury 1978:227–29; 1983:132–33, 142–46). However, these were not forthcoming.

As a result of the influx of foreign capital, consumer prices soon began to escalate. Before the October war, inflation had held steady at a moderate 8 percent, but afterward it grew to 25 percent.[9] High prices were further aggravated by the rising consumer demand due to remittances from foreign employment, by supply shortages stemming from public-sector production bottlenecks, and by obstacles to importing consumer goods such as foreign exchange restrictions and inadequate port and customs facilities (Waterbury 1978:231). Chronic inflation raised the cost of foreign investment and further discouraged legitimate domestic initiatives.

Another outcome of the "sound and fury" of economic activity initiated by the open-door policy was increased social polarization. In very short time, fabulous fortunes were made from commerce and smuggling, banking and currency scams, real estate swindles, and shoddy building construction. A parasitic elite emerged, consisting of advisers, experts, and consultants in the government, and intermediaries and merchants in the private sector, all of whom profited handsomely from widespread corruption, speculation, and profiteering. Meanwhile, the vast majority of Egyptians struggled just to remain solvent. Most remained heavily dependent on government consumer subsidies. Yet retail price controls that had been enacted to protect consumers were frequently transgressed by dishonest merchants and corrupt officials. Job generation remained sluggish as public-sector enterprises stagnated and new private- and joint-sector activities employed capital intensive technology instead of labor (Waterbury 1983:171–81; Hirst and Beeson 1981:207–10). Indicative, the chic new fashionable Cairene suburbs of Misr al-Jadīda, Maʿādī, and Muhandisīn beheld the rise of incredibly luxurious apartments, while the older inner-city neighborhoods of Shūbra, Bulāq, and Sayyida Zaynab saw only decay and neglect. Shantytowns were erected on former landed estates ringing the city, in places like Imbāba and Bulāq al-Dakrūr.

A third problem was that the open-door economy aggravated Egypt's chronic deficits in its balance of payments. The government import bill, especially for food, increased enormously, reflecting in part the precipitous rise in world energy prices, in part the steady growth in Egypt's population, but in large part the widespread stagnation that still afflicted domestic agriculture. Government revenues from exports declined as agricultural production deteriorated due to labor shortages, and industrial output remained static due to investment problems. The state was unable to draw upon domestic savings since its own banks were not securing foreign remittances which went instead into the "own-exchange" system of private importation and currency transactions, and later into private Islamic investment companies. Currency laws, credit regulations, and import requirements were revised time and time again so that the national banks could increase their deposits of remittances and so that the state could access and use this growing volume of hard currency. Meanwhile, in order to compensate for capital shortages, state officials relied on short-term commercial credit at very high interest rates (Waterbury 1978:305; Sadowski 1991:209).

Because of this poor economic performance, Egypt's balance of payments declined further while its national debt rose higher. As early as the spring of 1975, the IMF had drafted a stabilization plan to resolve these problems. As part of a larger U.S. Middle East peace initiative, the plan attracted much attention. But when U.S. diplomatic efforts faltered, Egypt sought short-term credit from Saudi Arabia and the Gulf states. Once these oil-producers agreed to ease Egypt's economic plight, the IMF plan was tabled.

Yet by 1976 Egypt had fallen behind in repaying its short-term debt. Fund-raising trips to the Gulf were arranged once again, but now Egypt's Arab bankers began insisting that Cairo comply with the IMF plan before they would extend further credit. Their lukewarm promises to contribute emergency aid, finance additional investments, and extend loans to cover debt servicing failed to provide sufficient capital. At last, that spring, the government capitulated and agreed to accept the IMF stabilization plan and its program of fiscal austerity.

The plan included currency devaluations, tax reductions, duty-free industrial zones, more joint ventures, higher land ownership ceilings, budget freezes, and subsidy reductions. Cairo adamantly rejected devaluing the pound and proposed instead a two-tier currency system. It initially refused to reduce consumer subsidies, arguing that it would contribute to rising inflation and to destabilizing the country. But IMF pressure forced the government to retreat (Waterbury 1978:306–10). In general, the IMF adjustments benefited exporters and foreign investors, but left the vast majority of Egyptian income earners and consumers destitute.

The countryside was completely overlooked, for it had become merely the source of low-cost food, export crops, cheap workers, and capital transfers. Rural laborers had left the countryside because of the low wages and harsh workloads generated by controlled farm prices, mandatory crop quotas, and compulsory harvest deliveries. In turn, they left behind production shortages in cotton and grain, covered over by low government prices and imperfectly compensated by high import volumes. The state was able to squeeze capital out of the countryside, but at the expense of increasing rural poverty, promoting rural-to-urban migration, swamping urban labor markets with low-wage workers, and raising the national debt to pay off its trade imbalances.

But neglecting the countryside, together with the great flurry of urban construction generated by the open-door policy, guaranteed an even larger exodus of rural labor, more agricultural production problems, and greater financial and political difficulties. From the perspective of the urban underclass, both the government's flawed open-door policy and the IMF stabilization program that intended to repair it were unsatisfactory since both guaranteed rising costs and stagnant incomes.

Legislative approval for the IMF plan was postponed until after the Parliamentary elections of October 1976. For Egypt's new electoral system threatened to expose state officials to harsh criticism from political opponents over their economic policies. Now for the first time since the 1952 revolution, more than the one political perspective was represented in the election campaign. The administration worried that too hasty an implementation of the stabilization plan would drastically affect the voting outcome (Waterbury 1978:314). As it turned out, it had little to fear from other politicians.

Back in 1971, immediately after the Corrective Revolution, President al-Sadāt had reorganized the ASU in order to make it less threatening. But the October war gave him a wider latitude unimaginable earlier. In April 1974, he proposed major modifications in the ASU that essentially expelled recalcitrant factions—workers, peasants, students, academics, and their advocates—who opposed his open-door policy.[10] Since the state was abandoning the public sector and relying instead on private-sector investments to generate jobs, profits, and commodities, those segments injured by this new policy who might protest and raise objections not only could prove embarrassing to the administration but could also upset the move to cooperative Fordism. Both would displease Cairo's benefactor, the United States, which had insisted not only on opening Egypt's trade door to the West but also on erecting an American-style party-based democracy. By implementing a multiparty system, the administration won acclaim from Washington and still effectively silenced all but the most agreeable opposition.

Since they were too large to be censured outright, these troublesome factions instead were muzzled by affiliating them with new political parties too weak to influence government policies and operations. Before the 1952 revolution, politics had been permeated by patron-client relations, but during the period of Arab socialism this paternalism had ceased. Now the honorifics, *bāy* and *bāshā*, reappeared, indicating that political success depended once again on displaying the right, servile deference required to access powerful government officials. Those not in the new ruling party were denied such access and were therefore neutralized. So silenced, many members of the underclass who had previously spoken out through various ASU departments (*amānāt*) were no longer able to bring attention to their critical conditions.

Like the United States before the Great Depression, Egypt too had no legitimate channel through which workers could articulate their demands for greater justice and equity, and through which the government could anticipate social turmoil beforehand. Without such an outlet, labor's simmering dissatisfaction began turning into a social pressure cooker that, undetected, could eventually cause major public outbursts. In the United States, the unrecognized but growing gap between income and consumption triggered a stock market crash and ushered in a decade of radical labor unrest. In Egypt, a similar gap sparked a series of demonstrations and attacks against the government. The first of these was the Cairo bread riots of January 1977.

The Cairo Riots of 1977

Shortly after the elections were over, the government announced on January 18, 1977, that in accordance with the IMF, it was reducing a number of essential subsidies and raising prices on basic consumer goods (Waterbury 1978:314). Egyptians in Cairo and other major cities reacted violently when they heard the news. Yahya Sadowski describes (1991:156) their angry response in detail:

> At 8:30 on the morning of January 18, demonstrations against the proposed price increases broke out among workers at the mills of the public sector Misr Textile Company in Helwan. They began a march [north] on downtown Cairo and were joined by workers from neighboring factories. By the time the march arrived at the Parliament building, its numbers were swollen by thousands of local university and high school students. Police attempts to disperse the crowd with tear gas only shifted the protesters into adjacent neighborhoods where they attracted a large following of poorer Cairenes. By evening the demonstrations had . . . turned violent. Protesters smashed shop windows, overturned trolleys and attacked police stations. Similar demonstrations had broken out in Alexandria on the same day. By the 19th they had spread to 17 smaller cities. In the provinces government offices, administration buildings, and governors' residences were attacked and burned. The police had long since lost any semblance of control and began firing directly into the crowd. For the first time since [January] 1952, regular army troops had to be called in to restore order. Even military intervention did not halt the violence. The demonstrations only subsided after 2:30 P.M. on January 20, when the radio broadcast the government's decision to reinstate subsidies and rescind all price increases. The government estimated that the protests had left 77 dead, 214 wounded, and thousands under arrest, but many Egyptians insist that the toll was several times larger. But a simple tally of dollars and death would not, in any case, indicate just how breath-

taking the confrontation had been for the majority of Egyptians. Violence on this scale signaled a revolutionary loss of faith in the government.

The January riots revealed the degree of discontent and dissatisfaction in Egypt's working classes that altogether alarmed state officials. The demonstrations were first organized by skilled laborers from the formal, state-owned industries. Only later did workers from the informal sector join in. Once confronted by the police, this clutter of protesters turned to riot. Nathan Brown once argued (1990:112–13) that although underlying complaints among peasants may be longstanding, such spontaneous outbursts of violence take place only when they are directly confronted with an immediate threat to their livelihoods. Once the proximate threat disappears, so too does the violence. Thus the singular demand of the Cairo rioters was to rescind the price increases and subsidy reductions despite the various other grievances of those employed in public-sector factories and informal-sector businesses. Once the radio announced their restoration, the immediate crisis vanished and so the rioting subsided. But the fundamental dissatisfaction that gave rise to it continued to simmer.

Ex-rural workers who had moved to cities to escape the double dilemma of *tarāḥīl* labor and farm work discovered that despite their higher wages, the cost of urban living was even greater. The limited achievements of the open-door policy had created only a tiny fraction of the jobs required by the growing majority and had not raised family incomes high enough to remain even with inflation. The services they had come to expect from the government as part of their entitlement—education, health, housing, training, transportation—were also not forthcoming, for government budgets either had not been restored since the "lean years" of the early 1970s or else had been cut under pressure from the IMF. Debt service consumed much of what little was left for social services.

The gap between the social classes continued to grow wider. The IMF stabilization plan only made matters worse. The price increases had failed, the old ones were soon restored, and eventually the conditional IMF loans were extended. Poor urban workers were momentarily silenced as their low incomes were once again able to cover the cost of subsidized consumption. But any hope of stimulating Egypt's agricultural sector was gone. Rural labor shortages continued to spoil state plans for agricultural self-sufficiency, and Egypt's fiscal predicament remained critical.

In 1979, Egypt's president was coaxed into signing the Camp David treaty in large part by U.S. promises of extended food aid to compensate for grain shortages (Richards and Waterbury 1990:145). In 1982, Egypt transacted one-sixth of all international wheat flour sales (*Wall Street Journal,* January 19, 1983, 32). By 1987 Egypt had become the fourth largest importer of wheat (Sadowski 1991:15). Within the year, 47 percent of the wheat consumed in Egypt was being imported (FAO 1990:47). In 1989, smaller riots erupted when bread prices were raised once again (Sadowski 1991:35–38). In November 1991, imported foodstuffs, including wheat, accounted for 70 percent of Egypt's total food consumption (*al-Wafd,* November 29, 1991). *Tarāḥīl* migrant farm workers who had once played a critical role in providing cheap foodstuffs were no longer cooperating. Their growing exodus, however, was generating more problems than just labor shortages. Egypt's entire economy and political autonomy were seriously limited by the difficulties in agricultural production.

The government had sought to increase the price of bread and other foodstuffs and decrease government subsidies that could have boosted agricultural production and reduced its dependency on foreign grain imports. Had food prices risen, higher crop prices could have translated into increased farm revenues that could have permitted better wages for rural workers. Had incomes also increased, both rural and urban workers could have afforded the more expensive consumption. Instead, the state capitulated to the IMF, which intended that higher prices go exclusively toward reducing Cairo's budget deficits and service its external debt. Egypt's labor force remained cheap. For more than just underwriting the consumption habits of the working class, subsidies had also permitted companies to reduce their wage bills and earn higher profits.[11] With the old policies restored, Egypt's entire business sector once again could breathe a sigh of relief and continue expanding its profits by cutting labor costs.

Moreover, any hope of improving economic conditions and changing state policy through legitimate channels such as labor unions or partisan parties disappeared once the administration reorganized the political system. Demonstrations, riots, and attacks against the government became the sole avenues of dissent. In the end, the government resumed its subsidies and received its international credit. Workers, however, both rural and urban, remained upset over the ever-escalating cost of living, the stagnation of incomes, and the uneven pace of job generation and economic development.

Earning a decent living in the countryside had become more difficult. *Tarāḥīl* workers had left to fill more promising construction jobs in the city, but improvement was possible only if their new effort = wage = price formula remained stable. The construction sector supplied steady but not necessarily permanent employment. Yet even more jobs were demanded.

Consumer prices increased without a corresponding rise in income or income sources. Additional dependents overwhelmed family budgets, which remained unrelieved by finding employment for its members. The troubles of the countryside had been replaced by similar difficulties in the city. In both cases, rural and ex-rural workers remained indignant over the limitations to their lives imposed by state policies.

Rural workers had once used *tarāḥīl* labor trips to escape gender-based wage cuts in the village, and then deserted *tarāḥīl* labor camps and returned home to escape corruption-generated hardships and exhaustion. However, this pendulum movement simply reinforced gender stereotypes at home and left those in the camps to work that much harder. Later, rural workers abandoned this oscillation and migrated to the cities when urban craftsmen emigrated to the oil-rich countries. But after their spontaneous outburst against inflation, underemployment, and joblessness subsided, they found themselves no better off than before. Thus, such movements and explosions were not just a matter of wage differentials; they also constituted responses to failures in controlling the effort = wage = price formula, which, however, did little if anything to permanently resolve the original problems.

In Egypt, state policies ensured that solutions would benefit the elite at the top of the social pyramid to the detriment of those at the bottom. At some point in the migratory movements of *tarāḥīl* workers from village to camp site, from countryside to city, laborers began to realize that their inability to control their labor, wages, and consumption stemmed from government policies and that the state was increasingly responsible for their poverty and powerlessness. The Cairo bread riot was the first of a number of protests against this central institution in their mode of regulation, although, of course, they did not describe it this way. Nevertheless, their resentment, and the reasons behind it, did not dissipate.

Indeed, the mob action of January 1977 soon began to coalesce into more organized forms of opposition but ones that still recalled the institutions of control practiced back in the countryside. Before, when the state had merely been a distant laissez-faire government, workers' conflict with local elites often tilted in their favor, using a paternalism that, while maintaining class distinctions, still netted workers enough benefits that the mutual yet asymmetric relationships involved in valorization could more or less continue uninterrupted. Yet once the state entered the fray, the battle lines became more sharply drawn. The state had a large, impersonal bureaucracy, with its ministries, security forces, and parties, its technocrats, generals, and expediters, and its propagandists, defenders, and opportunists. The lofty heights that separated these officials from the ordinary masses discouraged any paternalism across that line, although patrons and clients continued to link up together on either side to separately support or oppose government plans for national development. Open class conflict was not yet possible, for these vertical alliances still continued to obfuscate true class alignments. Even so, the contradictions of capitalism advanced to the point where ex-rural workers saw more clearly, if not their exploitation by capital, then at least their oppression by the state. This awareness sharpened their opposition and intentions even further.

8

Beating Plowshares into Swords, 1992

After January 1977, Egypt's economic performance remained disappointing despite the reinstatement of low food prices. Other prices continued to rise, incomes among the poor remained stagnant, and social polarization increased, resulting in even more popular discontent.[1] Overall, the countryside fared worse than the city, but while those in the villages responded silently through urban migration, those in the towns, with nowhere to go, reacted angrily with violence. Worldwide oil surpluses and falling petroleum prices after 1985 made the urban situation even more precarious. Many Egyptian emigrants returned home for good and foreign remittances declined. While some lesser-skilled domestic replacements were bumped back into part-time agriculture, many more workers remained in the city, un- or underemployed in construction projects, small informal workshops, and service jobs.

After mid-decade, crop production grew as price controls were gradually lifted. This encouraged mechanization and permitted wage increases for those still working in agriculture. Yet it was not enough. Egyptian agriculture had become, as Simon Commander concluded (1987:168), a sector of part-timers and moonlighters who temporarily returned to farming at night or on weekends. When I returned to Egypt in 1984, I found that there remained relatively few rural workers who inalterably shifted back and forth between village farming and *tarāḥīl* trips. Those still farming, even on a part-time basis, had local property interests; those without property had moved to town. Few saw agriculture as a viable career.

All segments of the rural community were involved in occupational diversification. The propertied strata of the village had taken advantage of ʿAbd al-Nāṣir's free education policy and sent their sons and daughters to public school and later on to urban universities so as to obtain better nonfarm employment. Those in the middle had mastered new skills in the army or trade schools; now they commuted between countryside and city, tending their village plots whenever they could. Those at the bottom who had once toiled as *tarāḥīl* workers had left the countryside altogether for seemingly better opportunities in towns and cities.

Yet the urban economy they encountered was no more encouraging than the rural one they had left behind, despite the potential for full-time employment and a higher standard of living. Insufficient investments and low job and income generation combined with inflation, social polarization, and political powerlessness to make urban life untenable. At first workers had protested these conditions by participating in spontaneous demonstrations and riots against high city prices and low urban incomes. But after 1985, political opposition became more organized. For those employed by large-scale factories and service organizations, this new opposition took the shape of job action and formal strikes against job insecurity and declining benefits. For those employed in small-scale informal-sector businesses, opposition took the form of a moral crusade that challenged government corruption and opportunism.

While the first group involved formal-sector workers born and raised in the city who belonged to hierarchically organized unions and political parties, the second included those transplanted from the countryside. Ex-rural laborers upset over their poverty linked up with equally discontented ex-rural university graduates, both unable to find appropriate employment, earn higher incomes, and achieve a better lifestyle in a stalled economy. United through strong bonds of paternalism, these two segments donned the garments of religious radicalism that sought to purify the government and purge it of the duplicity and fraud of what they saw as a parasitic and autocratic elite. In short they joined an Islamist movement that constituted the politics of rural-to-urban migration.

In 1992, the government responded to this opposition in an increasingly brutal fashion. The eruption of violence was particularly severe in the southern Saʿīd region, which Cairo routinely neglected when budgeting for the social services and assistance that meant the difference between survival and insolvency for those at the bottom of the social pyramid.

So far this study has concentrated primarily on the rural conditions that prevailed in Delta provinces like Minūfiya. But because social problems were more acute in the south, and because I was able to conduct additional research in al-Minyā, I wish to switch the focus of this analysis to the Saʿīd in order to understand just how much ex-rural laborers together with other ex-villagers influenced the recent turbulence in this region. The relatively greater underdevelopment of the south made labor's struggle with the state there all the more pronounced. It is this region, then, with its more extreme poverty and animosity, that comes under scrutiny in this chapter. Although the Saʿīd had its share of *tarāḥīl* labor, the Islamist movement there is not so much about rural workers as about what they did after they abandoned their dual employment and moved to the provincial cities and district towns of the south.

This chapter follows the continuing saga of *tarāḥīl* workers—now *ex*-migrant laborers—once they came to permanently reside in towns and cities, especially in those of southern Egypt. It begins by examining the global and national transformations that occurred after 1973 and left Egyptian workers in a difficult predicament. Previous efforts to establish what Alain Lipietz called a competitive peripheral Fordism had failed. They were now superseded by attempts to create a cooperative Fordism that required Egypt to collaborate with, rather than challenge, capitalism in the core. Egypt's unsuccessful adjustment to this new international division of labor aggravated a growing social polarization and an imperious elite, which generated both an autocratic government and a hostile popular response.

In the 1980s, the administration in Cairo was increasingly caught between the global forces of peripheral Fordism and the parochial vitality of the Islamist movement. On one side were the international financial community and political parties of local businessmen; on the other, a moderate Muslim Brotherhood and a successful Islamic investment sector. Pressure from the first group prompted the government to eliminate all rivals to its political and economic authority from among the second. Interfering with national elections ensured its political domination; closing down private Islamic investment companies guaranteed its financial supremacy. Even at the risk of alienating more Egyptians, the government cleared away the Islamic opposition so as to give it unbridled authority in dealing with international finance and domestic business. Caught between Islamist challengers and IMF bankers, the administration was not able to generate the popular consent needed for substantial economic growth and national development.

Religious opposition took the form of numerous Islamic associations, which at first were engaged simply in community development and charitable acts that benefited those at the bottom. The IMF-mandated reforms had reduced what little the state could spend for such activities as public schools and health clinics. The Islamic associations supplied the services the government was unable to provide. But then when the state closed down the Islamic investment companies that were funding these religious initiatives, took over private mosques and reallocated their charitable funds, and arrested and imprisoned dedicated Muslims who had been providing alternative resources, social services deteriorated even further. Members of the working classes were particularly hard hit. Ex-rural laborers and ex-rural professionals who had both joined the associations then united to transform fundamentally such unsatisfactory conditions. Denied access to legitimate political participation and subjected to increased government persecution, some Islamist groups turned to violence. Religious radicals who previously had just preached their opposition to the state turned into Islamic militants who began translating their words into holy combat. Today, my informants tell me, Egypt stands at the brink of a religious civil war that pits ex-villagers against their government.

A Would-Be NIC

Rising oil prices, recycled capital, emigrant workers, numerous construction projects, and rural labor shortages constitute key components in Egypt's adjustment to the post-1973 international division of labor outlined in chapter 1. But the adaptation extends well beyond rural workers creating deficits in food and export crops, and ex-rural workers participating in spontaneous riots to reinstate consumption norms. For stagnant agricultural production and vigorous informal-sector enterprises are merely symptoms of a yet larger crisis: an arrested development of peripheral Fordism held in check by the stalemate between labor and state economic planners.

Egypt's participation in the global economy essentially relies on three basic pillars—agricultural exports, nationalized import-substitution industries, and bank credit—to accumulate the foreign-currency reserves necessary to balance its trade payments, service its foreign debt, and finance economic investment. Settling trade and debt problems merely avoids pesky fiscal crises, but financing investments provides the country with an important engine of growth and development. Yet with all three pillars, workers critically constrained the state's position in the new international order and the emergence of cooperative peripheral Fordism. Discontented *tarāḥīl* migrant farm laborers damaged the first of these pillars by creating labor shortages and reducing crop production in cotton and grain. Underbudgeted and retrenched employees in public-sector companies undermined the second by easing up on their labor and restricting their output. And, finally, as consumers, these workers, along with other segments of Egypt's working class, began insisting on income increments to accommodate higher consumer costs inflated after subsidies were eliminated as a condition for receiving bank credit from the IMF. As workers and consumers reduced their effort and increased their demands, government policy makers became even more desperate for foreign currency as the need for economic growth increased.

Throughout the 1970s and 1980s, returning emigrants, their bumped-out colleagues, and the latter's female replacements in farming, were loathe to return to crop cultivation. No longer content to work in the fields, they remained employed instead in a lively construction sector, a burgeoning informal sector, and a brisk animal husbandry market. When male migrant farm laborers left *tarāḥīl* and agricultural employment, when their female and child replacements turned to livestock production and school, and when entire rural families moved to the city and stayed there, the cost of producing crops like cotton and grain rose substantially.[2] At the same time, the state continued to impose price controls—in the same decades, cotton remained one of the two crops still under state monopoly regulation—in order to subsidize domestic textile production, raise government revenues, and expand foreign currency reserves. In response, farmers shifted to other crops such as alfalfa, also a spring crop but one that is more profitably sold as fodder for unregulated meat production and one more easily cultivated by women. Finally, the appearance of synthetic materials and the success of cheaper competition in the periphery (Sudan and Uganda, for example) reduced the international demand for Egyptian cotton. As a result, the export of this "white gold" declined dramatically.

If export cotton failed to earn enough hard dollars, could industrial production succeed? Twice Egypt sought to create a viable Fordist manufacturing sector. The first significant experiment consisted of private efforts in the 1930s under Ṭalat Ḥarb and Aḥmad Abbūd, who took advantage of the economic recession in Europe to establish Egypt's first major industries. These deteriorated after World War II, when postwar declines in Britain and Egypt incapacitated the latter's manufacturing and agricultural economies. A second effort involved the large-scale government nationalizations ordered by President ʿAbd al-Nāṣir in the late 1950s and early 1960s. This attempt to achieve semi-peripheral status was derailed by the Six-Day war with Israel and the subsequent seven lean years of retrenchment. In the 1970s, President al-Sadāt's open-door policy sought to close down the dilapidated remnants of these losing endeavors and instead to attract foreign investors by selling off their assets. However, new capital-intensive competition from foreign markets, rigid government regulations, and outmoded production facilities kept Egypt's unsold public sector moribund.[3] While industrial performance continued to languish, selling off additional factories ran into strong opposition from Egypt's labor unions. Yet if there had been more industrial investment and more jobs, and if ex-rural workers had not provided such a large reserve army that swamped the competitive urban labor market, these factory workers would have been less apprehensive over the streamlining privatization entails.

At first industrialization was supposed to benefit from the tax on agricultural incomes and the transfer of capital out of the countryside. Yet after 1967, these revenues went instead to subsidize low-paid urban consumers and to reduce company wage costs. This kept urban labor cheap so as to attract more investment. Unfortunately, the proportion of urban poor rose substantially because of urban migration and the social polarization of the open-door policy. Subsidy costs increased accordingly.

Budget deficits, increased debt, and financial bailouts by the IMF forced Cairo to abandon this expensive program. Consequently, as consumer prices climbed, popular pressure began to demand corresponding increases in wages and salaries. Yet such income adjustments required greater productivity to avoid further inflation and more rapid job generation to avoid popular discontent. As their already precarious standard of living became further eroded by the steep rise in consumption costs and the added burden of unemployed dependents, workers and their families grew even more vocal in seeking higher incomes and more jobs. By the late 1980s, official unemployment hovered at a little over 12 percent. Yet for veteran workers, the rate rose to 22 percent due to the much lower rate of joblessness among lower-paid newcomers to the regular labor force (*al-Wafd*, November 13, 1991).

The state's record in employment and income generation remained uneven. It could not expand old industries or create new ones. Unable to accumulate foreign currency domestically from either industrial or agricultural exports, Cairo increasingly turned instead to outside resources. Wary of rising labor costs, labor force discipline, and widespread corruption, many foreign financiers hesitated. However, the abundance of core capital flowing into the periphery promised to overcome their initial reluctance.

Because of the economic recession of 1967 and the oil price rise of 1973, industrial investment in the core declined rapidly while it expanded dramatically in the periphery, either through direct corporate funding, institutional credit arrangements, or redistributed oil revenues. Since the early 1970s, the periphery has witnessed the emergence of several rich oil exporters (OPEC) and a number of newly industrializing countries (NICs).

Egypt is not a major OPEC oil producer or a member of the NIC club, although it certainly aspires to be, and has only sporadically benefited from transfers of core capital. At first, Cairo attempted to attract investment principally by relying on its ties to neighboring Arab petroleum producers. With the collapse of its chief regional rival, Lebanon, and the formulation of the open-door policy, the government had realistically expected greater investment activity to materialize after the mid-1970s. Its expectations were stymied, however, as most oil revenues bypassed Egypt and went instead into core banks first, and then later to more promising and profitable peripheral sites elsewhere. Further efforts to encourage Arab investment were frustrated by the 1979 Camp David Accords and Cairo's subsequent diplomatic estrangement from regional oil producers. Until reconciliation could be achieved, Egypt relied on U.S. assistance and renting out its large labor force.

Throughout the 1970s and 1980s, revenues from foreign aid, domestic oil production, declining cotton exports, stagnant industrial production, canal fees, and tourism were insufficient by themselves to promote further economic development. Workers' remittances, however, proved to be an important and substantial source of foreign currency and investment funds despite the government's initial reluctance. However, little of the generous incomes earned abroad were channeled through state banks. Rather, hard-currency remittances went instead into the private "own-exchange" system and Islamic investment companies, financing such investments as purchasing land, building housing, buying transport vehicles, and establishing small-scale service and manufacturing businesses in the informal sector, much of which drew even more workers out of agriculture (Assaad 1991:153).

Fortuitously, these individual initiatives financed economic ventures whose startup stimulated a great flurry of construction operations. The government also promoted building activities as it allocated national funds and utilized the small sums of foreign capital to erect housing for a growing urban population and to implement infrastructural projects for potential investors. All these undertakings conveniently matched the occupations of an experienced labor force increasingly repatriated in the mid-1980s by structural unemployment abroad[4] but still averse to full-time agricultural and *tarāḥīl* work in the village—a tenable position as long as urban jobs in construction, services, and the informal sector remained abundant.

Yet the government was unable to attract sufficient private investment, for despite this flow of foreign capital into Egypt, much of it financed high-yield operations in commerce, banking, real estate, and tourism instead of establishing solid labor-absorbing industrial projects. With domestic exports and foreign investment not forthcoming, the state turned to international sources of credit. However, the subsequent loans went to relieve the government's fiscal crises instead of financing additional jobs and incomes. Moreover, austere credit conditions required Cairo to eliminate consumer subsidies, reduce its national budgets, lower international exchange rates, raise domestic interest rates, and dismantle the public sector—all which made working-class lives and livelihoods even more untenable and made sustained state-led growth even less feasible.

Thus the futile quest for the hard currency necessary to finance economic development increasingly limited Egypt's options. Agriculture, state industry, labor remittances, foreign investment, and international credit were all viewed by the government as potential sources for the foreign capital that could underwrite its plans for peripheral Fordism and export-led growth. Unfortunately, this potential was seldom realized. The government was clearly troubled by the specter of the two Januarys—1952 and 1977—and sought to expand employment and income so as to avoid social unrest. Yet priority was more often than not given to the elites at the top of the social pyramid—wealthy businessmen, state planners, international bankers, shrewd politicians, powerful generals—before what little that remained was allocated for national growth. As a result, the sources of investment provided little in the way of benefit to the majority of Egyptians at the bottom. This generated at least two important consequences: the greater impoverishment of the Egyptian working classes, and their increasing awareness of the state's responsibility for their predicament.

Sowing Dragons' Teeth

For an increasing number of Egyptians, the corruption, polarization, and economic stalemate of the country's arrested development were becoming intolerable. The state had grown far too accommodating to the businessmen, bankers, speculators, and profiteers who benefited from the open-door policy, and had delivered far too little to compensate the rest of the population for lack of national growth. Unplanned riots intimidated officials, but only momentarily, and thus proved ineffectual in achieving fundamental policy changes. Without legitimate channels of protest, popular discontent soon took the shape of an Islamist movement that consisted of numerous, independent religious associations.

Initially, these associations were not hostile to the government. Indeed, from 1972 to 1977, the administration actually approved of their formation on Egypt's university campuses in its attempt to marginalize those on the Nasserist left who disagreed with the state's shift from supporting the public sector to promoting private capital. This encouragement climaxed in April 1975 when Islamist candidates won the national student union elections and defeated those who opposed the government's new development policies (Kepel 1985:chap. 5).

But even in their formative years, these associations could not be contained just within the bounds of safe academic discourse. One early group, Munazhzhamāt al-Taḥrīr al-Islāmiya, organized by Ṣaliḥ al-Siriya, mobilized cadets and officers at the national military academy in Heliopolis. In 1974 its attempted takeover of the academy presciently signaled the public appearance of an intense Islamist hostility to the Egyptian state. Nor did the associations remain limited to the halls of higher education. As campus leaders graduated, many established radical organizations outside the university. Shukrī Muṣṭafa, an agricultural engineering student from Assiyūṭ, later founded Jamāʿāt al-Muslimīn (also known as al-Takfīr wa al-Ḥijra), whose members lived together and worked in the poor urban neighborhoods of Cairo and other cities (Kepel 1985:77, 89).

At first this new brand of Islamic radicalism remained limited mostly to rural middle-class students and ex-students. It was not until after 1985, when the petroleum-induced recession hit Egypt, that it began to include members of Egypt's disaffected urban working classes, which contained large numbers of ex-rural laborers. What started then as a religious movement just among the educated later came to embrace unschooled members, including many former *tarāḥīl* workers, who had benefited from the philanthropy and expertise of these university graduates.

In 1977, the three abrupt policy reversals that occurred during my first year in Cairo—the January food riots, the July raid against the Jamāʿāt al-Muslimīn, and al-Sadāt's November trip to Jerusalem—turned several of these associations against the state. Sectarian strife in the southern provinces of al-Minyā and Assiyūṭ, and in the Cairo slum of al-Zāwiya al-Ḥamrā', further intensified their growing animosity. At first the administration remained somewhat indifferent to this opposition. Yet on August 1, 1981, commemorating the ʿId al-Fitr, over 100,000 members of different Islamic associations demonstrated in ʿAbdīn Square against al-Sadāt outside his presidential office. The following month, the government ordered large-scale arrests of Islamist leaders along with other political opponents, dissident writers, intellectuals, and popular leaders (Hiro 1989:77; Hirst and Beeson 1981:332–34; Ansari 1986:chap. 10).

A month later, during a military parade commemorating the October war, army soldiers belonging to the Islamic militant group al-Jihād assassinated Egypt's president. Once again, a new chief of state, Ḥusnī Mubarak, succeeded upon the death of the incumbent rather than upon his electoral defeat. The official patronage of these associations quickly ended and the battle soon commenced, a contest to win the hearts and minds of ordinary Egyptians, a struggle that eventually pitted the destitute against the elite. What had once been the spontaneity of random mob action henceforth grew into the more focused hostility of these Islamic associations against the state.

When Mubarak assumed office, the triple traumas of the June war, the January riots, and the October assassination combined to keep the new administration cautious and conciliatory during its first three years. It agreed to preserve the open door and to honor Camp David, thereby retaining the indispensable patronage of the United States. It also pledged to continue the democratization program begun by its predecessor. But while the government released hundreds of political opponents detained in the final month of the previous administration, it also quietly went about arresting scores of Islamic militants, concentrating particular attention on purging those in the military.

In April 1982, al-Jihād tried but failed to assassinate the new president as part of its attempt to establish an Islamic government (Hiro 1989:81). This led to even more government detentions. Subsequently, the organization divided in two. Al-Jihād, which followed the demagogic doctrines of ʿAbd al-Salām al-Faraj, was to operate principally in Cairo, while a new group, al-Jamāʿa al-Islāmiya—to be distinguished from the generic name that labeled all such religious associations[5]—appeared in the Saʿīd, heeding more the fiery rhetoric of ʿUmar ʿAbd al-Raḥmān. But this leadership split was merely tactical, for both agreed on the principles of overthrowing the state by force and establishing *sharīʿa*, or Islamic religious law. Such militancy increasingly found fertile ground, for as long as the government refused to permit the formation of an identifiable, religious-based political party, those who radically opposed state policy yet who chose to remain nonmilitant were increasingly frustrated by their inability to change the direction of national development.

The new president's grace period ended when parliamentary elections were scheduled for May 1984. But although the official secular parties offered no real danger, elements from the Islamist movement threatened to capsize the complacency of the administration. In order to sidestep the law forbidding religious parties, stealth candidates from the Muslim Brotherhood sought allies from among the conservative bloc, such as the Wafd and the so-called Liberal parties, in order to advance its moderate Islamist platform. Even so, the elections gave the ruling party an overwhelming victory.

This marked the real transition to the Mubarak era, for it allowed the president the latitude to appoint colorless technocrats to important cabinet and party positions and thereby place his imprimatur on the new government. The administration now finally emerged as a government in its own right, out from behind the shadows of both the Nassirist left and the Sadatist right, but nevertheless still faced with strong domestic pressures to yield power—primarily from a resurgent Islamic radicalism thwarted in even this mildest of attempts to gain greater influence over state policy (Springborg 1989:158–63; Hopwood 1991:185).

The rapid expansion of the Islamist movement was stimulated to a large extent by the growth of its financiers, the new Islamic investment companies. These private companies had been legalized by the open-door policy, but it was not until the 1980s that they began to play a major role in the nation's economy. Flush with hard-currency remittances from devout Egyptians working abroad, these operations soon challenged the stale and stodgy public banking sector that had long dominated, yet eviscerated, the nation's private investment and financial activities.

Government banks were primarily interested in making short-term credit available for large commercial export-import activities. Islamic investment companies, however, were willing to provide capital to numerous small-scale, informal-sector businessmen. These companies operated on the basis of Islamic commercial law, which was not unlike profit sharing. Creditors and depositors did not receive interest, which was forbidden, but instead shared the profit or loss incurred on moneymaking activities. Since technically such dividends were not a form of interest, they were not subject to state regulations, which kept official interest rates artificially low so as to ease government financial transactions. Depositors received shares that, when computed as rates of return, earned dividends of 25 percent annually—twice what the public banks offered. Creditors repaid according to the success of their operations (Sadowski 1991:231). The investment companies also automatically withheld a 2.5 percent deduction on all monetary transactions for charitable *zakāt* donations—what had only been a voluntary option with the government banks. This generated ample funds that were used to finance numerous community development projects implemented through recipient mosques by local Islamic associations established by educated and pious professionals. Thus the investment companies appealed to many devout Egyptian Muslims who respected the principles of Islamic finance that these operations followed, who benefited from these investments and transactions, and who supported the provision of social services that the companies' *zakāt* contributions financed.

But the state was not willing to accept this Islamic challenge to its banking monopoly quietly. Following the 1984 elections, the government mounted a major campaign to close nearly two hundred Islamic investment companies and to seize their foreign currency deposits. The government accused them of conducting unsound and even illegal transactions. But in fact these private efforts—no more improperly financed, Yahya Sadowski claimed (1991:248), than rival state institutions—were attacked because of their potential to outperform and even surpass government operations. Without this external competition, public banking operations were to remain narrow, limited, and unresponsive.

In January 1985, dozens of powerful Islamic investment officials were apprehended, triggering an abrupt shortage in foreign exchange. Coincidentally, oil prices began to fall, dropping by two-thirds in three months. Egypt's hard-currency reserves likewise declined. The government quickly found itself without the dollars it needed to pay for food imports and to compensate foreign creditors. This in turn provoked a major decline in the value of the Egyptian pound. Officials reacted by immediately implementing austerity measures aimed at tightening bank credit, regulating foreign currency transactions, limiting imports, and raising domestic prices. But these measures merely aggravated the situation. Fearing that these conditions would soon prompt riots like those in 1977, the state rescinded the measures, but still vowed to bring the Islamic investment companies under stricter government control (Sadowski 1991:233–47; Springborg 1989:53–54).

Certainly these two were competitors for a dwindling supply of hard currency, but there was more than just financial dominance involved. The Islamic companies were also underwriting worthwhile and successful development efforts that were gaining the Islamist movement new adherents and popular support. In its zeal to rein in the Islamic finance sector, the government also drastically cut the funds for countless community projects that were effectively delivering a wide range of important social benefits to poor urban workers and their families. Nothing was done to replace them.

In February 1987 the national Supreme Court annulled the 1984 Parliamentary elections because of voting irregularities. Parliament was dissolved and new elections were scheduled for May. The Islamic investment companies offered strong financial support for opposition candidates. Worried, even secular candidates assumed the verbal trappings of Islamic rhetoric. The government temporarily suspended its campaign against these companies. The IMF too postponed another bilateral agreement for fear it would upset the economy and help defeat cooperative politicians.

Already Islamist candidates had won elections to the executive boards in the professional syndicates for doctors, engineers, dentists, and teachers. In November 1985 student union elections in the faculties of science, engineering, medicine, dentistry, and pharmacy had given resounding victories to candidates from Islamic associations. The Muslim Brotherhood, Robert Springborg observed (1989:184), "demonstrated that it possessed the most broadly based, lavishly financed, and well organized opposition electoral machine in the country. It established itself as the core of the opposition to government in Parliament." It appealed to all classes, particularly to those alienated from the elite who controlled the secular parties, both right and left. Yet although the Muslim Brotherhood won significant gains at the ballot box, as long as it continued to be denied legal authority, many moderate Muslims were provoked into taking more radical positions. Those who already disagreed with the Brotherhood's mild centrist policies advocated an even more militant strategy. Many concluded from the overwhelming government victory in May that democracy was not an effective way to achieve their goals (Springborg 1989:163, 188, 227; Hopwood 1991:186).

Once the elections were over, the lull in the government campaign against the Islamic investment companies ended. It renewed its campaign in May 1987, coinciding with the signing of an IMF standby agreement negotiated to reschedule its national debt.

The IMF had negotiated four agreements with Cairo, starting with the 1962 accord that had helped undermine Arab socialism and including the 1977 settlement that had provoked the January riots. At first, the international financial community, including the IMF, World Bank, and the U.S. Agency for International Development, had encouraged Egypt's indebtedness. Then it used offers of conditional relief from its financial obligations, loan rescheduling, and foreign economic assistance to leverage the government into adopting policy reforms that expedited the entry of foreign capital. Far from solving Egypt's fiscal problems, twenty-five years of IMF assistance seemed to have made matters worse, although not without commercial and diplomatic benefit to those who contributed the bulk of the Fund's budget. Financial difficulties intensified, however, such that by 1987, Egypt was on the brink of a major recession. The IMF was the last resort.

When world petroleum prices fell after 1985, government revenues decreased substantially. The direct sale of domestic oil earned less income.

When other Arab oil producers cut their national budgets, regional assistance and investments declined. Many foreign construction projects were terminated or pared down, reducing their Egyptian expatriate labor force through attrition and replacement, and so workers' remittances declined as well. Suez canal transit revenues dropped as bigger, more efficient ships were rerouted to avoid the narrow channel. Thus overall foreign earnings decreased rapidly, and in 1987 Egypt faced the prospect of defaulting on its loan repayments.

International relief was sought, but now the IMF was not the only source of pressure for reform. Egypt's bilateral and private lenders were also insisting that Cairo implement the IMF-mandated reform package in order to receive more credit. The IMF conditions for extended credit and financial assistance insisted on an Economic Reform and Structural Adjustment Program (ERSAP) that required reducing budget deficits, reforming banking practices, and raising prices. The Fund again demanded, in the name of smaller government, that Egypt eliminate the state subsidies programs that otherwise encouraged greater private investment and restrained public discontent.

The IMF package proved extremely inflationary. First, it demanded higher exchange rates, which meant devaluing the Egyptian pound. This, the IMF argued, would improve Egypt's balance of trade, reduce its imports, increase foreign demand for its exports, and shift capital from the black to the official market. Second, the IMF insisted that interest rates rise to match or exceed the rate of inflation. This would enable state banks to attract more deposits and spur investment, but it would also raise the cost of credit to the government and cause numerous private bankruptcies. Finally, the IMF urged Egypt to cut its budget deficit by eliminating costly consumer subsidies and raising government tax revenues. In May 1987, after the Parliamentary elections, the administration relented, devalued the pound by 40 percent against the dollar, and froze consumer subsidies at their 1986 level. The IMF then agreed to an eighteen-month standby agreement that provided new lines of credit and a new timetable for repaying Egypt's $40 billion foreign debt.

The standard IMF procedure was to offer loans by degrees (tranches), rewarding progress in implementing reforms or penalizing delays and noncompliance. Soon IMF officials were complaining that Cairo was reneging on reducing subsidies, raising commercial exchange rates, and dismantling the public sector. Egyptian officials replied that already the IMF reforms were triggering social disorders like those that had erupted in 1977. Further pressure, they warned, would result in large-scale riots. To avoid an automatic cutoff of U.S. financial assistance, Cairo agreed to reduce fuel and food subsidies. Predictably, bread shortages appeared in January 1989 and were quickly translated into public protest (Sadowski 1991:35, 215–19; Springborg 1989:260, 266).

Economic disorder soon came to overwhelm more and more of the consuming public, including *tarāḥīl* migrant farm workers, but also ex-rural laborers, their urban colleagues, and even the heretofore comfortable middle class. Unable to legitimately influence government policy, many of the disaffected turned to other outlets for recourse. The secular left, already neutralized by two decades of marginalization, was unable to provide the leadership so urgently needed to shape and transform the widespread disaffection among the working classes. Instead, such guidance came from middle-class radicals who joined the Islamist movement and who galvanized mass discontent into a major challenge to the state. The proletarian core of their support came not so much from the organized labor located in large urban factories, but from the unorganized multitudes who, like ex-*tarāḥīl* workers but also like many other villagers, had flocked into the small district towns, provincial capitals, and urban interstices where they had found numerous jobs in small construction crews, unregistered workshops, and informal service activities.

The Islamist Solution to Structural Adjustments

In June 1989, an official IMF delegation arrived in Cairo to negotiate a new standby agreement to prevent Egypt from defaulting on its $40 billion debt. Safe on their own home turf, Egypt's savvy financial negotiators haggled and dickered, stretching out the countless number of committee meetings, postponing the final authorization. Signatures on the document were delayed. In the end, the IMF waited too long to settle. In August 1990, Iraq invaded Kuwait. The United States, eager to recruit Egypt into its international coalition, reversed its zealous support of the IMF, dropped its incessant insistence on economic and fiscal reform, and sought to ease Cairo's economic burdens. Egypt's participation in the 1990–91 Gulf war was further encouraged when the United States and its allies agreed to forgive $7 billion of Egypt's military debt and to persuade private creditors to write off another $10 billion (Sadowski 1991:218–19; Hooglund 1991:7). Both in 1979 with the Camp David treaty and in 1991 with the Gulf war, Egypt's diplomatic autonomy was seriously undermined by the financial problems generated by its economy's poor performance.

In January 1991, Egypt finally but reluctantly signed a still austere IMF agreement, which, predictably, resulted in substantial social unrest. Within the year, the extreme hardship of high price inflation was apparent to all. In 1992, Ramadan, the festive lunar month of religious fasting, fell in March. I was teaching in Alexandria at the time and it appeared then to be unusually haggard and sparse, as if lifted from a page out of Charles Dickens and nineteenth-century England. The swell of unhappy faces pressed against the shop windows, looking and longing, but seldom buying, the nuts, fruits, and candies reserved for this solemn occasion. Normally Ramadan is the exemplar month for nighttime feasting, yet this particular spring, the government was unable to keep Ramadan from turning into gloom. Ordinarily the Supply Ministry ensures that shelves are well-stocked and prices remain at reasonable levels. Yet, halfway through the month, even government stores ran out of basic necessities—an ominous sign indeed. More than the usual number of celebrants had to make do without the customary evening *iftār* (break-fast), the Ramadan cookies, and the new clothes. Worried, the government reported that the difficulties from the IMF's ERSAP would take three years to fix (*al-Ahrām,* May 26, 1992).

Industrial workers in the factory town of Helwan 15 miles south of Cairo decided not to wait. In January 1992, strikes in the cement and steel plants indicated just how anxious they had become toward rising prices and stagnant incomes. Laborers wanted a favorable decision on their bonuses: making them a higher proportion of their annual wage (20 percent instead of the government's offer of 15 percent), untaxed (the government taxed bonuses as regular income), and supplemented for those receiving additional training and for those at the end of their income scale. Meetings the following month with the prime minister were postponed until orders came down from above to convene (*al-Wafd,* March 18, 1992). Finally, President Mubarak announced a wage package that temporarily satisfied the discontented workers, but which was guaranteed to displease the more frugal IMF officials. Twenty percent bonuses were to be awarded in July 1992, and were to continue for five years, but would be taxed as part of annual earnings. Training bonuses and scale adjustments were added. Moreover, extra May Day bonuses of between 5 and 7 percent were announced later (*al-Ahālī,* April 9, 1992; *al-Ahrām,* May 1, 1992). Pressure from labor was beginning to force Egypt to forego plans to offer investors a cheap labor force. Those from urban factories were soon joined by workers employed in less formal enterprises, such as labor-only subcontractors and labor-intensive workshops, although their demands did not warrant such high-level council nor did they yield as satisfactory a response.

Given the growing economic hardship Egyptians were experiencing, it is not surprising that in the summer of 1992, strained tensions between Egypt's security forces stationed in the Saʿīd and angry and hostile Islamic militants erupted in gunfire, police raids, hot pursuit, arrests, and counterattacks. Initially the confrontation took place between Egyptian Copts and Muslims, but once the government security forces entered the fray, sights were turned on them instead. Police raided ammunition storerooms, and insurrectionists fought back with attacks on police headquarters. When bombs were found in one train car, the government ordered troops to occupy all coaches (*al-Ahrām,* October 7, 1992). Security forces blew up the homes of suspected outlaws. The Egyptian Saʿīd soon began to resemble an Occupied Territory.

In those areas more distant from the well-worn path of foreign visitors, where the local economy and its elite are much less dependent on tourism, outbreaks of violence soon took the shape of salvos discharged at foreigners. Although the number of incidents was very small, the sporadic shootings of German and Japanese tourists seriously threatened Egypt's tourism industry (*al-Ahrām,* November 12, 1992). Very quickly, cancellations began taking their toll, and the flow of hard currency began to dwindle. In 1992–93 tourism was reported to be down by 85 percent.[6] Soon the fighting began to explode in the poorer neighborhoods flanking Cairo. Trouble in Imbāba, a working-class suburb in northwest Cairo, resulted in the arrest of hundreds of Islamist activists, who were tried by military security judges instead of in civilian courtrooms (*al-Wafd,* October 28, 1992). But unlike the arrest and imprisonment of dissidents under ʿAbd al-Nāṣir and al-Sadāt, Egypt's religious prisoners were now given death sentences for their political crimes.

The ensuing battle set the state and its security forces against the many marginalized and pauperized by its adoption of IMF structural adjustments. Their enmity lay firmly rooted in the harsh economic conditions that divided the few well-to-do and break-evens from the multitudes going under and swamped by the tide of severe economic distress generated by government policy.

Arguably a more thorough strategy of overthrowing the state would rely instead on a socialist program from the left. Yet the left in Egypt was bankrupt, as in so many other countries, both developed and developing. Never able to truly escape its own class character, it nonetheless suffered unduly from twenty years of state repression since the death of ʿAbd al-Nāṣir.

In countries where the left has been crushed, removed, or eviscerated, either from within or without, unprogressive movements frequently arise to fill the void, often with demagogic leaders mobilizing the same popular discontent but diverting it instead into less threatening channels. These could lead to fascism—they certainly did in Europe—but in Egypt, the broad diversity of religious authorities and supporters and the diffuse quality of their uncoordinated associations provided a guarantee that the multiplicity of voices comprising the Islamist movement could prevent such an extreme outcome.

Religious movements are not automatically authoritarian. Liberation theology in Latin America, for example, grew out of the same soil of extreme poverty, economic stagnation, and failed modernization that Islamic radicalism in Egypt did and still remained progressive. Notwithstanding the prejudicial pronouncements of Egypt's state media, the Islamist movement contained many who proclaimed genuine, broadminded principles. They were, however, directed against the state and its supporters, whose monopoly over information therefore dominated the public's understanding of these religious radicals.

These radical organizations are reminiscent of the social protest movements Eric Hobsbawm documented (1959:chap. 2) for southern Italy before this region was incorporated into a unified modern nation. There, secret societies also brought together a disgruntled rural middle class and a discontented class of poor both displaced by the encroachment of nineteenth-century capitalism. Before the Italian Mafias turned criminal after 1860, its early actions may well have included acts of rebellion described by the state as illegal crimes (cf. Brown 1990:6–7). Egypt's Islamic associations were similarly characterized as "terrorist" organizations because they dared to challenge the legitimacy of the prevailing order.

The growth of these Islamic associations was particularly intense in the Saʿīd. Rural laborers in the south had benefited disproportionately from the government projects at Aswān and in desert land reclamation, and had stopped shifting between farm and *tarāḥīl* worksites much earlier than did their counterparts in the Delta. Since the rise of the regional petro-economy, skilled laborers in towns and cities up and down the southern Nile valley had emigrated abroad much sooner and in much larger numbers, opening up many more jobs for relocated rural laborers who then abandoned the countryside more thoroughly than in the north. But the greater proportion of Saʿīdīs working in Libya, Saudi Arabia, the Gulf, and Iraq made their return after 1985 even more problematic. Numerous repatriates bumped out their colleagues in the building trades, who then remained in town instead of returning to the countryside. This further expanded the quantity of those experiencing urban economic hardship. Poverty became much more intense in the south than in the rest of the country.[7]

The Saʿīd also remained much more underdeveloped than other parts of Egypt. Consequently, social discontent became much more pronounced. The south's greater emphasis on extended kinship relations meant literally a more clannish culture. Moreover, the Saʿīdī provinces of Sūḥāj, Assiyūṭ, and al-Minyā included a larger portion of Christian Copts, which guaranteed that sectarianism was not likely to subside. All these factors combined into generating a higher incidence of social turmoil in the south in the late 1980s and 1990s. Even so, by 1992, this unrest had begun to spread to the rest of Egypt as well.

From 1984 to 1986 I resided in al-Minyā city as the field office director for a U.S.-based community development organization. I was able to observe the economic and social conditions of the Saʿīd, visit local development projects, and discuss the Islamist movement with colleagues and their families. These personal friendships continued over the years. By the time I returned to Cairo in 1994, al-Minyā and the neighboring city to the south, Assiyūṭ, had become notorious hotbeds of Islamic radicalism and militancy. None whom I knew or later met were actually involved in militant Islamic activities, although many sympathized with the movement. Some had once belonged to radical Islamic associations but had quit. Some had relatives who had been arrested and imprisoned. For them, their families and jobs came first, and so they rejected militancy. Although tight state security limited research in al-Minyā to just casual visits and discussions, nevertheless I was able to comprehend the actual configuration of events, ideas, participants, groups, and policies that comprised both the Islamist movement in the Saʿīd and the government's response to it.

The radicalism of the Islamic associations in al-Minyā appealed to two social classes that both experienced the dislocation of rural-to-urban migration. One segment consisted of ex-rural but middle-class university students who had first come from diversified farm families and who had since graduated into an uncertain job market. These included well-educated but nonetheless alienated white-collar professionals—doctors, engineers, lawyers, teachers, accountants, bureaucrats—who were strongly supported by disgruntled members of the underclass, who found it increasingly difficult to stretch their limited incomes to cover rising consumption costs. This other segment, then, involved ex-rural workers who had migrated to the city and found employment in the construction, service, and informal sectors but who still remained destitute and impoverished.[8]

These two segments were strongly linked together through the pervasive bonds of paternalism, which emphasized personalized relations and reciprocity such that the favors and benefits from middle-class professionals were exchanged for the loyalty and support of working-class beneficiaries. They both joined religious association that re-created and reinforced the intimacy of a bygone village community, in contrast to urban organizations like professional syndicates and labor unions, the anonymity and coldness of which alienated these potential members.

University students from the countryside had benefited extensively from the new free education policies implemented by the ʿAbd al-Nāṣir administration. They were highly motivated and accomplished, and many participated in campus Islamic associations of the 1970s. Upon graduation, however, these students, especially those from the stigmatized south, discovered that despite their costly education—dearly paid for not only in money but also in the personal sacrifice of their families—the road to gaining better professional employment and achieving the higher-class status that leads inevitably to the capital city was blocked by the ascriptive wall of Cairene elite society. Frustrated when wealthy family connections took precedence over merit, many migrated to Libya, Iraq, and the Gulf to acquire the better incomes unavailable at home.

However, beginning in 1985, many of these professionals returned to the Saʿīd to stay. Many reactivated the piety and spirituality learned during their college days and reinforced while working abroad. They chose to emulate the life of the prophet Muḥammad, to grow beards and dress in white robes, and to perform charitable acts and good deeds that would bring them closer to their religion. But many remained thwarted in their quest for upward mobility. They therefore rechanneled their frustration into mobilizing an equally discontented ex-rural working class. The tone was one of moral outrage. The adversary became those who had been corrupted by opportunism and contact with Western authorities.

Here historical parallels prove fascinating. For as the first experiment with peripheral Fordism came to an end in the late 1940s, this interclass pattern pitting countryside against city and achievement against ascription found expression in highly trained military officers from the provinces overthrowing an entrenched but decadent palace oligarchy. In the 1970s, as the second attempt languished, this rural-urban paradigm took the distinctive shape of religious radicals from the countryside attacking an established but uncertain Westernized urban elite and its government.

Proletarianization and rural-to-urban migration had been taking place in Egypt for decades if not longer. But in the 1970s the exodus from the countryside increased rapidly after the seven years of economic stagnation that followed the June 1967 war and accelerated even further after the threefold increase in petroleum prices that followed the Egyptian-Israeli war of October 1973. Government price controls continued to limit farm incomes, gender segmentation continued to debase wages, and corruption-based speedups continued to overburden migrant farm workers. Ex-*tarāḥīl* workers migrated to the cities in large numbers and replaced emigrant workers in the construction sector, where the wages and organization attracted those who had previously been overworked and underpaid in the countryside. These laborers became attached to specific building contractors and small workshop owners through strong ties of paternalism, which they had once used back in their villages and which were again effective in the cities in order to guarantee employment opportunities on the one hand and, on the other, to preserve a readily available workforce even in periods of temporary inactivity.

After 1985, fewer skilled urban workers traveled abroad, and those who did came home sooner. Back in the Saʿīd, they mixed with their unskilled colleagues who had never emigrated. Together they sought work in a construction sector whose investments already were in decline. Patron-client relations allowed lesser-skilled laborers to stay tied to construction bosses and workshop proprietors despite growing unemployment so as not to return to their villages where conditions were even more hopeless. Many of these un- or underemployed workers became increasingly dependent on the charitable acts and good deeds of pious professionals. Constrained by high prices, low wages, and unemployed kin, they came to rely heavily on the largesse of private benefactors to get them through tight times. Such desperate circumstances firmly attached needy laborers to charitable professionals in ways that extended far beyond the specific welfare activities and benefits.

While one segment of the working class sought to change state economic policy through direct pressure, job action, and organized strikes such as those in Helwan, a second, much larger portion remained outside the domain of formal labor unions and their established channels of protest. Unable to pursue legitimate strategies for change, this second segment instead adopted the radical activism of this déclassé technocratic leadership. Those who joined and acted through the formal union organizations of public-sector factories were workers who, as Saad Eddin Ibrahim once pointed out (1980:447), came principally from an urban milieu. However, the vast majority of workers did not take part in these labor organizations since they were employed in the small, paternalistic enterprises commonly found in construction, informal businesses, and petty services, or else they were self-employed. Some belonged to unions, like the GUAMW, that simply no longer worked. Of this unrepresented or unorganized workforce, a large proportion originated from the countryside. Many who had been *tarāḥīl* migrant farm workers continued to be poor even after they had left their villages and found employment in the cities.

The social bonds between ex-rural technocrats and ex-rural workers were first forged in the countryside, where, at thousands of worksites, the mutuality of paternalism exchanged favors and privileges from employers for service and commitment from workers. When later employment shifted to small construction crews, service-sector activities, or small informal-sector businesses, workplace discipline continued to emphasize the personalized relations and reciprocity of paternalism. Such allegiances were then readily transferred to other benefactors even when they appeared outside the actual labor process.

Moreover, both professionals and workers subscribed to the values of a reinvented rural community. Middle-class village students attending urban universities for the first time in the history of their families were unfamiliar with the impersonality of large campuses, crowded classrooms, and indifferent professors. Rural workers moving into the city and finding employment in construction crews, workshops, and services were unaccustomed to the cold bureaucracy of government offices, large companies, and rapid commercial transactions. Nostalgia and uncertainty drove both groups into the more familiar, intimate surroundings of the Islamic associations.

Yet, ironically, the creed of these religious associations was not the same as what these villagers had left behind. Village Islam had been textured by the passive quietism of Sufism, saint shrines, and miracles. Urban Islamic associations rejected such "superstition" and instead exhibited the political activism of Salifiyism, legalism, and righteousness (Gilsenan 1992:chap. 10). The shift from rural to urban had been paralleled by a transformation from "traditional" to "modern." However, it was not a secular modernity but rather a religious one inherited from the doctrines of such Islamic intellectuals as Muḥammad ʿAbduh and Ḥassan al-Bannā.

These associations thus attracted ex-villagers by providing an intimacy reminiscent of the old rural community but in the process transposed their beliefs from tolerant submission to indignant radicalism. They united those who wished to practice a more devout and pious Islam with those who were in desperate straits, forming a core of religious activists and loyal supporters potentially useful for partisan action. Very few of these associations ever reached the violent intensity practiced by al-Jihād or al-Jamāʿa al-Islāmiya, although many members did switch associations once government persecution increased. Instead, most enthusiasts embraced a nonmilitant religiosity that advocated performing good deeds and pious acts on the one hand and bestowing devout blessings and grateful loyalty on the other.

Since the start of skilled-labor emigration after 1971, especially to such orthodox countries as Saudi Arabia and those in the Gulf, university-trained professionals who remitted their ample salaries home allocated a significant portion for performing Islamic good deeds, pious acts, and funding community-development and charity projects. In the early 1980s, such financing increased even further with the profit sharing and monetary transactions routed through the Islamic investment companies. Moreover, the supervision over the *zakāt* funds of local private mosques by like-minded colleagues guaranteed that the bulk of these donations would reach the surrounding communities and those in need.

The quantity and quality of these small development projects far outweighed the meager efforts of government programs or even the lavishly funded attempts by state-sponsored foreign agencies. In 1985, while living in al-Minyā, I had the opportunity to attend a regional conference of local development organizations that revealed the large proportion of Islamic efforts found in the Saʿīd. Of thirty participating agencies, four were foreign-funded. The remainder consisted of privately financed local associations that operated on a much smaller scale and budget, but with a much greater success rate in establishing important services that were not available from government line ministries. These associations provided hospital beds for the poor, low-cost health clinics, affordable housing, after-school tutoring, complimentary textbooks, clothing exchanges, veterinarian services, small-scale business assistance and low-cost credit, and guidance through the labyrinthine state bureaucracy for permits, licenses, and tax abatements. All of these constituted critically important services that the government in Cairo simply could not or would not provide.

Nor was the foreign community any more successful, in spite of its ample resources. Most foreign nongovernmental development agencies (NGOs) were located in the Saʿīd. Few operated in the Delta, although a small number of programs were active in the poorer neighborhoods of Cairo. Yet placing the majority of these NGOs in the south had not simply been a fortuitous decision by government officials in Cairo. For these agencies seemingly offered impressive showcase examples of secular development in a region where the alternative was strongly identified with Islam. But since secular foreign operations lacked the political insight and cultural skills necessary to successfully implement their programs, the smaller but more astute Islamic organizations were much more effective. Moreover, sympathetic bureaucrats employed in provincial offices often favored local Islamic initiatives over those misconceived by overseas home offices.

The vast scope of these Islamic development activities, subsumed under the name of good deeds and pious acts, delivered a wide range of important social benefits otherwise considered the duty of the state but which had not been forthcoming. Cairo had written off the south and neglected to provide essential social services. The gap was filled, not by a few inept foreign development agencies, but by the myriad of small community initiatives funded by labor remittances, *zakāt* funds, and Islamic investment companies, and intended to provide a strong Islamic presence.

Indeed, government schools in al-Minyā were so ineffective that many parents who had sacrificed family income in order to give their children an education were forced to sacrifice even more by enrolling them in after-school tutorial programs that could improve their chances for better scores on the Thānawiya ʿAmma examination.[9] (There was a common rumor that government teachers purposely undertaught their charges in the morning and then retaught them in the afternoon as private tutors in order to augment their low salaries.) In order to provide better instruction unavailable from the Education Ministry, a number of Islamic associations built and operated five private, comprehensive schools in al-Minyā. In a separate project, fifteen devout Muslim teachers joined together under the auspices of the Jamaʿiya al-Daʿwa al-Islāmiya to offer poor students private tutoring lessons at a nominal cost.[10]

Since the 1970s, the cost of health and medical services had risen enormously. Geography fundamentally determined the availability of these high-priced necessities. Cairo had more doctors per capita than many cities in the core. However, this left fewer available to service such places as al-Minyā city, district towns like Samalūṭ or Mallawī, or the surrounding countryside. The last was especially avoided by Egyptian medical school graduates; only those under obligation to the government to repay their scholarships spent time in the village before relocating to more prosperous urban clinics. Thus those who suffered the most from this maldistribution of medical specialists were also those who were least able to afford the cost of the few professionals who remained. Consequently, a group of Muslim doctors, pharmacists, and clinicians established the Jamaʿiya al-Muḥamadiya al-Islāmiya and staffed an Islamic clinic in al-Minyā. They charged a £E3.00 fee for examinations, treatment, and prescriptions when other doctors were charging £E15.00 for examinations alone. They also admitted any and all patients, "regardless of what was on their wrist"—a reference to the Coptic custom of etching a cross on their lower arm and an indication that the clinic was open to both Christians and Muslims alike.

Other associations had similar, yet more specialized projects. Jamaʿiya al-Tawḥid wa al-Nūr al-Khaīriya built an entire dormitory at al-Minyā University for rural students who did not have family in the city and therefore needed local accommodations. Jamaʿiya al-Hudā al-Khaīriya added a twenty-four-bed wing to one of the city's private hospitals exclusively reserved for indigent patients. Every month, the Jamaʿiya al-Ṣaḥwa al-Islāmiya distributed clothes, food, textbooks, and prescription medicine to neighborhood families. Arguably these endeavors just involved short-term charity, not long-term development, but such a debate is more academic than practical, for such projects provided beneficiaries with a range of services otherwise unavailable from large government or foreign offices. Many of the latter's development activities, despite their sophisticated planning, deteriorated in the long run due to mismanagement and improper funding, while those undertaken in the name of Islamic charity continued for as long as their endowment remained viable and their donors remained undetained.

In October 1992, an earthquake caused unusual devastation throughout Egypt. I was in Cairo conducting research on the GUAMW when it struck and damaged several poor urban neighborhoods. Old, neglected buildings were particularly susceptible, and the vibrations toppled a number of apartment complexes. When the general populace recovered from its shock, shelter, clothing, and food were foremost on people's minds. Yet the government was particularly slow in providing aid. Local Islamic organizations, on the other hand, rushed immediately to the stricken areas in order to deliver material assistance. Government officials defended their delay by pointing out that they needed time to investigate all the requests since many petitioners would present fraudulent claims to the government. The Islamic groups, however, had little need to investigate supplicants since they felt that few would lie before God. Observers I talked to noted that both sides were probably correct. A year later, when a long-term instability brought about by the earthquake caused large mudslides beneath the Muqaṭṭam hills on the east side of the capital, government troops were ordered to assist the victims without delay, worried that another public-relations blunder would once again help expand the influence of the Islamic opposition. The state also strongly discouraged aid and assistance except through the Egyptian Red Crescent (*al-Shaʿb*, October 20, 1992). This effectively eliminated any Islamic philanthropy.

All these private-sector achievements, initiated by Islamic associations of devout and pious believers, clearly surpassed government and foreign activities. Poor Egyptians received many essential services from these community projects, gratefully appreciated these efforts, and faithfully heeded the political message behind them. Pious acts of charity and community support made the difference in their lives between endurance and deprivation. This urban underclass gained tangible benefits from such programs, unlike the misdirected efforts of government offices or international agencies which mostly served the middle-class bureaucrats who staffed them. It was clear from visiting these projects and associations, and talking to their staff and members that these professionals were Muslims seriously committed to easing the lives of those they served. Many of their clients I learned were either unemployed, widowed, abandoned, or else, if they had jobs, were from informal-sector workshops, service-sector employment, and construction crews and who, before moving to al-Minyā, had frequently been villagers who had once worked as *tarāḥīl* migrant farm laborers.

The relationship between benefactor and beneficiary did not exhibit the professional condescension, high expense, and bureaucracy that otherwise discouraged the poor from approaching professionals in government or foreign offices. They were, after all, from similar origins—the countryside—and so together shared a common background. Their relationship was a familiar one based on close personal understanding. This informality, however, inhibited expansion were the size of these associations to grow to the point of anonymity. Nevertheless, as long as these projects remained small, both the poor and the professionals related to each other in intimate, unpretentious ways, though they remained aware of occupational, educational, and class differences. This mirrored the rural communities they had left behind, and the paternalism that had permeated the relationships they had participated in between those who were both equal and unequal at the same time. It was the major form of social control that had prevailed before the state had become such a major bureaucratic institution in regulating their lives and livelihoods. It was a more comfortable way of doing business.

The religious benefactors who helped out the poor and needy under the banner of Islam benefited in turn from the allegiance they won from doing their good deeds and pious acts. The devotion and loyalty these workers were accustomed to bestowing on their patrons above them in the workplace flowed beyond the workshop, building site, or janitor's room, and even spilled over from the evening-school lessons and the medical checkups to embrace the realm of radical activism within and outside the community. Whether these devout but déclassé professionals participated legally in community politics or else unlawfully in militant Islamic associations, their supporters found it easy to transfer the paternalism of the labor process beyond production to include these new patrons.

When Islamist technocrats entered political contests in the countless number of provincial, city, town, and district level election campaigns and partisan appointments, they received overwhelming support and loyalty from those they had once assisted. When pious but alienated professionals exhorted their followers to berate and attack the government for its fiscal corruption that had eliminated social services, working-class clients dutifully joined them and actively promoted their agenda. Thus poor laborers and ex-rural workers approved and followed those who had once helped them with difficult problems and who were now mobilizing support to strengthen their religious message and to establish an honest and virtuous administration. Paternalism sealed the bonds connecting the activist with the masses. So when the burning question turned to refashioning an otherwise unresponsive government and to end the corruption promoted by the IMF structural adjustments, then the fundamental reply simply became "Islam."

A number of Minyāwīs told me that a legal, religious-based, political party could absorb the angry and disaffected factions of ex-rural workers, small business owners, the self-employed, service-sector employees, students, and young, provincial white-collar professionals. Yet so long as the government denied this movement a legitimate channel for influencing state policy, they argued, the more its collective alienation turned to unlawful acts of violence.

After 1985, permanent labor repatriation, steady decreases in overseas remittances, and the government crackdown on Islamic investment companies generated major declines in funding the vital services that compensated workers for their lack of sufficient income. When the government took over local private mosques and appointed new clerics, it was doing more than just silencing opposition preachers. Before such action, the local committees of private mosques, composed of educated, middle-class members, decided on how the *zakāt* was to be distributed and chose which charitable activities were to receive financial support. Once the state controlled these mosques, however, it deposited most of their *zakāt* donations into government banks and decided where the little that remained was to be distributed, frequently resulting in a precipitous decline in funding for local social services.[11]

Then when the state failed to provide such assistance in turn, many

Saʿīdīs felt especially upset and indignant. They felt even more powerless when the political system prevented them from even voicing their concerns or further pressuring officials for better treatment. Throughout the late 1980s and 1990s, the growing political gap between elite secular parties on the one hand, and both frustrated provincial professionals and the unorganized urban working classes on the other, was mediated by local Islamic populist associations that then posed a serious challenge to the state.

In 1992 the government and its secular supporters mounted a major campaign against the Islamists who openly threatened its complacent and comfortable position underwritten by fraud and corruption. Already religious opponents dominated an impressive number of formal professional and university organizations. But discontent from the bottom of the social pyramid was beginning to incite the unorganized and to provoke even greater turmoil, especially throughout the Saʿīd but increasingly in Cairo as well. The government responded defensively and ruthlessly. Arrests and detention, extrajudicial executions and torture, and official denunciations followed one another in rapid succession. Compromise between the two sides seemed unthinkable.

Providing good deeds, charitable acts, and material welfare to those at the bottom of the social hierarchy seemed to be far removed from those engaged in senseless demagoguery or wanton terrorism. Indeed, the spiritual attitude and religious demeanor of the devout professionals I met in al-Minyā appeared beyond reproach. Yet the accumulative effects of constant government arrest, torture, and humiliation in the Saʿīd pushed many pious activists over the thin line that heretofore had separated them from those committed to violence. While some still remained hopeful that the political and election process would eventually establish a legitimate avenue for social change, a growing number moved beyond the limits of peaceful transformation as they began to realize that militancy offered the only practical way to fundamentally change the state and society.

Such a transition from pacifism to militancy was more frequently a response to state repression than due to any planned strategy for committing mayhem. The situation in Mallawī, a district town 80 kilometers south of al-Minyā, aptly illustrates how such good intentions change into violence. In 1991, al-Jamāʿa al-Islāmiya—and here it is difficult to distinguish between the generic term and the specific organizational offshoot of al-Jihād—began as a nonpolitical charitable association. At first its relation with the local town government was benign since its preoccupation with religious education and material welfare programs hardly constituted illegal crimes or acts of defiance. In May 1994, however, local security forces arrested two prominent members of the association, and while no mention of police misconduct was reported, the association's leader, Rajab ʿAbd al-Ḥakīm, an accountant by profession, was provoked enough to warn security officers to stop interfering with the group's activities. A week later, security forces "stormed Abdel Hakim's house and shot him." He died that evening in the hospital. Three months later, association members attacked the local police headquarters, launching what became a small civil war (*Middle East Times*, February 5–11, 1995). Throughout 1994 and 1995, Mallawī remained under strict martial law and a harsh twelve-hour curfew. What had once been harmless good deeds and pious acts had been transformed into militancy and bloodshed.

Throughout the Saʿīd, men wearing full beards and white robes and women dressed in the dark *naqāb,* the complete Islamic covering, were routinely arrested, questioned, humiliated (and perhaps tortured), and then jailed or released. Homes of suspected militants were bombed and burned. Few Saʿīdī militants came to trial—such a luxury was reserved mostly for their Cairene counterparts—but instead were fatally shot in police crossfire when security forces came to arrest suspects. Many families became heartbroken and terrified by this persecution. Neighborhoods became divided, sympathizing with those whose piety had earned them great admiration but frightened that their sympathy might make them suspect as well. Anger swelled, and, in response, many acts of police misconduct were repaid by outraged relatives—not through organized retribution but by individual acts of revenge. That most religious violence erupted in the Saʿīd may be more a testimony to this region's "tribal" practice of seeking revenge for the dishonor of family members—*al-tha'r*—rather than as an exceptional concentration of state repression. Police brutality also occurred in Cairo, Alexandria, and the Delta, but without this remnant of tribal tradition, such acts elsewhere went unavenged.

Islamic radicals took up the cause of opposing the corruption and injustice committed by the government in Cairo and by its representatives in the provinces. Those pushed to the extreme crafted an ideology based on religion that justified what the state called terrorism, but what the militants called holy combat against abuse and persecution. Based on the writings of Sayyid Quṭb, ʿAbd al-Salām al-Faraj, ʿUmar ʿAbd al-Raḥmān, and others, a militant Islam arose that appealed to those persecuted for performing good deeds and charitable acts, and for enacting the compassion decreed by the basic tenets of their religious beliefs, but which the state was now violating in its zeal to silence opponents.

Not all attacks against government forces were merely individual acts of retaliation for alleged injuries. Nor were they simply reactions provoked by the police harassment of otherwise blameless nonmilitant Islamic radicals. Informants reported that there may well have been clear cases of organized, intentional violence, perhaps even funded by foreign governments and sympathetic collaborators from outside Egypt. Firearms and ammunition certainly flooded the Saʿīd, yet this was not altogether new since old tribal vendettas, long antedating the rise of Islamic militancy, had once required such weapons for their execution (Abu Zayd 1965). Nevertheless, I was told that a good portion of the violence that erupted in southern Egypt involved resisting arrest by those who otherwise desired just to lead a righteous life and practice their faith in a more devout and concrete way, and retaliation for the abuse and suffering that occurred when these pious Muslims were taken into police custody.

Nor was the Islamist movement in the Saʿīd the same as that in Cairo. I was constantly amazed upon returning to the capital to realize how different the two were, as if they were taking place in two separate countries. In Cairo, militants had been arrested and imprisoned with much greater perseverance and much greater force, decimating their ranks at a much earlier date than in the south and thus leaving the stage of public debate to those who emphasized more cultural issues. The murder of the outspoken newspaper columnist Farag Foda, the assault on the Nobel prize–winning author Naguib Mahfouz, the censorship of the international film producer Yusif Shahine, the court-ordered divorce of the Cairo University philosophy professor Nasr Abu-Zeid—all were well-known luminaries whose cases reflected attacks against the free cultural expression so valued in the core and which followed the pattern of the Salman Rushdie affair in Iran. When I asked informants in al-Minyā about these "outrages," they replied that this was merely Cairene "silly business" concocted to distract people from the fundamental issues of injustice, corruption, and underdevelopment. For them the conflict was less cultural and much more economic and political. And while they acknowledged the spiritual failings of these celebrities, their newspaper articles, commercial films, and fiction and philosophy books were not considered relevant to life in the Saʿīd. Thus seen alternately from al-Minyā and Cairo, there appeared to be two separate, quite distinct, Islamist movements: an insurrectionist campaign in the south and a cultural crusade in the capital city.

In the aftermath of the earthquake of October 1992, when the prominent relief activities of the Islamic groups embarrassed the government, hundreds of Minyāwīs and Saʿīdīs were arrested under the pretext of suspicion or complicity (EOHR n.d.:2). From among the large number of those detained, a significant but unknown proportion crossed the line from nonviolence to militancy to enlist in the growing ranks of those who once had just performed good deeds and pious acts, but who were now provoked to engage in militancy and violence. Muslim radicals became Muslim militants, exchanging words for action in their campaign against a state that seemed unwilling to supply its citizens with their fundamental entitlements and basic social services, and against a state whose security forces committed what many viewed as ungodly acts against its own citizens.

Arrests and torture silenced many, especially those who participated in Islamic development associations. This reduced the provision of important welfare and charity services even more. Throughout the Saʿīd, communities witnessed major declines in the local development projects that were closely connected to committed Islamic associations. As successful programs and services closed for lack of funds and authorization, the government did not compensate by providing its own. Indeed, these Islamic efforts had first been initiated because of the very absence of government action. Subsequently, the state did not fill the vacuum left when it forced these associations and their members to suspend their activities. This in turn provoked even more anger and anxieties from those who had benefited from these charitable acts and good deeds. The termination of these religiously charged development projects, like the closing of their financiers, the Islamic investment companies and private mosques, made life in the Saʿīd even more difficult and precarious for its working classes.

Yet IMF adjustments and economic constriction continued to generate poverty and anger at the bottom, and corruption and opportunism at the top that together were eroding the state's ability to sustain solid economic growth and wearing down the government's legitimacy in creating a national consensus. Increasingly, only the state's security forces were able to buoy up the government's sagging authority. The Islamic opposition, unable to share power and alter the current configuration of economic policies and policy makers, turned instead to more militant means to achieve its political goals. In the end, the state continued operating much as before, yet ever fearful that once again, changes in the nation's top leadership would take place only after another funeral.

Tarāḥīl workers had once moved into the cities in order to improve their lives and livelihood. But their ambitions soon proved equally unfulfilled, for the same state that had made the village unbearable was now making the city just as intolerable. Still culturally attached to the countryside, they joined those organizations that embodied the social practices and transposed values of rural life. Yet in response to government repression, this discontented working class joined forces with an alienated professional class to demand the funding, services, and justice they felt entitled to, united together through the strong bonds of paternalism. The government in Cairo was slow to respond and when it did, restrictions from IMF's ERSAP prevented a satisfactory response. The world economy that had placed Egypt in a subordinate position did not encourage a better one.

Egypt remained thwarted in establishing a growth-oriented economy and an autonomous foreign policy, squeezed from one side by low agricultural and industrial exports, high food imports, reluctant investors, and the IMF and international creditors, and from the other side by disgruntled *tarāḥīl* migrant farm laborers, construction workers, recalcitrant factory employees, underpaid supervisors, irate consumers, and angry militants. The state did not promote its existing assets nor did it create new ones. Aggregate investment was not able to establish a sufficient number of economically viable industries that complemented production in the core. Egypt's diplomatic independence also became restricted just when a proliferation of hegemonic powers and investors—now including Germany and Japan—and domestic pressures required greater flexibility in order to successfully implement a new regime of cooperative peripheral Fordism.

Egypt's adjustment to the new global economy was not so much through the smooth initiatives of its state officials but by jerks, stammers, and stutters in response to popular pressure from its producers and consumers. As discontent grew among workers in *tarāḥīl* employment, agriculture, construction, informal businesses, industry, and many other sectors of the economy, Egypt's planners found it even more urgent but even more difficult to attract investment and achieve NIC status in an increasingly competitive world. Finding a comfortable niche in the new international division of labor has not been an easy task.

9

Frustrated Fordism: Bringing Labor Back into History and Theory

Before 1961, *tarāḥīl* workers continued to move back and forth between the two branches of Egypt's rural division of labor, more or less unaffected by the outside state except for its distant role as a silent night watchman who guarded property relations and social stability. Rural laborers worked in agriculture in the village until compelled by seasonal unemployment, family debt, and gender rivalries to leave on *tarāḥīl* work trips. Then they worked on "casual" labor projects in migrant work camps until forced by low wages, poor consumption, and corruption-generated speedups to return to their village. At distant worksites, migrants practiced stealth techniques, either directly or through cooperative supervisors, to reduce exhaustion, maintain income, and gain some respite. But these weapons of the weak did not adequately compensate workers for the extra effort they had to exert. Still, the ultimate weapon they wielded was to leave and find other jobs.

This pendulum movement proved contradictory, for it was unacceptable and tolerable at the same time. It was this pattern, after all, that underwrote rural capitalism by maximizing labor's effort, minimizing wages, raising consumption costs, but reducing the overall standard of living. This placed *tarāḥīl* workers in the unenviable position of being the lowest of the low. Yet at the same time it was a pattern of dual employment that workers themselves could control through the unequal but mutual relationships of paternalism. *Muqāwilūn* patrons needed laborers in order to make a profit; worker clients needed brokers in order to find a job. Each side used this "need" to extract what it could from the other. Thus laborers found themselves at a disadvantage at the bottom of the social hierarchy, but they were still able to use village patron-client relationships to gain some momentary benefits.

Workers and those in command fundamentally disagreed over the level of effort, wages, and prices each side supplied or demanded, yet both acted together to keep the state out of their local affairs by endorsing paternalism, which contrasted sharply with the state's impersonal, one-sided bureaucracy. The emergence of the state's direct role in managing the agricultural economy placed these local and previously unencumbered relations in jeopardy.

Although the new revolutionary government had legislated a radical land reform program in 1952, it had little effect on rural workers, or for that matter, on the countryside as a whole. It was not until after the Suez war, when the irregularities of High Dam and Tahrīr finances were finally resolved, that the state began to accelerate its direct interference in the countryside. In 1961, the combination of state policies for dam construction, desert land reclamation, property nationalizations, price controls, and agricultural cooperatives encouraged large numbers of discontented village workers to take up distant *tarāḥīl* labor. However, the wage increases and job improvements this employment offered did not always materialize, obstructed instead by unscrupulous labor brokers. After 1962, therefore, a number of provincial efforts attempted to unblock the rural labor market so as to persuade more workers to engage in *tarāḥīl* trips and to satisfy the tremendous demand for unskilled labor at Aswān and Tahrīr. These initiatives culminated in 1964, when the government established a national union for agricultural and *tarāḥīl* workers. However, this siphoned off even more workers from the countryside.

This movement of laborers out of farming left behind major failures in crop production. Consequently, the agricultural crisis of 1961 undermined the state's ability to implement the plans for industrial development and economic growth contained in its program of Arab socialism. The recession of 1965–66 and the country's inadequate foreign currency reserves left it ill prepared to defend itself in June 1967. State planners were repeatedly misled by erroneous assumptions about the unlimited supplies of unemployed rural workers, which blinded them to labor's crucial role in agricultural production.

After the Six-Day war, many *tarāḥīl* workers reluctantly remained in their villages, enduring seven lean years of retrenched state budgets and reduced employment. When the regional economy began to expand after 1973, they moved once again, this time rejecting both migrant labor *and* village agriculture and permanently leaving the countryside altogether. Discontented with their conditions at home, yet apprehensive about abandoning their birthplace, they migrated to the cities to find new urban jobs in the booming state-dominated construction sector, attracted by the similarities it shared with their previous occupations. They promptly filled jobs vacated by skilled craft workers who had pressed the government into authorizing their emigration.

As Anthony Giddens pointed out, once removed from the immediate vicinity where their problems first occur, the original agents no longer control the consequences of the difficulties they had originally provoked. The production shortages *tarāḥīl* laborers generated after 1961 were left behind to continue damaging Egypt's national economy even while the workers themselves turned to improving their lives by moving to urban areas to escape the dilemma of their dual employment.

Yet ex-rural laborers ended up no more satisfied with this solution than with their original predicament. A combination of limited, unsteady employment, low wages, and high prices generated by the confusion, corruption, and social polarization of the 1974 open-door policy made life just as precarious in the city as it had been back home in the village. Aspirations were thwarted, and ex-rural workers became increasingly angry over the stalled economy. This anger first erupted in the January 1977 food riots. The international financial assistance that was offered to resolve these problems instead made matters worse, placing government officials in the difficult position of enforcing austerity measures while restraining the hostility these policies generated. After the mid-1980s, when an oil-based recession hit Egypt, this hostility grew even greater. More and more it expressed itself through violence by righteous Muslims who had once just preached opposition to the government but who increasingly crossed the line into militancy and began to translate their vocal dissent into concrete action. The state's repression of their Islamic associations, its attack on the investment companies that financed their development activities, the seizure of locally controlled mosques and their *zakāt* funds, and the persecution and arrest of middle-class activists critically affected those workers at the bottom who had benefited from receiving income substitutes and services and who then became angry when these essentials disappeared and were not replaced. In 1992, this religious militancy escalated and attracted many who had been doubly dispossessed of both rural opportunities and urban necessities.

At first the troubles *tarāḥīl* workers generated were just economic, creating shortages in export and food crops, which had a lasting effect on the nation's economy and its ability to sustain long-term growth and development. Because farming continued to bear the major burden of financing Egypt's economy, their impact on agriculture critically affected the nation's overall wealth and well-being as well. Then, as rural workers became more removed in time and space from their original actions, as Giddens further suggested, other acts and events, caused by other agents, began to play a part in the country's development. Thus once supplemented by the actions of recalcitrant industrial workers, irate consumers, reluctant investors, and international bankers, these agricultural deficits and the problems they caused propagated throughout the economy to impede Egypt's advancement to more efficient levels of capitalism.

But the impact *tarāḥīl* workers made did not stop once they left their villages. Their relocation to the city continued to affect the economy. Industrial workers, otherwise secure in their permanent, contractual employment, became increasingly apprehensive over the ability of this new reserve army of urban un- and underemployed to replace them and to reduce their wages. Both formal- and informal-sector workers came to experience the limitations of a stalled economy, and both began protesting their unsatisfactory conditions—the former through negotiations, strikes, and demonstrations, and the latter through riots, defiance, and violence. As laborers and consumers, both segments opposed the direction Egypt's leaders were taking the national economy.

Once the government began to intervene in their jobs and way of life, *tarāḥīl* workers responded in ways that undermined the state's ability to achieve national development and to maintain legitimate authority. Their impact, therefore, also had a political dimension. The government, far from being a strong state, seemed unable to regulate their agency. Most state officials operated with a model of a social pyramid that lacked a proletarian base and therefore were unable to comprehend how those at the bottom could spoil and sabotage their well-made plans for national growth and autonomy. The result was a stalemate between the top of the pyramid, allied to international financial patrons, and the bottom, inspired by the growing success of the Islamist movement.

But this standoff meant more than just a weak state and a volatile labor force. It also indicated that, unlike other peripheral formations that after 1973 had turned into influential oil producers or newly industrialized countries, Egypt was not able to attract the investment and achieve the industrialization that not only could quiet those demanding more jobs and income but also create an economy based on peripheral cooperative Fordism. Thus the stalemate between labor and the state seriously undermined Cairo's ability to establish a viable Fordist regime.

In many respects Egypt's economy recalls the peripheral Taylorism of colonial economies that depend primarily on the export of local raw materials such as cotton. Here, the accumulation of capital still relies on extending the time laborers actually spend working, both by lengthening the workday and by reducing dead, unproductive time within the job. Inside contracting exists at many worksites whereby companies rely on independent labor brokers and foremen for organizing and supervising task assignments instead of depending on their own often underpaid bureaucrats. Production remains a labor-intensive process and one still strongly controlled by the paternalistic management of workers. Low-wage laborers living in or moving from the countryside continue to be cheaper than costly machinery imported from abroad, and arbitrary supervisors with few alternatives continue to be limited by the recisions and retrenchments of misallocated budgets. Equipment remains unused for want of spare parts or skilled operators. Instead, inoperative machinery is replaced by employing *tarāḥīl* workers and other part-time laborers. Efforts to establish a Fordism that relies on mechanized equipment have repeatedly lapsed back into the Taylorist use of unskilled laborers instead.

Egypt has made three attempts at creating a peripheral Fordism, first in the 1930s and later again in the 1950s. The first two endeavors were based on import substitution policies that involved domestic industries competing against similar production sites in the core and duplicating the latter's consumer goods and durables that then precluded importing them from abroad. Yet paradoxically these local firms came to rely heavily on foreign machinery and equipment, capital goods whose importation ultimately required transactions in hard currency. These efforts failed then because the state was unable to accumulate the necessary foreign currency to pay for such expensive technology transfers. Reductions in the export of cotton—Egypt's principal foreign exchange earner—and increases in the import of food—which drained the treasury of the dollars it did accumulate—were the outcomes of the poor performance of its agricultural sector. Both attempts at peripheral competitive Fordism languished for lack of the technology that could replace workers, improve productive efficiency, and generate profits through intensive capital accumulation.

Egypt's third attempt at peripheral Fordism has taken place since the mid-1970s. Because of the recession and deindustrialization in the core after 1973, a new type of economic development arose in the periphery, this time taking the shape of a cooperative Fordism. The goods and services that domestic manufacturers produced in free-trade zones and through subcontracting were now coordinated with and by multinational corporations headquartered in the core. Duplication still occurred, but this now became a means to undermine labor's control over producing the same commodity that was also manufactured in other peripheral factories. Shipment to assembly factories and final export to the core completed the cooperative arrangements that once had taken place just within a single core country but which were now distributed worldwide. The periphery's cheaper labor force permitted the accumulation of profits that were repatriated back to core countries whose economies were becoming increasingly service oriented as production was outsourced to these remote but more profitable sites.

This new type of peripheral Fordism did not just involve industrial production, however. Trade, contracts, technology transfer, state revenues, infrastructure, communications—all required complex commercial and diplomatic arrangements. Thus cooperative peripheral Fordism became synonymous with free-trade agreements, customs and tariff reduction, copyright and patent protection, fiscal and budgetary management, strong domestic taxation authority, currency and banking regulations, and privatization. Many of these demands were consolidated together into the IMF's economic reforms and structural adjustment programs that were imposed on peripheral countries as the price for their participation in the new global economy.

Far from generating new employment, the emergence of the new international division of labor created more unemployment instead. New industrialization in the periphery depended heavily on the existence of a large reserve army of labor to cheaply staff its factories and plants. This army of un- and underemployed kept wage levels low, but did not decline to any appreciable extent by being absorbed into the highly automated, capital-intensive production processes that came to characterize peripheral Fordism. Instead, the somewhat deceptive promise of better jobs induced even more workers to leave their villages, to crowd into shantytowns, slums, and informal businesses, and to join with others in waiting for the economy to grow. Investment, when it did happen, generated relatively few jobs. The reserve army expanded instead of contracted, making labor's situation all that more precarious (Fröbel, Heinrichs, and Kreye 1981:367–68).

The irony of establishing peripheral Fordism is that for the countryside, it essentially meant fulfilling the model first proposed by W. Arthur Lewis in 1954, which assumed unlimited supplies of rural labor and called for rationalizing and streamlining agricultural production and creating an industrial economy where investments would generate the employment necessary to absorb relocated rural workers. That is, for the emergence of this newest phase of capitalism, farming was to be mechanized and displaced rural workers were to be moved into urban industries.

Yet seasonally unneeded farm workers were not necessarily unemployed since they were already occupied in *tarāḥīl* labor. Nor were rural workers merely passive inputs that could be readily removed without damaging agricultural production. In applying the Lewis model to rural Egypt, the state never gave much consideration to coordinating the displacement of laborers from the countryside, their employment in urban enterprises, and the mechanization of agriculture. Contrary to Lewis's theory, the transfer of labor, crops, and capital from the countryside to the city did not take place easily, without misery for workers, or without harm to the national economy.

The first exodus of rural workers in the early 1960s left agriculture financially unable to bring them back, much less replace them by purchasing expensive machinery. The second wave of displacement since the early 1970s has not yet ended. But the rationalization of agriculture became limited just to part-time activities as propertied families diversified out of farming and propertyless workers stayed in the cities anticipating jobs in construction, services, and informal businesses. Only gradually were farm tasks mechanized, since this required the purchase of tractors and pumps that remained prohibitive for want of lenient credit terms and better crop prices, although remittances emigrants sent back to the village later helped defray the expense. Nor were field plots consolidated into efficient large-scale farms, since this meant changing the existing property-ownership laws and accumulating the capital that would make such concentration possible.[1]

Until then, agricultural production remained labor intensive and suffered from the lack of sufficient supplies of workers. As a result, the domestic consignment of food crops remained limited and required substantial imports to satisfy and pacify urban consumers. The transfer of capital initially intended to finance industrial development went instead to buying imported food and to subsidizing a low-paid urban workforce and its employers. Workers, cotton, grain, and savings eventually left the countryside, but the lack of coordination and foresight created serious difficulties for the entire national economy. Those government officials who promoted this exodus were unaware of the complexity of the technical division of rural labor and could only blame each other for the subsequent but nevertheless unexpected problems in agricultural shortages, urban disorder, and truncated development.

When the *tarāḥīl* alternative to farming expanded in size and wage levels in the early 1960s, workers did leave agriculture, although they did not appear in the city nor was their labor replaced by machine. Employment in

Aswān and Tahrīr momentarily postponed wide-scale migration to urban areas, fortunate perhaps since the factories that were to absorb relocated workers had not yet appeared, despite the indirect taxes on agriculture, foreign assistance, and nationalizations that were intended to revive and expand Egypt's industrial sector. But this merely postponed the crisis that would erupt when workers did move out of the countryside and before there were enough industrial jobs in the city to employ them.

After 1973, a new wave of departures from the countryside took place when the region's oil economy expanded. This time, with the High Dam completed, land reclamation in decline, and high-level corruption disrupting *tarāḥīl* labor, the only option left was to move to the city and seek new employment. But since industrial development still had not advanced, migrants found jobs instead in an expanding informal sector that involved the labor-intensive, low-productivity, extensive accumulation of a Taylorist regime. Labor's integration into the urban labor market remained incomplete until there could be a greater commitment of foreign and domestic capital to generate greater employment, higher wages, and more tolerable consumer prices. Yet the government was unsuccessful in attracting investments despite its economic policies and diplomatic initiatives. Its own revenues from exports, foreign aid, remittances, and international credit did not provide enough hard currency for further development since most of it went to settling trade and debt difficulties rather than financing new factories. Nor did the state's open-door investment plan and structural adjustments reform program create sufficient incentives for private investors, for these policies were frequently spoiled by the state's inability to eliminate corruption at the top and to persuade those at the bottom to cooperate.

Thus the Lewis model and the state policies it justified vastly underestimated the agency of rural workers and their ability to contest this theory in either village or city. These transfers were not painless for rural workers, nor were they without harm to agricultural production and the economy.

Supply problems in agriculture and chronic difficulties with Egypt's balance of trade, foreign currency reserves, and national accounts were in large part the result of rural workers leaving farming. Growth in population and per capita income notwithstanding (Richards and Waterbury 1990:140), Egypt's acute dependency on food imports—reaching as high as 80 percent in the 1980s—was caused by failures in agricultural production due to labor shortages. Numerous IMF standby agreements further testify to these problems, finally requiring in the 1990s the imposition of structural adjustments to force Cairo to put its financial house in order.

Nor was applying the Lewis model painless for rural and ex-rural workers. The first form of refusal and resistance appeared in overcoming the inertia of social ties and commitment to village life and leaving their home communities. Rural to urban migration generated considerable hostility, the attraction of bright lights notwithstanding. This anger occurred not in the countryside so much as in the city when, upon arrival, the bright lights dimmed. Opposition to the government's style of implementing peripheral Fordism first erupted in riots in January 1977, and later after 1985 fueled the rise of Islamic radicalism and militancy. Had the state and its international patrons allowed incomes to rise when it increased prices, workers could have afforded the more expensive consumption and accumulated the savings that would have generated a home market for purchasing the machinery and goods that the industrial sector manufactured. Instead, the lack of legitimate channels for protest and dissent compelled workers to use other means to present their demands and demonstrate their opposition.

Both spontaneous riots and militant organizations recall the rural politics that ex-villagers had left behind—first in the spontaneous outburst of "communal action" that reacted to immediate outside threats, then later in the establishment of paternalistic "secret societies" that defended the nation against dangers to a traditional way of life. But the indignation and anger generated by growing unemployment, economic difficulties, and inadequate services in the city transformed these practices into powerful urban weapons against the state. As the resentment and opposition from ex-rural workers and others steadily increased and multiplied, these weapons single-handedly prevented the nation's economic development from realizing the Lewis model or ushering in a third phase of peripheral Fordism.

Since 1961, *tarāḥīl* migrant farm workers from the countryside—representing the largest single segment of the national workforce—have prevented the country from joining the NIC club, thwarted its move toward peripheral cooperative Fordism, and obstructed the overall growth of capitalism. Rural workers have contributed to the state's financial misfortunes that have prevented substantial investment in enterprises that could generate employment and incomes. In the cities, ex-rural workers in the informal sector cumulatively have blocked the nation from advancing to newer forms of international capitalism. Their threat to the jobs and wages of those in the formal sector have provoked other workers to also oppose state plans for economic development through individual and collective action. The impasse between inflexible state officials and determined workers has obstructed Egypt's transition to peripheral Fordism. Thus rural labor has made a significant impact, albeit a negative one, on national development because it has been unfavorably affected in turn by the way these state programs were implemented. With state planners desperately running just to keep up with events, it seems clear that workers do matter in making Egypt's history and inhibiting its economic growth and development.

Regulation theory argues that the struggle between labor and those elites who ostensibly dominate it—employers, merchants, officials—constitutes the primary motor force of historical movement. This study of recent Egyptian history shows that while this is true in general, it is labor's struggle with the state in particular that has constituted the most important contest which moves society from one phase of capitalism to another, or, in this case, which has inhibited Egypt's advancement to peripheral cooperative Fordism. The state's attempts to insure social stability by planning for its steady growth have been foiled by labor's ambitions for a better life and livelihood, and its aspirations for greater control over its own efforts, wages, and consumption. Since 1961, workers' struggles with employers, brokers, supervisors, and merchants have become regulated by a yet larger institution, the state. Laborers then began to realize that while their earlier struggles had been local in nature—and therefore more susceptible to their own leverage—the more recent conflicts with state officials and bureaucrats proved more difficult, yet much more fundamental.

Although at first glance labor's subordinate position at the bottom of the social pyramid suggests a very weak ability to influence the state, in fact their aggregate and collective movement has had, indirectly, unintentionally, and without much acknowledgment, a major impact on Egypt's government and its policies of national development. Were a model of the monolithic and omnipotent state to be introduced—not so much the erroneous myth of an oriental despotism but even invoking the more objective versions presented by some marxists like Ralph Miliband (1969)—then its absolute ability to reproduce society would preclude any unforeseen transformations. Struggle, then, would cease altogether. This study has shown, however, that no matter how marginalized workers might be, their inherent ability to subvert the plans of those elites at the top who are nominally in charge gives them a critical agency that is difficult to ignore. The state, whether strong or weak, whether in the core, periphery, or semi-periphery, whether Taylorist or Fordist, is never so powerful that labor is completely unable to generate fundamental social change. To assume so is to enter the realm of propaganda rather than to formulate solid scholarly analysis.

Regulation theory further argues that these nuclear struggles between labor and those in command arise out of contradictions over the production and consumption that constitute the regime of accumulation, expressed here as a fluctuating parity among elements in the effort = wage = price formula. Conflicts over controlling valorization involve repeated attempts to define and redefine this equation in favor of one of two diametrically opposed sides. In such contests, workers and elites apply techniques and tactics that are prescribed by what is called the mode of regulation. In state- and class-based societies, this regulation is asymmetric, but seldom, if ever, is it completely one-sided.

In Egypt's villages, farm employers, merchants, and labor brokers used property relations, employment, finance and credit, work force composition, remuneration standards, technological stagnation, and market oligopsony to increase effort, lower wages, and raise profits. In turn, rural workers used patterns of kinship, collegiality, community solidarity—and the option of *tarāḥīl* labor trips—to raise incomes and improve their standard of living. Both used patron-client ties. At distant migrant labor camps, supervisors relied on their formal bureaucratic position, but, since such authority was weak, they also depended on the paternalism of inside contracting to impose their definition of valorization. Workers, for their part, also relied on paternalism in addition to using "weapons of the weak," labor gang solidarity, village employment, and the wider, outside labor market to refashion the effort = wage = price formula more to their liking. Thus each side had its repertoire of techniques derived from the mode of regulation that enabled it to try and shape the regime of accumulation according to its own interests. Some techniques prove more responsive to labor's interests than others and so workers struggle to preserve them as well. In Egypt, this meant reinforcing the local practices of paternalism and challenging the modern bureaucracies of the state.

Labor's tactics occasionally scored a win—what Miliband once called (1969:78) "ransom" or elite capitulation—but more often than not, they lost, though never so completely as to prevent their own reconstitution. The weaker ability of rural workers to control the two labor processes and their overall consumption compelled them to shift, pendulumlike, back and forth between the two branches of rural Egypt's technical division of labor, using patron-client ties to reduce momentarily the exhaustion, poverty, and austerity generated by *tarāḥīl* and village employment.

Before the direct intervention of the state, and while it still remained a distant and silent authority, workers contended mostly with just village elites. However, in the early 1960s, the Egyptian state intervened directly in order to control agricultural production. Paternalism lost its potency for both patrons and clients alike as officials and bureaucrats attempted to transfer labor, crops, and capital out of the countryside. Although the state sought to become the most powerful institution in the mode of regulation, rural Egyptians still retained the use of earlier economic and social institutions, even after they left the countryside and moved to the city. Paternalism in particular continued to provide a strong adhesive that linked together those villagers displaced and displeased by the encroachment of the state. Cairo's self-promotion as *the* single commanding authority collided directly with those unwilling to accept this dominance.

In the process, rural workers helped generate production shortages, trade problems, and financial difficulties, and ex-rural workers contributed to provoking urban disorder, government repression, and international uncertainty that have prevented the state from realizing its objective to maintain social stability through economic growth and national development. Although the social pyramid continues to function and capitalism continues to operate, the state's weak ability to establish a sound national economy has instead widened the pyramid's base and narrowed its top, and in turn has generated greater animosity between the two. The contradictions inherent in global capitalism have become more clearly delineated. As workers and consumers on the one hand and employers, merchants, and officials on the other have increasingly perceived and produced these contradictions, their actions, reactions, and struggles have constituted the substance of recent Egyptian history.

This history has been as much the result of those workers at the bottom of the social pyramid struggling to realize better lives as it has been the planned product of elites at the top who supposedly administered them. In the 1950s, Jamāl ʿAbd al-Nāṣir's stature rose to unprecedented heights. At home, he based his authority on building a High Dam at Aswān and on making the desert bloom at Tahrīr. Outside, he built his charisma on the policies of Arab socialism and foreign nationalization on the one hand, and pan-Arab nationalism and anti-imperialism on the other. But Arab socialism essentially failed after the 1961 agricultural crisis, and Arab nationalism was defeated by a June 1967 war undermined by economic crises. His successor, Anwār al-Sadāt reopened the door to foreign economic penetration in 1974 after the Crossing and superpower détente severely limited his policy options. The open-door policy relied heavily on foreign credit and assistance, but burdened by failures in producing food and export crops, and consequently by enormous import costs and a huge trade imbalance, it netted little that could advance the economic growth and political autonomy of the country. The social hostility it generated provoked both the 1977 riots and his own 1981 assassination. In the 1980s and 1990s, Egypt's third president, Ḥusnī Mubarak, has been burdened by the financial failures of both the public and private sectors. He has had to balance off international creditors intent on opening up Egypt to greater foreign penetration against domestic Islamic radicals outraged over the corruption and mismanagement of national economic policy. The costs have been high, risking more setbacks and even greater hostility. The result has been a loss of government legitimacy and perhaps even a religious civil war. In all cases the state has failed to go forward because it failed to take into consideration the aspirations and demands of those it ostensibly governs.

If workers like those who do or once did *tarāḥīl* labor can make a difference in the unfolding of Egyptian social history, can they and other workers also make a difference in the formulation of social theory? Regulation theory, in its efforts to explore the central question of capitalist transformation, returned to the holistic model of society that originated with Marx and which places particular emphasis on the struggle between historically and socially constituted class agents as the fundamental motor force of historical development. The marxism of Sartre and Althusser had denied labor any special agency in creating history, the former replacing workers with economically unanchored subjectivities, the latter dispensing with human agency altogether. Early regulation theory restored the centrality of labor's struggle with capital to the study of social change, borrowing widely from Italian workerist studies, theories of capitalist imperialism, and even from conventional economic theory.

Through its concepts of regimes of accumulation and modes of regulation, regulation theory is able to connect the everyday lives and labor of ordinary *tarāḥīl* migrant farm workers and their struggles for improvement with the larger trends of Egypt's political economy and national development. It links the micro-level activities of contests over controlling valorization with their macro-level consequences such as economic crises, regional wars, open-door policies, bread riots, civil disorder, and structural adjustments. This gives priority to the labor process and consumption, but it also recognizes both the preservative and transformative effects of economic, political, and cultural institutions. The continuous dialectical interaction of regimes and modes—effected by, through, and on workers—ultimately gives rise to the flow of socialized history.

Regulation theory does not assume a seamless, undifferentiated capitalism that remains static but for its initial emergence and its final disappearance. Instead it proposes a set of phases of capitalist development—Taylorism and Fordism, and its variants outside the core—that are able to more accurately track and measure capitalism's different moments of growth and decline. Regulation theory allows analysis to evaluate the contingent impact of class struggle by comparing concrete history to the proposed set of abstract development trajectories in order to better understand how labor's agency can critically affect the outcome of historical movement.

The rise of post-Fordism in the core has shifted the focus of scholarly analysis away from struggles occurring at the site of capitalist production as labor and work have become increasingly alienated and irrelevant. Instead research has examined those engaged in activities that reproduce capitalism in what Mario Tronti labeled (1971) the "social factory" outside the worksite. Scholarship has reduced its interest in the working class and has moved on instead to consider cultural projects and middle-class movements. But the emergence of these new planes of struggle should not imply the disappearance of the old arenas of conflict. Nor should the struggles over what Alain Lipietz called (1985:28–32) "value-added" downgrade or even erase those struggles over "value-creation." Both become important in explaining the development of post-Fordist history in the core. For even here, labor-capital contests still remain relevant, if in no other sectors than in producing food and constructing buildings, two areas that are still basic to social life and are, like in Egypt, operations still essentially done by hand. In the periphery, however, labor struggles over valorization still constitute, far and away, the most important domain where history is made, even while—and sometimes, because—these arenas have declined in the deindustrialized core.

If marxism is to be retained because of its widespread success in explaining the history of capitalist societies—and after all, capitalism still thrives globally—then its essential analytical techniques must be revived and reinforced. This means that it is necessary to reassert the social totality, to redraw the social pyramid in its entirety so that it includes workers, and to bring labor back into the picture of how societies are constituted, conserved, and changed. If we want to explain the trends of history and development, then it is becomes necessary to acknowledge that the workers' physical, occupational, organizational, and political movements are still important to our understanding and that their agency is still important to the making of history.

The capacity of *tarāḥīl* migrant farm workers to rearrange their spatial and social positions has decisively affected Egypt's historical development over the last three decades. I believe strongly that elsewhere, labor's movements have also produced similar results and will continue to do so.

NOTES

1. Regulating Rural Workers and Social Pyramids in Egypt

1. Ansari (1986:2). A page earlier he affirmed that "[r]uling elite models have helped a generation of scholars concerned with Middle East studies, but nowhere have they been so extensively applied as in studies of Egypt. . . . The elite-mass model has dominated the field without any rival."

2. The issue of rural homogeneity versus differentiation formed the crux of the debate between Teodor Shanin and Sidney Mintz, a proxy for the opposing approaches of Robert Redfield and Julian Steward's students (like Eric Wolf), and the even larger dispute between functionalists and marxists. Mintz (1973) criticized Shanin (1971) for analytically marginalizing such village groups as agricultural laborers, crafts producers, and pastoralists, who differ from the latter's definition of peasantry as a traditional, family-run agricultural community dominated by outsiders. Instead, Mintz argued, these groups constitute the very essence of historical social change in rural societies. While the Mintz-Steward-Wolf approach generated many worthwhile studies of Latin American peasants, it has not made significant headway among scholars of Middle East rural communities.

3. One book consistently cited by those who do explore the topic of *tarāḥīl* migrant farm workers is ʿAṭīyā al-Ṣīrfī's book *ʿUmmāl al-Tarāḥīl*, published in Cairo by Dār al-Thaqāfa al-Jadīda in 1975. When he wrote the book, al-Ṣīrfī was a tram conductor in the district town of Mīt Ghamr in Daqahliya Province and had no direct experience with these issues, although he claimed that since Mīt Ghamr was the major center of migrant-labor recruitment in the Delta, he witnessed many of the decisive events that led to organizing the workers' union discussed in chapter 6. However, in conducting documentary research about this union, I uncovered one page of al-Ṣīrfī's book (p. 114) reproduced from part of an *al-Akhbār* newspaper article (July 24, 1962, p. 5), although some numbers had been altered, which therefore made no sense in al-Ṣīrfī's text. Such plagiarism makes his book an unreliable source. Moreover, Mīt Ghamr was never an exceptional center for *tarāḥīl* labor recruitment, an activity prevalent

throughout rural Egypt, and although Daqahliya was an important province for organizing this union, other district towns proved more prominent in its early history.

4. For example, see Baldi (1972). I wish to thank Harry Cleaver for pointing out the similarities between Baldi and Aglietta's 1974 work.

5. These are not to be confused with the institutions found in the institutional approach referred to above. The term has broader applications in regulation theory that need not be limited to just bureaucratic organizations.

6. The labor process can be defined as the coordination of worksite activities and social relations whereby, over time, labor, under the formal direction of management and with the assistance of plans, skills, and tools, transforms raw materials and requests into useful, or partially useful, products and services (see Edwards 1979:11). This definition differs slightly from that of Marx, who defined (1967:78) the "elementary factors of the labor process" to include "1, the personal activity of man, i.e., work itself; 2, the subject of that work; and 3, its instruments." This has since become the orthodox definition of the forces of production (organization, raw materials, and means of production). The first definition adds three crucial elements: 4, workers; 5, managers; and 6, coordination and management, i.e., control. This interpretation then combines both the forces *and* the relations of production inside the labor process. See Toth (1993) for a broader discussion of these issues.

7. Tracing a trajectory of capitalist development borders on historicism or evolutionism, both anathema in marxist studies. Regulation theory differs, however, in that this trajectory is not automatic or deterministic but rather contingent. It suggests what *might* happen, and then, should the model not be realized, it allows us to ask why such developments did *not* take place.

8. Since this phase first appeared in Britain and not the United States, the name Babbagism would be more accurate since the theories of Charles Babbage anticipated those of Frederick Taylor by more than half a century (Braverman 1974:85).

9. According to the Organization of Economic Cooperation and Development, NICs are peripheral countries in which manufactured products represent 25 percent of gross domestic product and at least 50 percent of exports (Lipietz 1987:74).

10. Geoffrey de Ste. Croix pointed out (1984:100) that neither explicit consciousness of class identity nor collective political activity are necessary ingredients for class and class struggle as long as there is exploitation and resistance to it together within a framework of the relationships of control over the means and labor of social production.

2. *Tarāḥīl* Migrant Farm Labor

1. Rural women and girls are recruited into gangs of unskilled wage laborers, but their employment invariably involves only *local* day labor in village agriculture. *Tarāḥīl* work, on the other hand, as the term is used here, is exclusively performed by men. This gender segmentation of the rural workforce is a critical element in *tarāḥīl* labor and is examined in chapter 3.

2. Idrīs published his novel *al-Ḥarām* in 1959. It prominently publicized this otherwise marginal group of destitute workers. His dramatic imagery of Saʿīdī *tarāḥīl* laborers aroused a great outcry of sympathy from among urban reformers who previously had not considered this neglected portion of Egypt's impoverished labor force. Paradoxically, both the novel and its cinematic adaptation depict female migrants as a central motif of the fictional story. This may have once been true of *tarāḥīl* migrants from the south since its short single agricultural season and underdeveloped economy could have forced many workers, male and female, to go north when farm work was finished at home. However, since the 1950s, migrant labor in the Saʿīd had essentially disappeared, stopping the flow of both men and women—if, indeed, female participation was ever more than just a romantic plot. Judging by the stronger codes of female seclusion practiced by the more tribal south, female *tarāḥīl* workers seem very implausible despite the popular beliefs created by Idrīs.

3. According to government labor regulations, Egyptian workers are considered temporary if they are hired for two months or less. Then, by law, they must be discharged for a week before they can be rehired by the same employer and still remain casual laborers. This status reduces the legal and financial responsibility the company assumes toward workers (Koch et al. 1978:52).

4. Labor contracts in land-reclamation employment specified safe transportation, permanent shelter, nonwork service personnel, bedding, and food supplied from the UN World Food Programme. These work benefits were initially inspired by the model labor camp experiments in Wādī Natrūn in the early 1960s and later included in labor regulations under pressure from the General Union for Agricultural and Migrant Workers.

5. These percentages are derived from a survey I conducted in 1981 of 398 *tarāḥīl* workers from Minūfiya Province working at the Mariout Reclamation Company. Although not entirely representative of the national *tarāḥīl* population—migrant farm labor profiles vary by province and region—the figures do emphasize the overwhelming youthful trend among all *tarāḥīl* migrant farm workers in the 1980s and 1990s.

6. Hearth members combine remunerated field work and camp tasks in various amounts in order to form viable work and consumption units. In joint hearths, which include seniors, juniors, and boys, all members are responsible for field work but seniors are relieved of doing camp tasks, which are performed instead by younger workers. In junior-only hearths, all members complete regular work and overtime assignments and share camp chores among themselves. In "loner" hearths, old workers do a minimum amount of waged work and a minimum amount of camp chores. Boys, who are always attached to an elder's hearth, engage in set-up and clean-up work and perform the maximum amount of camp chores.

7. In my survey of 398 workers, there were 58 senior workers who were forty years or older. Of these, 25 workers (constituting 23 hearths, 43.10 percent of the total) came with nephews or sons—20 of them (18 hearths) came with only their sons alone, and 5 of them (5 hearths) came with both sons and nephews; 3 workers (3

hearths) came with their younger brothers and cousins; 8 workers (5 hearths) came as single senior foremen related to younger retinue leaders; 4 workers (2 hearths) came with an unrelated peer (defined as a colleague within two years of age); and 18 workers (18 hearths, 31.03 percent of the total) came as "loners." Of these "loners," 9 workers were actually accompanied by younger relatives residing in other hearths, with kinsmen as distant as a worker's brother-in-law's son, and 9 workers lacked any relatives whatsoever and therefore constituted true loners.

The average size of a foreman's hearth was 5.6 members (based on 5 hearths), while the size of other hearths in which senior workers lived was 2.5 members (based on 26 hearths). When the hearths of intermediate task leaders were subtracted from this second group of 26, the common hearth size declined to 2.3 members. Thus the foreman's hearths were more than twice the size of the common senior worker's hearth. This retinue supported the decisions he made and orders he gave, lending allegiance and authority to his commands.

8. Michael Burawoy found (1985:chap. 4) a similar pattern of intergenerational tension at the Red Star Factory in Budapest. Speedups in this unvarnished piece-rate system provoked two responses, depending on whether workers belonged to the senior or junior generation. Older workers staged slowdowns in order to exact workload concessions. Younger workers instead wanted to maximize earnings without regard to cutting piece rates. This recalls Claude Meillassoux's notion (1973) of gerontocratic exploitation. What Burawoy missed, however, is similar to what was missing in Meillassoux's writing: age segmentation between senior and junior workers is never permanent. Juniors eventually become seniors, and the older generation paves the way for younger workers. What the elderly generation bequeaths quickens the time the young take when they go on to establish their own alternative income sources later as they mature. In Egyptian migrant farm labor, a permanent gerontocratic disparity does not exist because of these long-term exchanges between the two generations.

9. The "internal store" refers to early attempts by Taylorist companies to control consumption before it later became appropriated by the state as part of its Keynesian policies under Fordism. Other examples include company stores, trading posts, local *pulperias,* mine compounds, "ticket systems," and company scrip. Here I use a phrasing that parallels Michael Burawoy's "internal labor market" and "internal state" (1979), which are hallmarks of Fordism. The "internal store" of Taylorism dissolved once Burawoy's "internal labor market" and "internal state" arose under Fordism as more efficient mechanisms of labor control.

10. These dishonest merchants are comparable to the cheating shopkeepers Breman found (1985:215) among cane cutters in Gujarat, India; the ridiculing store owners Wolf heard about (1956:228) from coffee workers in San José, Puerto Rico; and the racist townspeople Friedland and Nelkin observed (1971:37–50) among African-American migrants in the United States. Such prejudice helps maintain the monopoly that "internal stores" have in controlling the effort = wage = price formula of migrant farm labor.

3. Exporting Unskilled Farm Labor

1. Both Bent Hansen (1969) and Alan Richards (1982) challenged the conventional calculations concerning surplus labor. Yet despite analyses that critically revised and drastically lowered this percentage, even these economists failed to appreciate the full impact of Egypt's technical division of rural labor on agricultural production and work.

2. The horizontal axis is the calendar year; the vertical axis is the number of working days per month. Two calculations were made. One includes Friday, the Islamic Sabbath, as a workday, the other excludes Fridays. Piercing the shaded portion means using up all non-Sabbath workdays; going beyond it means that, even including Fridays, the month is completely occupied with work.

3. Evaluating nonmale participation in agriculture must be done cautiously. The 1960 census reports the ratio of females to the total agricultural labor force at 6.2 percent, while the 1973 Labor Force Sample Survey states it was 2.3 percent (Mohie-Eldin 1982:241). Yet Egyptian census data notoriously underestimate the amount of female labor and overestimate the amount of child labor used in agriculture. The problem may be located in the very generation of census data itself: in the inquiry about individual female family member activities by outside male enumerators. A farm household head may be reluctant to confess that women bring in incomes when confronted by the local middle-class schoolteacher who frequently serves as enumerator. Census estimates of female participation (3–10 percent) and child involvement (upward of 90 percent) are commonly considered too low and too high, respectively (Fitch et al. 1980:15). Saunders and Mehenna (1986:112) offer four reasons for the extremely low estimates of female participation: (1) the seasonality of women's work; (2) its casual character; (3) its low prestige; and (4) its inclusion in what is normally considered "housework." Beneria (1982:120) concludes that the absence of reliable data is a major problem in evaluating the female contribution to domestic economies. Concurring with Saunders and Mehenna, Beneria also adds that the conventional definitions of labor and its contributions need rethinking. Not only is what constitutes marketable labor questionable, but also "homework" can include productive and reproductive tasks essential to carrying on income-generating farm work. For Egypt, participation rates need serious revision before analyses can be judged reliable.

4. The Labor Process among *Tarāḥīl* Workers

1. Data for this section was collected during two years of fieldwork among *tarāḥīl* workers from two villages in Minūfiya Province. Ironically, data collection replicated Taylor-like "time-motion" studies by measuring work time, size of output, area or volume assigned, and staffing practices. Few ordinary workers fully grasped the dynamics of task assignments since they seldom remained at the same site or stayed with the same labor gang. Most were too exhausted for extensive

interviews anyway. If there was a "full-time" *tarāḥīl* worker, it was the foreman, whose knowledge provided the main source of information.

2. This is somewhat troubling to those more accustomed to time payments instead of piece-rate wages. For if "time means money" then income becomes based on time spent on the job rather than the amount that has to be completed. Thus, disregarding time in such circumstances seems a sacrilege. Yet time rates are more appropriate to Fordism than piece rates since filling work time and raising productivity is determined by management, which speeds up the labor process through its distant control of assembly-line machinery and equipment. Those reared on Fordism may find the indifference to time in Egypt irritating. Nevertheless, *tarāḥīl* laborers work hard and expend much effort, regardless of whether this is seen as a "fast tempo" or a "big amount."

3. The reference is to Frederick Taylor's intentions to both reduce gaps—"filling the pores"—in the workday and to lengthen it as techniques of extensive capital accumulation of absolute surplus value. The term originally came from Marx (1967:410).

5. The Stillbirth of Arab Socialism, 1961

1. In 1960, agriculture represented 30 percent of Egypt's gross domestic product, manufacturing 14 percent, and commerce 10 percent (United Nations 1967:569, table 181). Agriculture's share remained relatively constant until the early 1980s. By the end of that decade, its proportion of GDP had dropped to 15 percent, about the same level as manufacturing (United Nations 1995:181, table 23).

2. Muḥammad Sālim (1977) reported that labor's share of total crop costs in 1977 was 44 percent for cotton, 25 for wheat, and 35 for rice. Alan Richards (1991) reported that in 1988 this proportion was 61 percent for cotton, 45 for wheat, and 42 for rice. Of course these percentages depend on other factor costs and on domestic and world prices. Nevertheless, such figures underscore the critical need for workers in cotton production and for other crops as well.

3. Radwan and Lee calculated (1986:30) that in 1977 agricultural income constituted 51 percent of all rural incomes. A comparable figure for 1960 is difficult to obtain. For 1960 I computed the agricultural GDP per farm worker (£E91.96) as a proportion of the national GDP per rural resident (£E164.10), using figures cited in Hansen and Radwan (1982:31). This resulted in a ratio of 56 percent, which is similar to, but somewhat larger than, the 1977 number.

4. These proportions agree with the data I obtained in 1980 from interviews with 33 older workers from Minūfiya Province working in land reclamation: 14 (42.42 percent) never had land; 7 (21.21 percent) once had land; 4 (12.12 percent) had indirect access to land; 8 (24.24 percent) owned or rented land. Thus we see that almost two-thirds (63.63) had no land while one-third (36.36) had access to it, although "access" here does not necessarily mean formal landholding—that is, someone with a *hiyāza*, or a legal-use deed. Three workers had relatively large farms (1.5, 4, and 6

faddāns) but were unable physically to work at home. The others averaged 10.8 *qīrāṭs* (1 *faddān* equals 24 *qīrāṭs)*, which was entirely too small to be viable.

5. It is not always possible to get economic data for the same years. Mahmoud Abdel-Fadil's 1961 figures for land holdings (1975:14) are the closest to the census year of 1960 as can be obtained.

6. These were the Labor Force Sample Surveys for 1971, 1974, 1976, 1977, 1978, and 1980, published by the Central Agency for Public Mobilization and Statistics (CAPMAS) in May of each of these years.

7. Hansen and Radwan's 50 percent estimate of rural workers engaged in local day labor (1982:121) appears high considering the "shame" of local work mentioned above, its infrequent availability through paternalistic contractors, and the long commuting distances traveled to arrive at urban recruiting areas at dawn.

8. The IMF initially demanded an even greater devaluation of 50 piasters to the dollar but finally compromised at 43.5 (Hansen and Nashashibi 1975:106).

9. In 1969 the International Labour Office (ILO) in Geneva and the Institute of National Planning (INP) in Cairo concluded that substantial labor redundancy existed in rural Egypt. This opinion was based on research conducted in 1963, a year when many rural workers had returned once again to the countryside, but which sharply contrasted with the adjacent years 1961 and 1964, when labor-induced agricultural crises occurred.

10. The first stage consisted of excavating a diversionary channel on the east bank of the Nile, installing turbine generators, and building upstream and downstream coffer dams. The second stage involved building the actual dam itself, grafting it onto the coffer dams, which would sandwich a cement mountain anchored by a concrete curtain extending 800 feet down to bedrock (Little 1965:78).

11. Average agricultural wages from 1951 to 1958 remained relatively constant at 11 piasters a day. In 1959 they rose 1 piaster. The average rural day wage for 1960 is not known, but in 1961 its value was 12.6 piasters (Abdel-Fadil 1975:66). A monthly income of £E10.00 from working at Aswān turns out to be 42 piasters a day for a six-day workweek, four weeks a month. If laborers work seven days a week, the daily wage declines to 36 piasters a day. Still, wages at the High Dam were more than three times those in agriculture.

12. For all practical purposes, figures for the numbers of workers at Aswān and related projects do not exist. The ILO estimated (1969:79) that 155.2 million man-days and £E80.8 million in wages were involved in the High Dam project and another 215.2 million man-days and £E100.7 million in wages were spent on related irrigation and drainage projects and for construction of new Nile barrages. Yet the report does not indicate the specific period under discussion, the various skill levels, or the amount of day rates. Abdel-Fadil, using the same ILO report, calculated (1975:126) that the High Dam offered 45.6 million man-days of casual employment. Assuming a twenty-four-day work month and three years of employment, he determined that 527,663 "casual laborers [were] likely to have benefited from the new employment

opportunities opened up by the construction stage of the High Dam and other dependent projects." He then cites an ILO report that lowers this estimate to 300,000. Abdel-Fadil's higher estimate constitutes 22 percent of the 2.39-million-man *tarāḥīl* workforce (see page xxx above) while the lower estimate represents 13 percent of this labor force.

6. Groundwork for the Six-Day Disaster

1. Compare this number to the calculation computed in chapter 5 of 2.39 million *tarāḥīl* workers recruited from a total of 3.42 million rural laborers, who in 1960 were in need of extra work.

2. The GUAMW focused only on laborers in land reclamation companies and disregarded both those working on the Aswān High Dam—which by 1964 was nearly finished—and migrants employed in the private sector.

3. These were the districts of Mīt Ghamr, Ajā, al-Sinbalāwīn, Dikirnis, al-Mansūra, and Shirbīn.

4. Abāzha's preoccupation with communism emerged during a 1992 interview and may have referred specifically to the participation of Aḥmad al-Rifāʿī, the second president of the GUAMW, a career GUAMW organizer, and a member of the Egyptian Communist Party.

5. Baradāʿī (1972:23). These figures fall within the range of wage levels for manual labor stated in note 11 in chapter 5, although the difference between farm and construction wages was less related to Employment Office negotiations than to the sharp rise in the national demand for unskilled workers. However, the 22-piaster figure is well below the 42 piasters estimated for daily High Dam wages, although the two ought to be equal within the same national labor market. The discrepancy may be due to imperfections in the labor market, incorrect calculations for the Aswān figure, levels posted just for large Aswān constructions companies, or reductions in the wages actually paid *tarāḥīl* workers in Buḥayra once commissions, fees, and mandatory living expenses were deducted.

6. Productivity was measured daily by camp supervisors, who reported increases ranging from 44 to 140 percent, depending on the task. Workers were compared to a "control" group of migrants located adjacent to the Wādī Natrūn camp but who did not receive special treatment.

7. Unquoted portions paraphrase the literal translation of the Arabic text.

8. Shawqī Salāma, who was later identified as a major labor broker (*al-Akhbār*, September 30, 1968).

9. The law required organizers to register *at least* a minimum of thirty workers in a single village in order to establish a local union committee.

10. Hopkins must have meant 4,000 *union committees*. The "branch" was an organizational term later reserved for GUAMW activities operating at the provincial level.

11. This total differs from Hopkins' count of twenty-one (see above). *Al-Akhbār* reported (July 13, 1964) the election of twenty union executives: ten officers, including the president, and ten board members.

12. Two years later, the GUAMW held a conference at the potentially explosive Shihāb al-Dīn reclamation site near Daqahliya. However, recommendations were extremely mild, asking only that employment operations rely on provincial authorities. No radical demands were made and none were adopted (*al-Jumhūriya,* March 15, 1968).

7. Sowing the Seeds of Urban Discontent

1. Messiha (1980:13). In 1966, 51 percent of all work permits for foreign employment were granted to schoolteachers, followed by managers and merchants (22 percent) and medical practitioners (10 percent). Skilled craftsmen received only 7.6 percent of these work permits (Dessouki 1978:9).

2. *Al-Ahrām* reported (July 7, 1974) that "the professions prohibited from traveling are: carpenters, plasterers, ironmen (for concrete reinforcement), white washers, painters, window and door carpenters, electricians, sanitary window makers, hot brick layers, lathers, iron kreetal, tile layers, tile makers, porcelain tile layers, high voltage electricians, mechanical operators, metal workers, repairmen, air conditioner electricians, drivers, regular workers, and porters."

3. In 1960, 2.39 million rural workers engaged in *tarāḥīl* labor (see chapter 5). By 1973, the number had declined to 1.5 million, and by 1980 it had decreased even further to 0.8 million.

4. The Egyptian Ministry of Housing estimated that the value of output per worker in the construction sector, in constant 1979 prices, fell by 50 percent from the early 1960s to the late 1970s due to a decline in labor skills (General Organization for Housing 1981, vol. 2:121).

5. Unfortunately, government statistics measure only those who engaged in interprovincial movement to Cairo, Alexandria, and the three canal-zone cities. Migration also took place within the provinces, from villages to neighboring district townships to nearby provincial capitals, but these figures do not appear in the national census material. Moreover, as transportation improved, many villagers commuted daily or weekly to urban jobs, as demonstrated by the huge, homeward bound crowds at the Aḥmad Ḥilmī taxi and microbus station in Cairo every Thursday afternoon.

6. The public sector included forty-seyen construction companies. In 1979, 27 percent of their operations was subcontracted to the private sector (General Organization for Housing 1981, vol. 2:26).

7. The exact number of private-sector contractors is not known. The General Organization for Housing (1981, vol. 2:29) estimates that in 1980 they numbered between 20,000 and 25,000 firms. Koch et al. reports (1978:39) that in 1977, 12,000 to

15,000 general and specialty contractors existed, with an additional 6,700 labor-only contractors operating in Cairo alone. In 1966, there were 3,000 registered labor-only contractors, a number that declined to 1,600 in 1971 and then rose to 6,700 in 1977. This included only those who were registered labor contractors—a small, though constant, proportion of all labor contractors (Ashley and Selim 1980:62). This trend agrees with the fluctuations in construction wages for the same years.

8. In 1984, public-sector firms directly employed 20 percent of the construction labor force, half the share it held in 1972. (Of these firms, just three accounted for 60 percent of public-sector employment, with one firm alone employing 42 percent of public-sector workers.) Large private firms of ten persons or more employed only 1 to 2 percent of the workforce. Thus small, informal firms contained nearly 80 percent of the workers, an increase of one-third over its share in 1972 (Assaad 1991:131).

9. From 1970 to 1972, the consumer price index for food alone rose 8 percent. Yet in just one year, 1974, the index jumped 16 percent and by the end of the decade had risen to 120 percent of its 1974 levels (United Nations 1981, 1988).

10. For a list of those speaking out against the dismemberment of the ASU, see Waterbury's description (1978:253–54) of the parliamentary hearings that were held in September 1974.

11. Folker Fröbel, Jürgen Heinrichs, and Otto Kreye concluded (1981:322–23) that cheap labor constitutes the most significant factor encouraging foreign investment in free production zones and world market factories. Since foreign capital also invests in the periphery under less accommodating terms—subcontracting, import substitution, regular industrial- and service-sector development—the need for a cheap, docile workforce is all that much more pressing.

8. Beating Plowshares into Swords

1. Despite the reinstatement of official low food prices, by the end of the decade the total consumer price index had risen 48 percent, and the consumer price index for food alone had risen 49 percent (United Nations 1981:721, table 168; 1988:170, table 37).

2. See note 2, chapter 5.

3. Egypt has had some success with exporting ready-made garments, an industry closely tied to its domestic textile manufacturing and subsidized cotton production. However, with the consolidation of the European Economic Community and the opening of Eastern Europe, this market may be in jeopardy (*International Herald Tribune,* December 2, 1994).

4. *Structural* unemployment refers to those secular changes that permanently reduced employment opportunities abroad. In the mid-1980s, oil gluts and lower consumption reduced world prices for oil. National economies that relied on such revenues slowed down. A number of development projects were canceled. Others seeking cheaper wage costs replaced Arab workers with less troublesome counter-

parts from Korea and the Philippines. Skilled Egyptian workers were also replaced by more experienced North Africans, who left the European labor market because of the influx of East Europeans and the rise of ethnic prejudice and who then sought employment in Libya and the Gulf. Finally, the success of numerous manpower training programs in the Gulf began to permanently replace Egyptian workers with domestic ones. Should Arab oil economies expand again in the future, these structural changes preclude a significant return of Egyptian workers to the levels of the 1970s and early 1980s.

5. Patrick Gaffney indicated (1994:329–30) that the Islamic Association al-Jamāʿa al-Islāmiya in al-Minyā was preceded by the al-Jamʿiya al-Islāmiya, also translated as the Islamic Association, but with a slightly different nuance in the Arabic. This is also the generic term for any Islamic religious association. The confusion is not just among foreign speakers; informants in al-Minyā also found it difficult to distinguish in government publications among these two distinct organizations and the generic term.

6. The assertion that Islamist attacks against foreigners occur only in areas where the local economy and its elites are not affected was contradicted on November 17, 1997, when six Islamists murdered fifty-eight tourists and four Egyptians in Luxor. Both the nature of the location—Egypt's premier tourist attraction—and the severity of the incident tempted many to question whether, in fact, the murderers were really Egyptian despite the evidence that they were from the al-Jamāʿa al-Islāmiya. The enormous decrease in foreign tourism, however, followed earlier patterns of provoking economic disruption in order to achieve political goals.

7. In the early 1990s, the portion of those in the Saʿīd living under the poverty line reached as high as 40 percent, according to a Shūra council report (*al-Wafd*, February 19, 1995).

8. Ibrahim (1980:430–32) and Ansari (1986:chaps. 9 and 10) assert that the militant Islamic leadership of the 1970s and early 1980s primarily involved highly educated, middle-class migrants from the countryside. This identification of class, origins, and profession agrees with the detailed information I collected in al-Minyā in the mid-1990s. Informants and visits there also identified the occupational background and the working-class character of many of the rank-and-file participants who have joined these religious associations since 1985.

9. The Thānawiya ʿAmma, borrowed from the French educational system, constitutes the large comprehensive examination at the end of high school that determines the discipline, and hence the occupation, of beginning college students. The Scholastic Aptitude Test (SAT) in the United States is a similar testing device, although it is much less decisive.

10. The names of these religious associations are fictitious.

11. One informant told me that when the mosque he attended had been private, 80 percent of the *zakāt* funds went to the community and 20 percent covered administrative costs. Once it became a government mosque, however, these percentages, he said, were reversed.

9. Frustrated Fordism

1. In 1992, Parliament legislated a new owners-renters law for rural real estate that went into effect in October 1997. It was intended to promote such consolidations, but at the risk of expelling many small farmers from their already tenuous position in the countryside, channeling them either into rejuvenated *tarāḥīl* labor gangs or else into the crowded urban informal sector (*al-Wafd*, November 2, 1992).

Bibliography

Books and Articles

Abdel-Fadil, Mahmoud. 1975. *Development, Income Distribution, and Social Change in Rural Egypt, 1952–1970.* London: Cambridge University Press.

Abd al Nāṣir, Jamāl. 1964. "Address by President Gamal Abdel Nasser at [the] Popular Rally in Aswan on the Occasion of the High Dam Celebrations, January 9, 1963." In *Speeches and Press Interviews, January–December, 1963,* 11–38. Cairo: Information Department, United Arab Republic.

Abu Zayd, Ahmad. 1965. *al-Th'ār: Dirāsa Anthrūbūlūjiya bī Ahdī Qurā al-Sa'īd* [Retaliation: An Anthropological Study of Some Villages in the Saʿīd]. Cairo: Dār al-Maʿārif.

Aglietta, Michel. 1979. *A Theory of Capitalist Regulation: The U.S. Experience.* Translated by David Ferbach. London: Verso. First published as *Régulation et Crises du Capitalism* (Paris: Calmann-Lévy, 1974).

Ansari, Hamied. 1986. *Egypt: The Stalled Society.* Albany: State University of New York Press.

Antoun, Richard. 1968. "On the Modesty of Women in Arab Muslim Villages: A Study in the Accommodation of Traditions." *American Anthropologist* 70, no. 4 (August):671–97.

Ashley, David B., and Tarek Selim. 1980. "Resources and Contractors in Egypt: A Review." In *Management of the Construction Industry in Egypt, Seminar Proceedings, January 19–20, 1980,* 45–73. Cairo: Joint Research Team on the Housing and Construction Industrial, Cairo University, and Massachusetts Institute of Technology.

Assaad, Ragui. 1991. "Structure of Egypt's Construction Labour Market and Its Development since the Mid-1970s." In *Employment and Structural Adjustment: Egypt in the 1990s,* edited by Heba Handoussa and Gillian Potter, 125–65. Cairo: American University in Cairo Press.

Baldi, Guido. 1972. "Theses on Mass Worker and Social Capital." *Radical America* 6, no. 3 (May–June):3–21.

Baradāʿī, Hussayn. 1972. *'Ummāl al-Tarāḥīl fī Miṣr* [*Tarāḥīl* Workers in Egypt]. Cairo: Majalāt al-ʿAmal, Kitāb al-ʿAmal. No. 103. September.

Beinin, Joel, and Zachary Lockman. 1987. *Workers on the Nile: Nationalism, Com-*

munism, Islam, and the Egyptian Working Class, 1882–1954. Princeton: Princeton University Press.

Beneria, Lourdes. 1982. "Accounting for Women's Work." In *Women and Development: The Sexual Division of Labor in Rural Societies,* edited by Lourdes Beneria, 119–48. New York: Praeger.

Bianchi, Robert. 1989. *Unruly Corporatism: Associational Life in Twentieth-Century Egypt.* New York: Oxford University Press.

Boserup, Ester. 1970. *Woman's Role in Economic Development.* New York: St. Martin's Press.

Braverman, Harry. 1974. *Labor and Monopoly Capital: The Degradation of Work in the Twentieth Century.* New York: Monthly Review Press.

Breman, Jan. 1985. *Of Peasants, Migrants, and Paupers.* Oxford: Clarendon Press.

Brown, Nathan. 1990. *Peasant Politics in Modern Egypt.* New Haven: Yale University Press.

Burawoy, Michael. 1985. *The Politics of Production.* New York: Verso Press.

Buttrick, John. 1952. "The Inside Contract System." *Journal of Economic History* 12, no. 3 (Summer):205–24.

Central Agency for Public Mobilization and Statistics (CAPMAS). *Baḥth al-ʿImāla bī al-ʿAyyina* [Labor Force Sample Survey]. Cairo: Arab Republic of Egypt. Various years.

———. 1978a. *Statistical Indicators for the Delta.* Cairo: Arab Republic of Egypt.

———. 1978b. *The General Census of Residents and Residences. 1976. Population Census. Detailed Results.* Cairo: Arab Republic of Egypt.

———. 1978c. *Population and Development: A Study of the Population Increase and Its Challenge to Development in Egypt.* Cairo: Arab Republic of Egypt.

———. 1991. *Statistical Yearbook.* Cairo: Arab Republic of Egypt.

Choucri, Nazli. 1980. "Construction and Development: The Effects of Labor Migration." In *Management of the Construction Industry in Egypt. Seminar Proceedings. January 19–20, 1980,* 75–88. Cairo: Joint Research Team on the Housing and Construction Industry, Cairo University, and Massachusetts Institute of Technology.

Choucri, Nazli, Richard S. Eckaus, and Amr Mohie-Eldin. 1978. *Migration and Employment in the Construction Sector: Critical Factors in Egyptian Development.* Cairo: Cairo University–Massachusetts Institute of Technology, Technology Adaptation Program. October.

Cleland, Wendell. 1936. *The Population Problem in Egypt.* New York: Columbia University Press.

Cleaver, Harry. 1979. *Reading Capital Politically.* Austin: University of Texas Press.

Collier, Jane Fishburne. 1974. "Women in Politics." In *Woman, Culture and Society,* edited by Michelle Rosaldo and Louise Lamphere. Stanford: Stanford University Press.

Commander, Simon. 1987. *The State and Agricultural Development in Egypt since 1973.* London: Ithaca Press.

Connell. R. W. 1979. "A Critique of the Althusserian Approach to Class." *Theory and Society* 8, no. 3:321–43.

Cuddihy, William. 1980. *Agricultural Price Management in Egypt.* Staff Working Paper no. 388. Washington: World Bank. April.

Davis, Eric. 1983. *Challenging Colonialism: Bank Misr and Egyptian Industrialization, 1920–1941.* Princeton: Princeton University Press.

Department of Statistics and Census. 1963. *1960 Census of Population.* Volume 2, *General Tables.* Cairo: United Arab Republic. July.

Dessouki, Ali E. Hillal. 1978. *Development of Egypt's Migration Policy, 1952–1978.* Project on Egyptian Labor Migration. Cairo: Cairo University–Massachusetts Institute of Technology, Technology Adaptation Program. December.

de Ste. Croix, Geoffrey. 1984. "Class in Marx's Conception of History, Ancient and Modern." *New Left Review,* no. 146 (January–December):94–111.

Dunlop. John. 1949. "The Development of Labor Organization: A Theoretical Framework." In *Insights into Labor Issues,* edited by Richard Lester and Joseph Shister, 163–93. New York: Macmillan.

Edwards, Richard. 1979. *Contested Terrain: The Transformation of the Workplace in the Twentieth Century.* New York: Basic Books.

Egyptian Organization for Human Rights (EOHR). N.d. [ca. 1994]. *Aliyāt Intāj al-'Unf fī Miṣr: Asiyyūṭ, Ḥāla Namūdhajiya* [Tools of the Production of Violence in Egypt: The Assiyūṭ Case Study]. Cairo: EOHR.

Fitch, James, Sinia M. Aly, and Adel Mostafa. 1980. "Recent Trends in Agricultural Policy." Manuscript. Cairo: Ford Foundation. June 28.

Food and Agriculture Organization. 1990. *Production Year Book: World Development Report.* Rome: FAO.

Friedland, William H., and Dorothy Nelkin. 1971. *Migrant: Agricultural Workers in America's Northeast.* New York: Holt, Rinehart and Winston.

Fröbel, Folker, Jürgen Heinrichs, and Otto Kreye. 1981. *The New International Division of Labour.* Translated by Pete Burgess. New York: Cambridge University Press.

Gaffney, Patrick. 1994. *The Prophet's Pulpit: Islamic Preaching in Contemporary Egypt.* Berkeley: University of California Press.

Galby, Aly Abd El Razek, Mohammed Abdou Mahgoub, and Raouf Moustafa Ismail. 1980. *The Egyptian Society's Attitudes Towards Manual Labor.* Translated by Layla Ahmed Touba. Alexandria: Anthropology Department, Faculty of Arts, Alexandria University.

General Organization for Housing, Building, and Planning Research, the Steering Committee of the Ministry of Housing, and the World Bank. 1981. *Construction/Contracting Industry Study: Final Report.* 3 vols. Cairo: Arab Republic of Egypt, Ministry of Housing. July.

Giddens, Anthony. 1984. *The Constitution of Society.* Berkeley: University of California Press.

Gilsenan, Michael. 1992. *Recognizing Islam: Religion and Society in the Modern Middle East.* New York: I. B. Tauris.

Goldberg, Ellis. 1986. *Tinker, Tailor, and Textile Worker: Class and Politics in Egypt, 1930–1952.* Berkeley: University of California Press.

Goldschmidt, Arthur. 1988. *Modern Egypt: The Formation of a Nation-State.* Boulder: Westview Press.

Gordon, David M., Michael Reich, and Richard Edwards. 1982. *Segmented Work, Divided Workers: The Historical Transformation of Labor in the United States.* Cambridge: Cambridge University Press.

Government of Egypt. 1961. *Parliament Records.* First Legislative Portion. Third Regular Meeting. Eleventh Session. May 8.

Halliday, Fred. 1984. "Labor Migration in the Arab World." *MERIP Reports* 14, no. 4 (May):3–10.

Hammam, Mona. 1986. "Capitalist Development, Family Division of Labor, and Migration in the Middle East." In *Women's Work: Development and the Division of Labor by Gender,* edited by Eleanor Leacock and Helen Safa, 158–73. South Hadley, Mass: Bergin and Garvey.

Hanafi, Mohamed Nazem. 1973. *Surplus Labour and the Problem of Disguised Unemployment in Egyptian Agriculture.* Memo no. 1054. Cairo: United Arab Republic, Institute of National Planning. December.

Hansen, Bent. 1969. "Employment and Wages in Rural Egypt." *American Economic Review* 59, no. 3 (June):298–313.

———. 1972. "Economic Development of Egypt." In *Economic Development and Population Growth in the Middle East,* edited by Charles A. Cooper and Sidney S. Alexander, 21–89. New York: Elsevier.

Hansen, Bent, and Mona El-Tomy. 1965. "The Seasonal Employment Profile in Egyptian Agriculture." *Journal of Development Studies* 1, no. 4 (July):399–409.

Hansen, Bent, and Karim Nashashibi. 1975. *Egypt: Foreign Trade Regimes and Economic Development.* New York: National Bureau of Economic Research.

Hansen, Bent, and Samir Radwan. 1982. *Employment Opportunities and Equity in Egypt.* Geneva: International Labour Organisation.

Harik, Ilya. 1974. *The Political Mobilization of Peasants.* Bloomington: Indiana University Press.

Hiro, Dilip. 1989. *Holy Wars: The Rise of Islamic Fundamentalism.* New York: Routledge.

Hirst, David, and Irene Beeson. 1981. *Sadat.* London: Faber and Faber.

Hobsbawm, Eric. 1959. *Primitive Rebels: Studies in Archaic Forms of Social Movements in the Nineteenth and Twentieth Centuries.* New York: Norton.

Hooglund, Eric. 1991. "The Other Face of War." *Middle East Report* 21, no. 171:3–7, 10–12.

Hopkins, Harry. 1969. *Egypt: The Crucible. The Unfinished Revolution of the Arab World.* London: Secker and Warburg.

Hopkins, Nicholas S. 1983. "The Social Impact of Mechanization." In *Migration, Mechanization, and Agricultural Labor Markets in Egypt,* edited by Alan Richards and Philip L. Martin, 181–97. Boulder: Westview Press.

———. 1987. *Agrarian Transformation in Egypt.* Boulder: Westview Press.

———. 1993. "Small Farmer Household and Agricultural Sustainability in Egypt." In *Sustainable Agriculture in Egypt,* edited by Mohamed A. Faris and Mahmood Hasan Khan, 185–95. Boulder: Lynne Rienner.

Hopwood, Derek. 1991. *Egypt: Politics and Society, 1945–1990.* New York: HarperCollins.

Ḥussain, Ḥusnī. 1971. "'Ummāl al-*Tarāḥīl* fī al-Arḍ al-Jadīd" [*Tarāḥīl* Workers in the New Lands]. *al-Ṭālīʿa* (Cairo) 7, no. 1 (January):26–29.

Ibrahim, Saad Eddin. 1980. "Anatomy of Egypt's Militant Islamic Groups: Methodological Note and Preliminary Findings." *International Journal of Middle East Studies* 12, no. 4 (December):423–53.

———. 1996. "Cairo: A Sociological Profile." In his *Egypt, Islam, and Democracy: Twelve Critical Essays,* 93–133. Cairo: American University in Cairo Press.

Idrīs, Yūsif. 1984. *al-Ḥarām.* Translated by Kristin Peterson-Ishaq. Washington: Three Continents Press.

International Labour Office. 1969. *Rural Employment Problems in the United Arab Republic.* Geneva: International Labour Office.

Jessop, Bob. 1982. *The Capitalist State: Marxist Theories and Methods.* New York: New York University Press.

———. 1990. "Regulation Theories in Retrospect and Prospect." *Economy and Society* 19, no. 2 (May):153–216.

Kepel, Giles. 1985. *The Prophet and the Pharaoh: Muslim Extremism in Egypt.* London: Al Saqi Books.

Koch, Janet A., Tarek Selim, and Omar el Gamal. 1978. "Organization and Operation of the Construction Industry." In *The Housing and Construction Industry in Egypt: Interim Report Working Papers 1978,* 3–93. Cairo: Joint Research Team on the Housing and Construction Industry, Cairo University, and Massachusetts Institute of Technology.

Korayem, Karima. 1979. "The Agricultural Price Policy and Implicit Taxation of Agricultural Income." Paper presented to the Lisbon Conference on Egyptian Income Distribution, October 29–November 21, 1979. Published in *The Political Economy of Income Distribution in Egypt,* edited by Gouda Abdel-Khalek and Robert Tignor. New York: Holmes and Meier, 1982.

LaTowsky, Robert. 1984. "Egyptian Labor Abroad: Mass Participation and Modest Returns." *MERIP Reports* 14, no. 4 (May):11–18.

Lewis, W. Arthur. 1954. "Economic Development with Unlimited Supplies of Labour." *Manchester School of Economic and Social Studies* 22, no. 2 (May):139–91.

Lipietz, Alain. 1982. "Towards Global Fordism?" *New Left Review,* no. 132 (March–April):33–47.

———. 1985. *The Enchanted World: Inflation, Credit, and the World Crisis.* Translated by Ian Patterson. London: Verso Press.

———. 1987. *Mirages and Miracles.* London: Verso Press.

Little, Tom. 1965. *High Dam at Aswan: The Subjugation of the Nile.* New York: John Day.

Littler, Craig R., and Graeme Salaman. 1982. "Bravermania and Beyond: Recent Theories of the Labour Process." *Sociology* 16, no. 2 (May):251–69.

Marx, Karl. 1967. *Capital.* New York: International Publishers.

Meillassoux, Claude. 1973. "The Social Organization of the Peasantry: The Economic Basis of Kinship." *Journal of Peasant Studies* 1, no. 1.

Messiha, Suzanne A. 1980. *Export of Egyptian School Teachers to Saudi Arabia and Kuwait: A Cost-Benefit Analysis.* Cairo Papers in Social Science, vol. 3, monograph 4. Cairo: American University in Cairo Press.

Miliband, Ralph. 1969. *The State in Capitalist Society.* New York: Basic Books.

Mintz, Sidney. 1973. "A Note on the Definition of Peasantries." *Journal of Peasant Studies* 1, no. 1 (October).

Mohie-Eldin, Amr. 1966. "Agricultural Investment and Employment in Egypt since 1935." Ph.D. diss., London University.

———. 1982. "The Development of the Share of Agricultural Wage Labor in the National Income of Egypt." In *The Political Economy of Income Distribution in Egypt,* edited by Gouda Abdel-Khalek and Robert Tignor, 236–67. New York: Holmes and Meier.

Nash, June C. 1985. "Deindustrialization and the Impact on Labor Control Systems in Competitive and Monopoly Capitalist Enterprises." *Urban Anthropology and Studies of Cultural Systems and World Economic Development* 14, nos. 1–3:151–82.

Nutting, Anthony. 1972. *Nasser.* New York: Dutton.

O'Brien, Patrick. 1966. *The Revolution in Egypt's Economic System.* London: Oxford University Press.

Offe Claus. 1975. "The Theory of the Capitalist State and the Problem of Policy Formation." In *Stress and Contradiction in Modern Capitalism: Public Policy and the Theory of the State,* edited by Leon N. Lindberg, Robert Alford, Colin Crouch, and Claus Offe, 125–44. Lexington, Mass.: D.C. Heath.

Paige, Jeffery. 1975. *Agrarian Revolution: Social Movements and Export Agriculture in the Underdeveloped World.* New York: Free Press.

Posusney, Marsha. 1991. "Workers Against the State: Actors, Issues, and Outcomes in Egyptian Labor/State Relations, 1952–1987." Ph.D. diss., University of Pennsylvania.

Radwan, Samir, and Eddy Lee. 1986. *Agrarian Change in Egypt: An Anatomy of Rural Poverty.* London: Croon Helm.

Richards, Alan. 1982. *Egypt's Agricultural Development, 1800–1980.* Boulder: Westview Press.

———. 1991. "Agricultural Employment, Wages, and Government Policy in Egypt during and after the Oil Boom." In *Employment and Structural Adjustment: Egypt in the 1990s,* edited by Heba Handoussa and Gillian Potter, 57–93. Cairo: American University Press.

Richards, Alan, and John Waterbury. 1990. *A Political Economy of the Middle East: State, Class, and Economic Development*. Boulder: Westview Press.

Rishād, Muḥammad. 1968. *Iḥtarnā lī al-Falāḥ: al-Thawra wa al-ʿUmmāl al-Zarāʿīn wa al-Tarāḥīl* [We Select for the Peasant: The Revolution and Agricultural and Tarāḥīl Workers]. Cairo: Ministry of Culture/ Egyptian General Organization for Composition and Publication/Arab Book House for Printing and Publishing, Newspaper Branch. Vol. 2, no. 10. April.

Rugh, Andrea. 1985. "Women and Work: Strategies and Choices in a Lower-Class Quarter of Cairo." In *Women and the Family in the Middle East*, edited by Elizabeth Fernea, 273–92. Austin: University of Texas Press.

Saab, Gabriel. 1967. *The Egyptian Agrarian Reform, 1952–1962*. London: Oxford University Press.

Sadowski, Yahya. 1991. *Political Vegetables: Businessman and Bureaucrat in the Development of Egyptian Agriculture*. Washington: Brookings Institution.

Sālim, Muḥammad. 1977. *Iqtiṣādiyat al-Zirāʿa al-Miṣriya* [Economics of Egyptian Agriculture]. Internal Memo no. 566. Cairo: Institute of National Planning.

Saunders, Lucie Wood, and Suhair Mehenna. 1986. "Unseen Hands: Women's Farmwork in an Egyptian Village." *Anthropological Quarterly* 59, no. 3 (July):105–14.

Scott, James. 1985. *Weapons of the Weak: Everyday Forms of Peasant Resistance*. New Haven: Yale University Press.

Shanin, Teodor. 1971. "Peasantry: Delineation of a Sociological Concept and a Field of Study." *European Journal of Sociology* 12, no. 2.

al-Shināwi, ʿAbd al-ʿAzzīz Muḥammad. 1958. *al-Sukhra fi Ḥafr Qanāt al-Sūwaīs* [The Corvée in Excavating the Suez Canal]. Alexandria: al-Maʿārif al-Ḥadītha.

Springborg, Robert. 1979. "Patrimonialism and Policy Making in Egypt: Nasser and Sadat and the Tenure Policy for Reclaimed Lands." *Middle East Studies* 15, no. 1 (January):49–69.

———. 1982. *Family, Power, and Politics in Egypt: Sayed Bey Marei—His Clan, Clients, and Cohorts*. Philadelphia: University of Pennsylvania Press.

———. 1989. *Mubarak's Egypt: Fragmentation of the Political Order*. Boulder: Westview Press.

Stevenson, Mary Huff. 1978. "Wage Differences Between Men and Women: Economic Theories." In *Women Working: Theories and Facts in Perspective*, edited by Ann Stromberg and Shirley Harkess, 89–107. Palo Alto: Mayfield Publishers.

Taylor-Awny, Elizabeth. 1987. "Labour Shortage in Egyptian Agriculture: A Crisis for Whom?" In *Peasants and Peasant Societies: Selected Readings*, edited by Teodor Shanin, 2d ed., 166–73. Oxford: Basil Blackwell.

Thurow, Lester. 1975. *Generating Inequality*. New York: Basic Books.

el-Togby, Hassan Ali. 1976. *Contemporary Egyptian Agriculture*. New York: Ford Foundation.

Toth, James. 1987. "Migrant Workers in the Egyptian Delta." Ph.D. diss., SUNY–Binghamton.

———. 1991. "Pride, Purdah, or Paychecks: What Maintains the Gender Division of Labor in Rural Egypt?" *International Journal of Middle East Studies* 23, no. 2 (May):213–36.

———. 1993. "Manufacturing Consent and Resistance in Peripheral Production: The Labor Process among Egyptian Migrant Workers and Egyptian National Development." *Dialectical Anthropology,* no. 18 (Summer):291–335.

Tronti, Mario. 1971. *Operai e capitale* [Labor and Capital]. Torino: Giulio Einaudi.

United Nations. 1967. *Statistical Yearbook, 1966.* Statistical Office of the United Nations, Department of Economic and Social Affairs. New York: United Nations.

———. 1981. *Statistical Yearbook, 1979/80.* Department of International Economic and Social Affairs. New York: United Nations.

———. 1988. *Statistical Yearbook, 1985/86.* Department of International Economic and Social Affairs. New York: United Nations.

———. 1995. *Statistical Yearbook, 1993.* Department for Economic and Social Information and Policy Analysis, Statistical Division. New York: United Nations.

Voll, Sarah P. 1979. "Egyptian Land Reclamation since the Revolution." Unpublished report for the U.S. Agency for International Development, January 10. Partially reprinted in *Middle East Journal* 34, no. 2 (Spring 1980):127–48.

Wallerstein, Immanuel. 1974. *The Modern World System: Capitalist Agriculture and the Origins of the European World-Economy in the Sixteenth Century.* New York: Academic Press.

———. 1984. *The Politics of the World-Economy: The States, the Movements, and the Civilizations.* New York: Cambridge University Press.

Waterbury, John. 1978. *Egypt: Burdens of the Past, Options for the Future.* Bloomington: Indiana University Press.

———. 1979. *Hydropolitics of the Nile Valley.* Syracuse: Syracuse University Press.

———. 1983. *The Egypt of Nasser and Sadat: The Political Economy of Two Regimes.* Princeton: Princeton University Press.

———. 1991. "Peasants Defy Categorization (as Well as Landlords and the State)." In *Peasants and Politics in the Modern Middle East,* edited by John Waterbury and Farhad Kazemi, 1–23. Miami: Florida International University Press.

Weyland, Petra. 1993. *Inside the Third World Village.* London: Routledge.

Wilmington, Martin W. 1971. *The Middle East Supply Centre.* Albany: State University of New York Press.

Wolf, Eric. 1956. "San José: Subcultures of a 'Traditional' Coffee Municipality." In *The People of Puerto Rico,* edited by Julian Steward. Urbana: University of Illinois Press.

World Bank. 1989. *Social Indicators.* Baltimore: Johns Hopkins University Press.

Newspapers and Magazines

al-Ahrām (Cairo).
al-Akhbār (Cairo).
al-Ahālī (Cairo).
al-Sha'b (Cairo).
al-Wafd (Cairo).
al-Masā' (Cairo).
al-Jumhūriya (Cairo).
Akhir Sā'a (Cairo).
Majalāt al-'Amal (Cairo).
Majallāt al-Thaqāfa al-'Ummāliya (Cairo).
Rūz al-Yūsif (Cairo).
The Middle East Times (Cairo).
The Wall Street Journal (New York).
International Herald Tribune (Paris).

Interviews and Personal Communications

Wajīh Abāzha, June 22, 1992. Cairo.
Adil Afifi. September–December 1980. Cairo.
Aḥmad al-Rifā'ī. July 22, 1992. Cairo.
Anwār Salāma. July 7, 1992. Cairo.

Index